MARITIME LAW

ATTORNEY THOMAS WILLIAM WINSLOW

This Book is dedicated to the woman dedicated to me, my wife, Lauren, who is always there to support me as we work to support our community. To my children for whom I work to nurture my community, so that my community can nurture them. To my parents who always served me so that I may serve God.

Table of Contents

Acknowledgements 1

PART ONE:
The Conversion Non-Conversion 2

I. Introduction. 3

II. Overview of the Doctrine of Maintenance and Cure 6

    A. Historical Origin   6

    B. Persons Entitled to Maintenance and Cure   7

    C. Duration and Extent of Benefit   8

    D. Defenses   10

        1. Willful Misconduct   10

        2. Failure to Disclose Preexisting Illness   11

        3. In the Service of the Ship   11

        4. Maximum Medical Cure   12

III. Maximum Medical Improvement 12

    A. Paving the Road from Reed to Vella   13

IV. Survey of the Federal Circuit Courts of Appeal. 16

V. What is Curative Care? 31

VI. What is Palliative Care?. 32

VII. Human Rights Analysis of Access to Pain Treatment and
Palliative Care 35

    A. The Right to the Highest Attainable Standard of Health   36
    B. Pain Treatment, Palliative Care, and the Right to be Free
    from Cruel, Inhuman, or Degrading Treatment   37

VIII. Conclusion. 39

PART TWO:
Where Does the Tow Line Break?. 42

I. Introduction. 43

    A. What is Towage?   44

II. Salvage—Pure and Contract. 47

    1. Pure Salvage   48

        a. Marine Peril   49
        b. Service Voluntarily Rendered   49
        c. Effort Must be Successful   50

    2. Contract Salvage   53

III. Towage Versus Salvage 56

IV. Peril in Groundings 58

V. A Case Review of Other Potential Towage
Versus Salvage Situations 63

    A. Evanow v. M/V Neptune, 163 F.3d 1108, 1111-19
    (9th Cir. 1998):   63
    B. The Flottbek, 118 F. 954, 960-65 (9th Cir. 1902):   65
    C. The Catalina, 105 F. 633 (5th Cir. 1900):   66
    D. Mississippi Valley Barge Line Co. v.
    Indian Towing Co., 232 F.2d 750, 751-55 (5th Cir. 1956):   67
    E. The Joseph F. Clinton, 250 F. 977, 978-80 (2d Cir. 1918):   67

F. La Rue v. United Fruit Co., 181 F.2d 895, 896-99
(4th Cir. 1950):   69

G. Magnolia Petroleum Co. v.
Nat'l Oil Transp. Co., 286 F. 40 (5th Cir. 1923)   71

H. The Kennebec, 231 F. 423, 424-27 (5th Cir. 1916):   72

VI. Conclusion 73

PART THREE:
The End of the American Small Port:
A Prospectus on the End of Small Ports in the United States 76

I. Introduction 77

    A. Maritime Commerce Over the Last 100 years   77

        1. Panama Canal   77

        2. Containerization   79

    B. American Small Ports—"Emerging Harbors"   84

        1. The Port of Georgetown, South Carolina   84

        2. America's Small Ports and Harbors Are Suffering   86

    C. American Dredging Policy   87

        1. The Harbor Maintenance Trust Fund   88

        2. The Future Dredging of the U.S. Small Ports   94

    D. Securing funding for the American Small Port   97

        1. The Port of Charleston, SC   97

        2. The Port of Georgetown, S.C,   100

        3. Comparison   101

    E. The Need of the American Small Ports to
American Maritime Policy   102

        1. Economy of Small Town Port Communities   102

        2. Emergency   105

3. Natural Disaster 105

4. Man Made Disaster 106

5. Terrorism 107

6. National Security 108

F. Saving the American Small Port 111

1. Emergency Readiness 111

2. Port Specialization (niche) 112

3. Using the American Small Port to Refresh the Merchant Marine 113

G. Conclusion 115

PART FOUR:
Carolina Gold **118**

I. Introduction. 119

II. Current Status of Wind Energy in the United States 122

III. Who Regulates? 128

A. History 129

B. Modern Developments 130

C. State Jurisdiction 132

IV. The Coastal Zone Management Act: Reconciling Local Interests with National Priorities. 133

V. Starting the Offshore Energy Process 136

A. State Participation 138

B. Offshore Regulatory Task Force 139

V. Applicable Maritime Regulations and Laws 142

A. The US Energy Policy Act and 30 CFR § 585—"RENEWABLE ENERGY AND ALTERNATE USES OF EXISTING FACILITIES ON THE OUTER CONTINENTAL SHELF" 143

VI. More on the Mineral Management Services Alternative Energy
Regulations.. 147

VII. More than just Regulations – American Cabotage 153

    A. The Jones Act   155
    B. Other Maritime Cabotage Laws   157
    C. Waiver Authority   159

VIII. Placement matters: The United States Continental Shelf 161

    A. United Nations Convention on the Continental Shelf 165
    B. Outer Continental Shelf Lands Act Amendments   169
    C. Application of Federal Law to OCSLA Resources:
    Oil, Gas, and Minerals   172

IX. OCSLA Applied to Alternative Energy Projects............. 188

    A. OCSLA Should Not Be Forced to fit the
    Development of Wind Energy on the OCS   189

X. Other Potential Laws that may impact the Installation of
Offshore Energy 190

    A. The Migratory Bird Treaty Act   190
    B. Bald and Golden Eagle Protection Act   191
    C. The Endangered Species Act   193
    D. The National Environmental Policy Act   196
    E. The National Wildlife Refuge Systems
    Administration Act   197
    F. The National Historic Preservation Act   200

XI. The OCS and Wind Resources: Proposed Legislation:
H.R. 793 and H.R. 5156 203

XII. Conclusion 207

Acknowledgements

I acknowledge my team members at Winslow Law who give their hearts and souls to serve our clients, and I want to acknowledge our clients and community for trusting us to serve them.

PART ONE

The Conversion Non-Conversion

The Misconception of Cure's Maximum Medical Improvement

I. Introduction

In 1975, the Supreme Court spoke regarding the *maximum medical improvement* (*MMI*) defense in *Maintenance and Cure* with *Vella v. Ford Motor CO.*[1] Vella, a seaman aboard a Great Lakes vessel, slipped and fell on an oily floor plate, striking his head on an electrical box on April 4, 1968, while replacing an engine room deck plate. At his trial, on April 27, 1972, an otolaryngologist testified that the plaintiff's condition, a vestibular disorder, which damaged the balancing mechanism of the inner ear, could have been caused by the blow to the head and that it was incurable. The case came before a district court jury, which awarded the seaman *maintenance and cure* in the amount of $5,848. The ship-owner moved for a judgment notwithstanding the verdict on the ground that the award was not within the permissible scope of *maintenance and cure.* The district court denied the motion, stating that *maintenance and cure* continues until such time as the incapacity is declared to be permanent. The Court of Appeals for the Sixth Circuit reversed.[2] The Supreme Court reversed the Court of Appeals.[3]

Justice Brennan, writing for the Court, pointed to the humanity of the maritime law's *maintenance and cure* doctrine and its effect of giving the seamen a sure remedy devoid of most of the exceptions and delays, which ordinarily hamper or defeat illness and injury claims.

The Court stated:

> Denial of *maintenance and cure* when the seaman's injury, though in fact permanent immediately after the accident, is not med- ically diagnosed as permanent until long after its occurrence would obviously disserve and frustrate the "combined object of encouraging marine commerce and assuring the well-being of

---

1 Vella v. Ford Motor Co., 421 U.S. 1, 95 S. Ct. 1381, 43 L. Ed. 2d 682, 1975 A.M.C. 563 (1975).

2 Vella v. Ford Motor Co., 495 F.2d 1374, 1975 A.M.C. 81 (6th Cir. 1974), judgment rev'd, 421 U.S. 1, 95 S. Ct. 1381, 43 L. Ed. 2d 682, 1975 A.M.C. 563 (1975) and vacated in part, 519 F.2d 1403 (6th Cir. 1975); Cox v. Dravo Corp., 517 F.2d 620 (3d Cir. 1975).

3 Vella v. Ford Motor Co., 421 U.S. 1, 95 S. Ct. 1381, 43 L. Ed. 2d 682, 1975 A.M.C. 563 (1975).

seamen." A ship-owner might withhold vitally necessary *maintenance and cure* on the belief, however well or poorly founded, that the seaman's injury is permanent and incurable. Or the seaman, if paid *maintenance and cure* by the ship-owner, might be required yments if it is later determined that the injury was permanent immediately after the accident. Thus, uncertainty would displace the essential certainty of protection against the ravages of illness and injury that encourages seamen to undertake their hazardous calling. Moreover, easy and ready administration of the ship-owner's duty would seriously suffer from the introduction of complexities and uncertainty that could "stir contentions, cause delays, and invite litigations."[4]

Recently, a string of cases in federal district courts across the country have started to push the cure *MMI* yet again in favor of protecting the seaman. In July 1996, the United States District Court for the Southern District of Florida in *Costa Crociere v. Rose*,[5] circumvented the Supreme Court's permanency rule when it denied a ship-owner's request to terminate *maintenance and cure* for a seaman diagnosed with an incurable and permanent kidney disorder.[6] The issue in Costa Crociere was whether the ship-owner remained obligated to pay for the seaman's dialysis treatment or a possible organ transplant, since the seaman had reached the point of *maximum medical improvement* as defined by Vella.[7] Refusing to be restricted by the permanency confines of Vella, the Costa Crociere Court declared that a ship-owner's obligation to provide *maintenance and cure* should continue until it has been medically determined the injured or ill seaman can no longer improve his/her overall medical condition and not just the specific disease or ailments

---

4 Vella v. Ford Motor Co., 421 U.S. 1, 95 S. Ct. 1381, 43 L. Ed. 2d 682, 1975 A.M.C. 563 (1975).
5 Costa Crociere v. Rose, 939 F. Supp. 1538 (S.D. Fla. 1996).
6 Costa Crociere v. Rose, 939 F. Supp. 1538, 1558-1559 (S.D. Fla. 1996).
7 Costa Crociere v. Rose, 939 F. Supp. 1538, 1539 (S.D. Fla. 1996). The Court in Vella sought guidance from both Farrell v. United States, 336 U.S. 511 (1949) and Article IV, Paragraph I of the Ship owner's Liability Convention, Oct. 24, 1936, 54 Stat. 1696, T.S. No. 951, when it held that maintenance and cure should continue until the point the seaman's incapacity is declared to be permanent. See Vella v. Ford Motor Co., 421 U.S. 1, 5 (1975).

from which he suffers.[8] The Costa Crociere decision marked the Florida Court's first exploration of the doctrine of *maintenance and cure* in the context of an incurable, life threatening disorder.[9]

Haney v. Miller's Launch, Inc.[10] is a revolution in cure application out of the Eastern District of New York that may set forward thinking for many courts. It recognizes that the traditional view is that medical treatment solely to reduce pain and suffering does not fit within the definition of cure. This Court held that in the view of modern medicine and in terms of contemporary views of the public, pain amelioration is a part of cure and should subject the employer to provide the cost of "palliative medical attention to reduce pain, even after physical injuries have been corrected to the extent practicable."[11]

In *Mabrey v. Wizard Fisheries, Inc.*,[12] the Western District of New York held that a ship-owner is required to pay for the plaintiff's pain management treatment and ongoing mental health care as related to his shoulder injury until it is determined that the plaintiff has reached maximum medical cure for his shoulder injury. The defendant had argued that the pain management treatment is palliative and not part of its cure obligation. In rejecting the argument that the cost of palliation should be segregated and excluded, the Court relied on a statement by the First Circuit in *In re RJF Intern. Corp. for Exoneration from or Limitation of Liability*:[13] "Some segregation would be silly— imagine excluding pain medicine from the setting of a bone…."

The most difficult issue is presented where a patient has reached the maximum medical cure in the sense that his/her condition cannot be improved further, but the failure to continue to provide treatment will result in a worsening of his/her condition. Does the duty to cure include measures needed to prevent deterioration? Suppose without treatment, such as

---

8 Costa Crociere v. Rose, 939 F. Supp. 1538, 1550 (S.D. Fla. 1996).

9 Costa Crociere v. Rose, 939 F. Supp. 1538, 1549 (S.D. Fla. 1996).

10 Haney v. Miller's Launch, Inc., 773 F. Supp. 2d 280, 2011 A.M.C. 1931 (E.D.N.Y. 2010).

11 Haney v. Miller's Launch, Inc., 773 F. Supp. 2d 280, 283 2011 A.M.C. 1931 (E.D.N.Y. 2010).

12 Mabrey v. Wizard Fisheries, Inc., 2008 WL 110500 (W.D. Wash. 2008).

13 In re RJF Intern. Corp. for Exoneration from or Limitation of Liability, 354 F.3d 104, 2004 A.M.C. 355 (1st Cir. 2004).

dialysis treatment, the patient will die, but his/her condition is incurable in the sense that neither dialysis nor any other treatment will cure or improve his/her condition? If the alleviation of pain improves a patient's life, is that curative? While it may seem that cure *MMI* is a set premise, it appears that the courts may be converting to a new understanding of what *maintenance and cure* truly means.

II. Overview of the Doctrine of Maintenance and Cure

It is a longstanding rule of maritime law "that when a seaman becomes ill or suffers an injury while in the service of a vessel, he is entitled to *maintenance and cure*."[14] *Maintenance* represents the seaman's right to food and lodging, while *cure* includes the right to necessary medical expenses.[15] Both of these benefits are available to the seaman until he reaches *maximum recovery*, or *maximum cure*.[16]

A. Historical Origin

The doctrine of *maintenance and cure* derives from ancient maritime codes, such as the Laws of Oleron,[17] the Laws of Wisbuy,[18] the Law of the Hanse Towns,[19] and the Marine Ordinances of Louis XIV.[20] According to the ancient Laws of Oleron, when "sickness seizes on any one of the mariners, while in the service of the ship, the master ought to set him ashore, to provide lodging and candlelight for him, and also to spare him one of the ship-boys, or hire a woman to attend him."[21]

14Benedict on Admiralty §42, at 4-5 (Gelpi Sullivan Carrol & Gibbens P.L.C. ed., 7th ed. rev. 1997).

15 Thomas J. Schoenbaum, Admiralty and Maritime Law §6-28, at 348 (2d ed. 1994).

16 Thomas J. Schoenbaum, Admiralty and Maritime Law §6-28, at 348-49 (2d ed. 1994).

17 Laws of Oleron art. VII, reprinted in 30 F. Cas. 1171, 1174 (1897).

18 Laws of Wisbuy art. XIX, reprinted in 30 F. Cas. 1189, 1191 (1897).

19 Laws of the Hanse Towns art. XLV, reprinted in 30 F. Cas. 1197, 1200 (1897).

20 Marine Ordinances of Louis XIV tit. 4, art. XI, reprinted in 30 F. Cas. 1203, 1209 (1897).

21 Laws of Oleron art. VIII, reprinted in 30 F. Cas. at 1174.

The obligation to provide *maintenance and cure* first appeared in American maritime common law in Harden v. Gordon.[22] In Harden, Justice Story concluded that such a policy would benefit not only seamen, but ship-owners and the country as well.[23] Justice Story reasoned that the doctrine of *maintenance and cure* would increase the willingness of seamen to put to sea at low wages and at the same time strengthen the bond between seamen, their ship, and their country, while simultaneously ensuring ship-owners' interest in the welfare of their crews.[24] Regardless of the truth of his projection, it is evident that seamen have reaped a great benefit from Justice Story's decision.[25]

B. Persons Entitled to Maintenance and Cure

The right to *maintenance and cure* may be asserted by anyone classified as a Jones Act seaman.[26] The classification includes any employee who has a connection, substantial in both duration and nature, to a vessel or identifiable group of vessels in navigation.[27] The employee must also "contribute to the function of the vessel or to the accomplishment of its mission."[28] The right to qualify for *maintenance and cure* "has been granted to, among others, hairdressers, horsemen, bartenders, musicians and barbers."[29] However, to receive *maintenance and cure*, the seaman must suffer an injury or illness during the course of his/her employment.[30]

The illness or injury does not have to result from performing specific duties on the vessel as long as it occurs while the seaman is "in the service

---

22 Harden v. Gordon, 11 F. Cas. 480, 482 (C.C.D. Me. 1823) (No. 6,047).

23 Harden v. Gordon, 11 F. Cas. 480, 482 (C.C.D. Me. 1823) (No. 6,047).

24 Harden v. Gordon, 11 F. Cas. 480, 483 (C.C.D. Me. 1823) (No. 6,047).

25 Benedict on Admiralty §42, at 4-5 (Gelpi Sullivan Carrol & Gibbens P.L.C. ed., 7th ed. rev. 1997).

26 Thomas J. Schoenbaum, Admiralty and Maritime Law §6-28, at 348-49 (2d ed. 1994).

27 Chandris, Inc. v. Latsis, 515 U.S. 347, 368, 1995 AMC 1840, 1856 (1995).

28 Chandris, Inc. v. Latsis, 515 U.S. 347, 368, 1995 AMC 1840, 1856 (1995).

29 1B Benedict on Admiralty §42, at 4-5 (Gelpi Sullivan Carrol & Gibbens P.L.C. ed., 7th ed. rev. 1997).

30 1B Benedict on Admiralty §42, at 4-11 (Gelpi Sullivan Carrol & Gibbens P.L.C. ed., 7th ed. rev. 1997).

of the vessel."[31] Regardless of his/her location, a seaman is considered to be in the service of the vessel as long as he/she is answerable to the call of his/her employer.[32]

C. Duration and Extent of Benefit

The traditional rules surrounding *maintenance and cure* held that the benefit was available only until the end of the voyage or until the contract of employment terminated.[33] However, in 1938, the Supreme Court changed the rule in *Calmar Steamship Corp. v. Taylor*.[34] In Calmar, Justice Stone stated

> It is plain that in many cases these purposes [to provide for the unfortunate seaman and to induce him to accept maritime employment] will not be accomplished if the owner's duty to furnish *maintenance and cure* ends with the voyage. If the injury or illness outlasts it, the seaman may still be left helpless and uncared for in a foreign port. Even if he is returned to the home port the inducement to the owner to care for the health and safety of seaman during the voyage and the inducement to seamen to take the necessary risks of a hazardous calling will be materially lessened. The chances of their prompt restoration to a service, whose preservation is in the public interest, will be diminished if the right to *maintenance and cure* ends with the voyage.[35]

Justice Stone continued by stating that "the right to *maintenance and cure*

---

31 1B Benedict on Admiralty §42, at 4-9 (Gelpi Sullivan Carrol & Gibbens P.L.C. ed., 7th ed. rev. 1997).

32 See Macedo v. F/V Paul & Michelle, 898 F.2d 519, 520-21, 1996 AMC 1368, 1368-70 (1st Cir. 1989) (holding that a fisherman who was injured on a Sunday pleasure jaunt between trips was entitled to receive maintenance and cure because he was subject to being called in to work on Sundays).

33 Benedict on Admiralty §42, at 4-30 (Gelpi Sullivan Carrol & Gibbens P.L.C. ed., 7th ed. rev. 1997).

34 Calmar S. S. Corp. v. Taylor, 303 U.S. 525, 58 S. Ct. 651, 82 L. Ed. 993 (1938).

35 Calmar S. S. Corp. v. Taylor, 303 U.S. 525, 528-529, 58 S. Ct. 651, 82 L. Ed. 993 (1938)

[continued] for a reasonable time after the voyage…'reasonable time' being appraised with reference to the special circumstances of each case.'"[36]

Eleven years after Calmar, the United States Supreme Court revisited the issue of *maintenance and cure* in *Farrell v. United States*.[37] In Farrell, the Court stated that *maintenance and cure* payments are due to a seaman only until he reaches a maximum cure.[38] The justification for this limitation was given by Justice Jackson:

> Maintenance and cure is not the only recourse of the injured seaman. In an appropriate case he may obtain indemnity or compensation for injury due to negligence or unseaworthiness and may recover, by trial before court and jury, damages for partial or total disability. But *maintenance and cure* is more certain if more limited in its benefits. It does not hold a ship to permanent liability for a pension; neither does it give a lump-sum payment to offset disability based on some conception of expectancy of life.[39]

Thus, the duty to provide *maintenance and cure* exists until *maximum medical improvement* is reached[40] or until it is determined that the condition has been cured or that it is incurable or of a permanent character.[41] Cure, however, does not extend to alleviating symptoms of the condition—only to its actual improvement.[42] *Maintenance and cure* payments for treatments, which only arrest further progress of the disease, or are merely palliative treatments have been rejected by the courts after a seaman has reached the point of total disability.[43] However, if a seaman has been found to have reached maximum cure such that *maintenance and cure* benefits have stopped, the seaman may reassert a demand for benefits if new medical techniques become available that will improve his/her condition.[44]

---

36 Calmar S. S. Corp. v. Taylor, 303 U.S. 525, 58 S. Ct. 651, 82 L. Ed. 993 (1938)
37 Farrell v. United States, 336 U.S. 511, 515-519, 1949 AMC 613, 617 (1949).
38 Farrell v. United States, 336 U.S. 511, 515-519, 1949 AMC 613, 617 (1949).
39 Farrell v. United States, 336 U.S. 511, 515-519, 1949 AMC 613, 617 (1949).
40 Farrell v. United States, 336 U.S. 511, 515-519, 1949 AMC 613, 617 (1949).
41 Vella v. Ford Motor Co., 421 U.S. 1, 5, 1975 AMC 563, 566 (1975).
42 Cox v. Dravo Corp., 517 F.2d 620, 626 (3d Cir. 1975).
43 Cox v. Dravo Corp., 517 F.2d 620, 626 (3d Cir. 1975).
44 Cox v. Dravo Corp., 517 F.2d 620, 626 (3d Cir. 1975).

D. Defenses

An employer has four possible defenses against a claim for *maintenance and cure*. First, the employer may assert that the seaman's injury or illness is the result of engaging in willful misconduct.[45] Second, the employer may show the seaman failed to disclose a preexisting illness.[46] Third, the employer may argue that at the time of incurring the injury or illness, the seaman was not in the service of the vessel.[47] Fourth, the employer may argue that the seaman has reached maximum medical cure.[48]

1. Willful Misconduct

When illness or injury is caused solely by the willful misconduct of the seaman, regardless of when the willful misconduct occurred, the employer will escape liability for *maintenance and cure*.[49] Historically, such instances of willful misconduct have been limited to injuries or illnesses resulting from extreme drunkenness, or alcohol abuse,[50] or from the contraction of venereal disease.[51] Although intoxication was, at one time, considered willful misconduct, it can now be thought of as "a classic predisposition of sailors ashore,"[52] thus removing it from the list of activities constituting willful misconduct.[53]

---

45 Aguilar v. Standard Oil Co., 318 U.S. 724, 731, 1943 AMC 451, 457 (1943).

46 Benedict on Admiralty §42, at 4-20 (Gelpi Sullivan Carrol & Gibbens P.L.C. ed., 7th ed. rev. 1997).

47 Farrell v. United States, 336 U.S. 511, 516, 1949 AMC 613, 617 (1949).

48 1B Benedict on Admiralty §42, at 4-20 (Gelpi Sullivan Carrol & Gibbens P.L.C. ed., 7th ed. rev. 1997).

49 Thomas J. Schoenbaum, Admiralty and Maritime Law §6-28, at 348-49 (2d ed. 1994).

50 Jardins v. Foss Maritime Co., 1993 AMC 2233, 2239 (W.D. Wash. 1993) (denying seaman maintenance and cure for illness developed solely as a result of his alcohol abuse); see also Aguilar, 318 U.S. at 731, 1943 AMC at 457 (citing Barlow v. Pan Atlantic S.S. Corp., 101 F.2d 697 (2d Cir. 1939); S/S Berwindglen v. Hooten, 88 F.2d 125 (1st Cir. 1937); Lortie v. American-Hawaiian S.S. Co., 28 F.2d 819 (9th Cir. 1935); Oliver v. Calmar S.S. Co., 33 F. Supp. 356 (E.D. Pa. 1940)).

51 Aguilar v. Standard Oil Co., 318 U.S. 724, 731, 1943 AMC 451, 457 (1943).

52 Aguilar v. Standard Oil Co., 318 U.S. 724, 731, 1943 AMC 451, 457 (1943).

53 Aguilar v. Standard Oil Co., 318 U.S. 724, 731, 1943 AMC 451, 457 (1943).

However, intoxication can still arise as willful misconduct if an element of willfulness is shown.[54]

Even though a valid argument can be made that contraction of a venereal disease is analogous to intoxication in that it springs from classical predisposition of sailors ashore, no court has ever allowed *maintenance and cure* for such an illness.[55] Justice Rutledge, in Aguilar v. Standard Oil Co.,[56] pronounced that "[o]nly some wilful misbehavior or deliberate act of indiscretion suffices to deprive the seaman of his protection . . . . [One of] [t]he traditional instances [is] venereal disease."[57] Justice Rutledge's position still stands as the final word on the subject.

2. Failure to Disclose Preexisting Illness

If a seaman knowingly conceals an illness or injury when entering the employment of a vessel, "he may be denied *maintenance and cure* if the malady becomes aggravated during the course of the voyage."[58] However, the rule does not apply "if the seaman had a latent physical defect and was without reasonable grounds to anticipate a manifestation of its disabling effect [while in the service of the ship]."[59]

3. In the Service of the Ship

A seaman asserting a claim for *maintenance and cure* must prove the injury arose or the illness manifested itself during the seaman's service of the ship.[60] If an injury or illness arises or manifests prior to employment or at a time when the seaman is not subject to the call of the ship, the employer has no duty to provide *maintenance and cure*.[61]

---

54 Quaker City v. United States, 1 F. Supp. 840, 843 (E.D. Pa. 1931)).
55 Quaker City v. United States, 1 F. Supp. 840, 843 (E.D. Pa. 1931)).
56 Aguilar v. Standard Oil Co., 318 U.S. 724, 1943 AMC 451, 457 (1943).
57 Aguilar v. Standard Oil Co., 318 U.S. 724, 731, 1943 AMC 451, 457 (1943).
58 Benedict on Admiralty §46, at 4-20 (Gelpi Sullivan Carrol & Gibbens P.L.C. ed., 7th ed. rev. 1997).
59 Benedict on Admiralty §42, (Gelpi Sullivan Carrol & Gibbens P.L.C. ed., 7th ed. rev. 1997).
60 Farrell v. United States, 336 U.S. 511, 516, 1949 AMC 613, 617 (1949).
61 Thomas J. Schoenbaum, Admiralty and Maritime Law §6-31, at 355 (2d ed. 1994).

4. Maximum Medical Cure

An employer's duty to provide *maintenance and cure* does not extend indefinitely.[62] When the injury or illness is diagnosed as incurable, regardless of whether the injured seaman will need to continue with periodic examinations and treatments for life, the employer's duty to provide *maintenance and cure* ends.[63]

As a defense, *maximum medical improvement* rests upon the definition imposed by an expert physician in the determination of whether the seaman can medically improve or further treatment is purely palliative. Many times the levels/types of care are intertwined and what that maximum level is could be difficult to determine.

III. Maximum Medical Improvement

The defense of *maximum medical improvement* will be used by nearly every employer once the seaman has established his/her right to *maintenance and cure*. The *maximum medical improvement* will cut off the payment of cure; however, the burden of proof shifts to the ship-owner to demonstrate that the seaman has reached the point of *maximum medical improvement*.[64] *Maximum medical improvement* is a medical determination, not a legal one;[65] and, as a matter of procedure, the rule requires the ship-owner to seek a declaration stating the seaman has reached the point of maximum medical cure from the seaman's treating physician.[66] The ship-owner must then file an action under the Declaratory Judgment Act[67] to determine whether he can terminate the seaman's benefits.[68]

---

62 Farrell v. United States, 336 U.S. 511, 515, 1949 AMC 613, 617 (1949).

63 Lindgren v. Shepard S.S. Co., 108 F.2d 806, 807, 1940 AMC 741, 743 (2d Cir. 1940).

64 Costa Crociere v. Rose, 939 F. Supp. 1538, 1548 (S.D. Fla. 1996).

65 Breese v. AWI, Inc., 823 F.2d 100, 104-05 (1987). See also, Tullos v. Resource Drilling Inc., 750 F.2d 380, 388 (5th Cir. 1985) (emphasizing the termination of a seaman's right to maintenance and cure should be based on an unequivocal medical determination).

66 Thomas J. Schoenbaum, Admiralty and Maritime Law, n.9, at 307 (2d ed. 1994). (citing Gillikin v. United States, 764 F. Supp. 261, 268 (E.D. N.Y. 1991)).

67 28 U.S.C. § 2201 (1994).

68 Lancaster Towing, Inc. v. Davis, 681 F. Supp. 387, 388 (N.D. Miss. 1988).

A. Paving the Road from Reed to Vella

Throughout history, courts have adopted various formulations of *maximum medical improvement*.[69] In 1832, the Circuit Court for the District of Massachusetts in *Reed v. Canfield*[70] established the majority rule, which lasted more than a century. In Reed, a seaman suffered frostbite while rowing to shore from the defendant's ship.[71] In determining when the obligation to provide *maintenance and cure* should cease, the Court declared in dicta[72] that the ship-owner was "liable only for expenses necessarily incurred for the cure; and when the cure is completed, at least so far as the ordinary medical means extend, the ship-owners are freed from all further liability."[73] The decision in Reed, however, was not universally recognized.[74] Other courts held that a ship-owner's duty to provide *maintenance and cure* extended no longer than the seaman's right to wages under his/her employment contract.[75]

In 1938, the United States Supreme Court in *Calmar S.S. Corp. v. Taylor*[76] temporarily resolved this debate by declaring *maintenance and cure* should continue for a "fair time" after the voyage.[77] The seaman in Calmar was

---

69 Costa Crociere v. Rose, 939 F. Supp. 1538, 1548 (S.D. Fla. 1996).

70 Reed v. Canfield, 20 F. Cas. 426 (C.C. Mass. 1832) (No. 11, 641). While attempting to delineate the extent of the ship owner's obligation, Justice Story wrote: 'The sickness or other injury may occasion a temporary or permanent disability; but that is not a ground for indemnity from the ship-owners. They are liable only for expenses necessarily incurred for the cure; and when the cure is completed, at least so far as the ordinary medical means extend, the ship-owners are freed from all further liability...'.

71 Reed v. Canfield, 20 F. Cas. 426 (C.C. Mass. 1832) (No. 11, 641).

72 Reed v. Canfield, 20 F. Cas. 426 (C.C. Mass. 1832) (No. 11, 641). The main issue in Reed was whether the ship-owner was obligated to provide the seaman maintenance and cure since he did not injure himself during the actual voyage and the vessel was not abroad. The fact the voyage had ended and the vessel was anchored in port did not preclude the seaman from claiming maintenance and cure.

73 Reed v. Canfield, 20 F. Cas. 426, 429 (C.C. Mass. 1832) (No. 11, 641).

74 William H. Welte, Maintenance and Cure: The Third Count of The Seaman's Complaint, 7 Suffolk Transnat'l L.J., 1, 40, n. 71 (1983).

75 Atlantic, 2 F. Cas. 121, 132 (S.D. N.Y. 1849) (No. 620) (holding that an injured seaman had no claim against ship-owner once the obligation to pay the seaman's wages terminated); Nevitt v. Clarke, 18 F. Cas. 29, 32 (S.D. N.Y. 1846) (No. 10, 138) (holding that a seaman's right to maintenance and cure is concurrent with his right to wages).

76 Calmar S. S. Corp. v. Taylor, 303 U.S. 525, 58 S. Ct. 651, 82 L. Ed. 993 (1938)

77 Calmar S. S. Corp. v. Taylor, 303 U.S. 525, 531, 58 S. Ct. 651, 82 L. Ed. 993 (1938)

diagnosed with Buerger's Disease, an incurable and fatal disease affecting the veins and arteries.[78] Faced with the issue of whether the ship-owner was obligated to provide a lump sum payment to finance the seaman's medical treatment for the remainder of his life, the Court determined "the award of a lump sum in anticipation of the continuing need of *maintenance and cure* for life or an indefinite period is without support in judicial decision."[79] The Court reasoned that lump sum payments were difficult to calculate; and, in the case of Buerger's disease, such determinations could not be measured by reference to mortality tables.[80] The Court also cautioned that an improvident seaman might be induced to spend his/her award on things unrelated to medical care;[81]and the Court concluded, "we can find no basis for saying that, if the disease proves to be incurable, the duty extends beyond a fair time after the voyage in which to effect an improvement in the seaman's condition as reasonably may be expected to result from nursing, care, and medical treatment."[82]

While the Supreme Court in Calmar attempted to clarify the ambiguities "concerning the duration of a ship-owner's obligation to provide *maintenance and cure*, the Court's use of such words as fair and reasonable still failed to provide a definitive solution to the problem."[83] In 1949, however, the Supreme Court clarified the duration issue in *Farrell v. United States*[84] where a seaman suffered both total and permanent blindness and post-traumatic epileptic convulsions after falling into a dry-dock.[85] Confronted with the inevitable consequence of the seaman requiring medication to ease headaches and epileptic convulsions for the remainder of his life, the Court upheld the lower Court's determination that "the duty of a ship-owner to furnish *maintenance and cure* does not extend beyond the time when the maximum cure possible

---

78 Calmar S. S. Corp. v. Taylor, 303 U.S. 525, 526, 58 S. Ct. 651, 82 L. Ed. 993 (1938)
79 Calmar S. S. Corp. v. Taylor, 303 U.S. 525, 530, 58 S. Ct. 651, 82 L. Ed. 993 (1938)
80 Calmar S. S. Corp. v. Taylor, 303 U.S. 525, 531, 58 S. Ct. 651, 82 L. Ed. 993 (1938)
81 Calmar S. S. Corp. v. Taylor, 303 U.S. 525, 531, 58 S. Ct. 651, 82 L. Ed. 993 (1938)
82 Calmar S. S. Corp. v. Taylor, 303 U.S. 525, 531, 58 S. Ct. 651, 82 L. Ed. 993 (1938)
83 William H. Welte, Maintenance and Cure: The Third Count of The Seaman's Complaint, 7 Suffolk Transnat'l L.J., 1, 40, 43 (1983).
84 Farrell v. United States, 336 U.S. 511 (1949).
85 Farrell v. United States, 336 U.S. 511, 512-513 (1949).

has been effected."[86] On reaching its decision, the Court relied on Article IV of the Ship-owner's Liability Convention,[87] limiting a ship-owner's liability to the time at which the ill or injured seaman has been cured or until his disease or injury is declared permanent.[88]

Article IV of the Ship-owner's Liability Convention was not the only factor considered by the Court in Farrell. In addition, the Court also reasoned that *maintenance and cure* was intended to provide only limited benefits to the seaman,[89] and "does not hold a ship[owner] to permanent liability for a pension; neither does it give a lump sum payment to offset disability based on some conception of life expectancy."[90]

The Court emphasized that *maintenance and cure* was not the only recourse available to the injured seaman.[91] Under the appropriate circumstances, the Court suggested, a seaman could obtain indemnity or compensation for his/her injuries through the Jones Act or on a claim for unseaworthiness.[92] Consequently, the Farrell Court denied the injured seaman's claim for future benefits even though it recognized that he/she would require treatment for the remainder of his/her life.[93]

Finally, as previously discussed, in 1975, the Supreme Court in *Vella v. Ford Motor Co.*[94] reaffirmed Farrell and examined how best to determine the point of *maximum medical improvement*.[95] The Vella Court considered how to determine the point of *maximum medical improvement*.[96] Concerned that a ship-owner might withhold needed benefits based on the mistaken belief

---

86 Farrell v. United States, 336 U.S. 511, 512-513 (1949).

87 Article IV, Paragraph I of the Ship-owner's Liability Convention, Oct. 24, 1936, 54 Stat. 1696, T.S. No. 951, when it held that maintenance and cure should continue until the point the seaman's incapacity is declared to be permanent. See Vella v. Ford Motor Co., 421 U.S. 1, 5 (1975).

88 William H. Welte, Maintenance and Cure: The Third Count of The Seaman's Complaint, 7 Suffolk Transnat'l L.J., 1, 40, 44 (1983).

89 Farrell v. United States, 336 U.S. 511, 519 (1949).

90 Farrell v. United States, 336 U.S. 511, 519 (1949).

91 Farrell v. United States, 336 U.S. 511, 519 (1949).

92 Farrell v. United States, 336 U.S. 511, 519 (1949).

93 Farrell v. United States, 336 U.S. 511, 519 (1949).

94 Vella v. Ford Motor Co., 421 U.S. 1 (1975).

95 Vella v. Ford Motor Co., 421 U.S. 1, 4(1975).

96 Vella v. Ford Motor Co., 421 U.S. 1, 2 (1975).

the seaman had reached maximum cure when, in fact, the seaman was still susceptible to curative treatment, the Court suggested *maximum medical improvement* should be determined pursuant to a medical diagnosis of permanency.[97] The Court reasoned a ship-owner's denial of *maintenance and cure,* when the seaman's injury though permanent at the time of the accident, "is not medically diagnosed as permanent until long after its occurrence, would obviously disserve and frustrate the combined object of encouraging marine commerce and assuring the well-being of seamen."[98]

Currently, the United States Supreme Court stands for the proposition that a ship-owner's duty to provide *maintenance and cure* terminates once the seaman's condition is either cured or diagnosed as permanent.[99] Lower court application of the permanency standard has proven somewhat difficult, especially since injuries and ailments are often distinct and susceptible to different forms of treatment.[100] Lower courts, which are often confronted with this type of situation, have found it necessary to evaluate each case on a fact-specific basis.[101] Consequently, while the line of cases extending from Reed to Vella may have paved the road to require a diagnosis of permanency in *maximum medical improvement* determinations, lower court application of the permanency rule has clearly created a minor revolution of cure.

IV. Survey of the Federal Circuit Courts of Appeal

First Circuit

The most recent first circuit case is *Whitman v. Miles,* decided in 2004.[102] On July 17, 2000, while working as a cook on a Miles' ship, the *S/V Timberland,* Whitman had to be driven to a hospital after falling several times on the ship, burning herself while cooking, and experiencing other symptoms including fatigue, cold, numbness, and incontinence.[103] Following an MRI, Whitman

---

97 Vella v. Ford Motor Co., 421 U.S. 1, 5 (1975).
98 Vella v. Ford Motor Co., 421 U.S. 1, 5 (1975).
99 Vella v. Ford Motor Co., 421 U.S. 1, 4 (1975).
100 Costa Crociere v. Rose, 939 F. Supp. 1538, 1549 (S.D. Fla. 1996).
101 Costa Crociere v. Rose, 939 F. Supp. 1538, 1549 (S.D. Fla. 1996).
102 Whitman v. Miles, 387 F.3d 68 (1st Cir. 2004).
103 Whitman v. Miles, 387 F.3d 68, 70 (1st Cir. 2004).

was diagnosed with multiple sclerosis (*MS*), an autoimmune disease that causes a person's immune system to attack healthy tissue in the body.[104] Testimony revealed that treatment would, at best, slow or arrest the progression of her *MS* but would not reverse her symptoms or improve her condition beyond the point of maximum medical recovery.[105]

Whitman further argued that her depression was a distinct ailment from her *MS*, giving rise to its own claim for *maintenance and cure*; however, the Court ruled that she had failed to produce any evidence that she began to suffer from depression while in the service of the ship, an element on which she would have the burden of proof at trial.[106] Further, the alternative argument that Whitman's depression is a symptom of her *MS* would not alter her eligibility for *maintenance and cure* as then it would not be a curative treatment.[107]

The Court concluded that palliative treatment or curative treatment for subsequent manifesting illnesses is not covered.[108] Further, the Court deemed that a physician does not have to use the magic words *permanent* or *incapable of being improved* to terminate cure in a diagnosis for a disease that is clearly incurable.[109]

Second Circuit

Messier, a career tugboat seaman, was assigned to work on a Bouchard vessel called the tug Evening Mist.[110] The plaintiff claimed that on the evening of October 23, 2005, while in service, he fell climbing down a ladder and suffered back pain.[111] He sought medical care and was diagnosed with a *probable back sprain*.[112] Messier's back injury was apparently minor, and the pain

---

104 Whitman v. Miles, 387 F.3d 68, 71 (1st Cir. 2004).
105 Whitman v. Miles, 387 F.3d 68, 71 (1st Cir. 2004).
106Whitman v. Miles, 387 F.3d 68, 74 (1st Cir. 2004).
107 Whitman v. Miles, 387 F.3d 68, 75 (1st Cir. 2004).
108 Whitman v. Miles, 387 F.3d 68, 75 (1st Cir. 2004).
109 Whitman v. Miles, 387 F.3d 68, 75 (1st Cir. 2004).
110 Messier v. Bouchard Transp., 688 F.3d 78, 80 (2d Cir. 2012), as amended (Aug. 15, 2012), cert. denied, 133 S. Ct. 1586, 185 L. Ed. 2d 578 (U.S. 2013).
111 Messier v. Bouchard Transp., 688 F.3d 78, 80 (2d Cir. 2012), as amended (Aug. 15, 2012), cert. denied, 133 S. Ct. 1586, 185 L. Ed. 2d 578 (U.S. 2013).
112 Messier v. Bouchard Transp., 688 F.3d 78, 81 (2d Cir. 2012), as amended (Aug. 15, 2012), cert. denied, 133 S. Ct. 1586, 185 L. Ed. 2d 578 (U.S. 2013).

associated with it quickly subsided. But the resulting medical examinations revealed B-cell lymphoma.[113]

The Court found that the obligation to provide *maintenance and cure* does not furnish the seaman with a source of lifetime or long-term disability income.[114] As a seaman is entitled to *maintenance and cure* only until he/she reaches maximum medical recovery.[115] Put another way, *maintenance and cure* continues until such time as the incapacity is declared to be permanent. However, where a seaman has reached the point of maximum medical cure and *maintenance and cure* payments have been discontinued, the seaman may, nonetheless, reinstitute a demand for *maintenance and cure* where subsequent new curative medical treatments become available."

As the Court of Appeals for the Second Circuit appears not to have specifically ruled on whether payments to relieve pain and suffering are appropriate under the *maintenance and cure* doctrine, a lower district court took up the torch in the previously described *Haney v. Miller's Launch, Inc.* What follows is the verbatim dictum from the Court resulting in its revolutionary decision.

> On occasion courts in this circuit have held that a sailor was entitled to curative, but not palliative treatment for pain. Those decisions rely on precedent that is somewhat ambiguous on the issue. *See, e.g., McMillan,* 885 F.Supp. at 461 ("The rule of law which must be applied in this Circuit dictates that as long as the seaman's condition is susceptible to curative as opposed to palliative treatment, the ship-owner is liable for *maintenance and cure.*") (citing *Berke v. Lehigh Marine Disposal Corp.,* 435 F.2d 1073, 1076 (2d Cir.1970)); *Desmond v. United States,* 217 F.2d 948, 950 (2d Cir.1954), *cert. denied,* 349 U.S. 911, 75 S.Ct. 600, 99 L.Ed. 1246 (1955); *Vella v. Ford Motor Corp.,* 421 U.S. at n. 4, 95

---

113 Messier v. Bouchard Transp., 688 F.3d 78, 82 (2d Cir. 2012), as amended (Aug. 15, 2012), cert. denied, 133 S. Ct. 1586, 185 L. Ed. 2d 578 (U.S. 2013).
114 Messier v. Bouchard Transp., 688 F.3d 78, 83 (2d Cir. 2012), as amended (Aug. 15, 2012), cert. denied, 133 S. Ct. 1586, 185 L. Ed. 2d 578 (U.S. 2013).
115 Messier v. Bouchard Transp., 688 F.3d 78, 83 (2d Cir. 2012), as amended (Aug. 15, 2012), cert. denied, 133 S. Ct. 1586, 185 L. Ed. 2d 578 (U.S. 2013).

S.Ct. 1381; *Nasser,* 191 F.Supp.2d at 317 (allowing payment for "all reasonable medical curative (i.e. not palliative) expenses incurred", citing *McMillan, supra,* at 461).

The Supreme Court has not squarely addressed the issue of whether "cure" encompasses palliative care. In *Vella* the Court held that a ship-owner's duty to provide *maintenance and cure* ends when medical diagnosis is made that the seaman's injury was permanent and incurable. 421 U.S. at 5–6, 95 S.Ct. 1381. It expressly reserved decision on the issue of payment for pain and suffering. "[I]t is not necessary to address the question whether the jury award might also be sustained on the ground that the ship owner's duty in any event obliged him to provide palliative medical care to arrest further progress of the condition or to reduce pain, and we intimate no view whatever upon the ship owner's duty in that regard." *Id.* at 6, n. 4, 95 S.Ct. 1381; *see also Farrell v. United States,* 336 U.S. 511, 69 S.Ct. 707, 93 L.Ed. 850 (1949) (permanently disabled seaman not entitled to *maintenance and cure* payments after his condition was diagnosed as hopeless).

In *Berke,* the Court of Appeals for the Second Circuit held that treatment for aggravated bronchitis was not part of the vessel owner's "cure" obligation because it would only "relieve the symptoms but would not permanently improve the condition." 435 F.2d at 476. Though it considered and rejected the Third Circuit's now overruled position that "cure" covers payments for pain relief, *see id.* n. 3, the Court of Appeals for the Second Circuit issued no specific holding regarding the validity of payments for pain and suffering.

Maintenance and cure, on the grounds that a condition was incurable, were denied in *Desmond,* 217 F.2d at 950 ("If incurable, the ship-owner has no further liability, whether or not the patient requires additional treatment to restrain degeneracy or relieve pain."); *see also Lindgren v. Shepard S.S. Co.,* 108 F.2d 806, 807 (2d Cir.1940) (reversing judgment for *maintenance and cure* since treatments to prevent relapse do not "effectuate further cure"); *Muruaga v. United States,* 172 F.2d 318, 321 (2d Cir.1949) (reversing a judgment for *maintenance and cure* to a victim of an incurable cardiovascular disease because treatment has provided "all the improvement to be expected in an incurable disease").

Apparently in the Second Circuit where a defendant's negligence aggravates a plaintiff's preexisting condition (causing plaintiff to experience new pain); defendant is liable in full for the treatment of the resulting pain. *See Milos v. Sea–Land Serv. Inc.,* 478 F.Supp. 1019, 1023 (S.D.N.Y.1979), *aff'd without op.,* 622 F.2d 574 (2d Cir.1980).

Courts in other circuits have held that treatment to relieve pain is "palliative" and does not support *maintenance and cure* payments since reduction of pain or its intensity does not affect the underlying medical problem. *See, e.g., Whitman v. Miles,* 387 F.3d 68 (1st Cir.2004) ("[T]reatment that is more than simply palliative, and would improve [the seaman's] medical condition ... is enough to support an award of *maintenance and cure* in aid of permanent improvement short of a complete cure. (internal quotations and citation omitted)"); *Cox v. Dravo Corp.,* 517 F.2d 620, 627 (3d Cir.1975) (overruling *Neff v. Dravo Corp.,* 407 F.2d 228 (3d Cir.1969)) (vessel and cargo owner are not required to insure against the cost of palliative or preventive care); *Stanovich v. Jurlin,* 227 F.2d 245, 246 (9th Cir.1955) (holding "palliative" is not covered by* meaning of "cure" since it is defined as "to ease without curing"); *Lopinto v. Crescent Marine Towing,* No. Civ.A. 02–2983, 2004 WL 1737901, 2004 U.S. Dist. Lexis 13405 (E.D.La. Aug. 2, 2004); *Sefcik v. Ocean Pride Alaska,* 844 F.Supp. 1372, 1373 (D.Alaska 1993) ("A vessel owner must only pay for curative, as opposed to palliative, medical treatment.");

see also, e.g., Robert Force, *Admiralty and Maritime Law* 90 (Fed. Jud. Center 2004) (citing *Farrell v. United States,* 336 U.S. 511, 69 S.Ct. 707, 93 L.Ed. 850 (1949), for the proposition that "an employer has no obligation to provide maintenance and cure payments for palliative treatments that arrest further progress of the condition or relieve pain once the seaman has reached the point of total disability"); Grant Gilmore & Charles L. Black, Jr., *The Law of Admiralty* 299 n. 52b (2d ed. 1975) (" 'Cure' in the phrase '*maintenance and cure*' originally meant 'care.' One of the odd by-products of the Farrell case is that the meaning of 'cure' has now shifted to that of recovery from disease or injury."). Gilmore and Grant explain that *Farrell* does not create, any time limit on the duration of the ship owner's liability, so long as there is a chance of improvement in the claimant's condition. The majority opinion in Farrell seems to take the position that 'cure' means improvement, or the possibility of improvement, and that Farrell could not recover medical expenses necessary to maintain him in his present condition without further deterioration. *Id.* at 299.

Current general medical practice raises doubts about these hoary limitations on medical treatment to alleviate the kind of persistent pain and suffering Haney is allegedly experiencing. New theories on medical treatment for pain relief, and an evolving sense of the importance to doctors and patients of well-being and quality of life issues, include pain management. Palliative care is now encompassed in the notion of recovery and maximum improvement. The medical profession has a specialty for pain medicine and an association dedicated to fostering advocacy, research and training in the field. *See* American Academy of Pain Medicine ("AAPM") (representing physicians practicing in pain medicine). The AAPM notes that "[t]he practice of pain medicine is multi-disciplinary in approach, incorporating modalities from various specialties to ensure the comprehensive evaluation and treatment of the pain patient." *See* AAPM, Mission Statement, *available at* http://www.painmed.org/ (last visited Nov. 15, 2010) (indicating that pain medicine crosses numerous fields including anesthesiology, internal medicine, neurology, neurological surgery, orthopedic surgery, physiatry (rehabilitation physicians who treat nerve, muscle, and bone injuries), and psychiatry). Physicians note that "[p]ain is one of the most common reasons people seek medical care." Richard M. Mularski et. al., *Measuring Pain as the 5th Vital Sign Does Not Improve Quality of Pain Management,* 21 J. of Gen. Internal Med. 607, 607 (2006) ("[C]hronic pain has been estimated to be under treated in up to 80% of patients in some settings."). "Uncontrolled pain not only results in unnecessary suffering, but compromises the care of underlying diseases and can lead to depression, decreased enjoyment of life, and less productivity." *Id.*

When a patient is assessed for treatment at a medical facility it is now standard practice to measure the individual's pain along with his temperature, pulse, respirations and blood pressure. *See* Veterans Health Admin., *Directive 2009–053: Pain Management, available at* http://www1.va.gov/PAINMANAGEMENT/docs/ VHA09PainDirective.pdf (last visited Nov. 15, 2010) (discussing "Pain as a Fifth Vital Sign" initiative); *see also* Mularski et al., *supra,* at 611 ("Additional interventions are needed to improve providers [sic] awareness of patients' pain and to increase the rates at which they provide appropriate therapy."). *See also, e.g.,* American Academy of Pain Management, *Assessing and Treating Low Back Pain An Interview with Bruce Nicholson M.D.,* 15 The Pain Practitioner 3, 17–21 (Fall 2005) (discussing numerous treatment options for back pain including medical, surgical and other non-invasive therapies); Sepulveda et. al., Palliative Care: The World Health Organization's Global Perspective, 24 J. of Pain and Symptom Mgmt. 2 (Aug. 2002) (discussing importance of developing palliative care systems to improve quality of life of sick and injured); Pub. L. No. 106–386 (Oct. 28, 2001) (declaring the calendar decade beginning in January 1, 2001 the Decade of Pain Control and Research).

One problem with compensation for pain is that so much of it is subjective and incapable of a precise objective evaluation. *See, e.g.,* Marcia L. Meldrum, *A Capsule History of Pain Management,* 290 J. of the Am. Med. Assoc. No. 18, Nov. 12, 2003 at 2470 (2003) ("Pain is a complex clinical problem. Assessment depends on verbal report, and the patient's physical perceptions may be modified by cognitive and affective factors.").

The cost of maritime insurance may possibly be increased by a change of law to include pain alleviation in "cure." The same issue exists with respect to compensation for injuries and tort law generally. There appears no reason why adequate control against excessive recoveries cannot be provided in admiralty cases.

Whether pain is included in medical treatment may be a question of fact for the jury. It is time to reconsider the old rule, now out of the main stream of medical practice. In any event, the probable need for further surgery suggests that in the instant case treatment may not have been completed even in its traditional sense."[116]

Haney v. Miller's Launch, Inc. may turn out to be the case that forces action to occur on the conversion of the mentality that palliative care is not curative. As discussed, the care of a patient is often intertwined and not easily separated. If the Court allows an employer to classify medical care and defund the treatment plan, the implications may result in a disastrous regression of the patient's ultimate maximum cure potential.

---

116 Haney v. Miller's Launch, Inc., 773 F. Supp. 2d 280, 283-94 (E.D.N.Y. 2010).

Third Circuit

Plaintiff William O'Connell was employed as a merchant seaman aboard the M/V Gopher State, a vessel owned by the United States Maritime Administration (*MARAD*) and operated by defendant Interoceanic Management Corporation (*IOMC*), as an agent for the United States.[117] On July 19, 1991, onboard the Gopher State, O'Connell accidentally severed the tendon in his left little finger while operating a grinding wheel.[118] Despite two surgical procedures and a skin graft, O'Connell will never regain full use of his little finger, which is permanently deformed.[119]

The Court did not enter into the discussion of what is the role of palliative; however, they did rule that an employer's obligation to furnish *maintenance and cure* continues "until the seaman has reached the point of maximum cure, that is until the seaman is cured or his/her condition is diagnosed as permanent and incurable."[120]

Fourth Circuit

On August 13, 2008, the Asian Spirit was navigating in the Chesapeake Bay en route to the Port of Baltimore where it was scheduled to load a cargo of motor vehicles.[121] Plaintiff Aggarao was working to raise floor panels in the ship in preparation for receipt of the cargo load.[122] As the crew began raising the floor panels, Aggarao was crushed between a deck-lifting machine and a pillar.[123]

While the Court does not address *MMI* within the dicta of its order, they do note it in the footnotes. They cite the general maritime law in stating that a seaman's fitness for repatriation is not determinative of his/her right to *maintenance and cure*; rather, the obligation to provide *maintenance and cure* persists until he/she *attains* maximum cure, defined as the point at which he/she is either cured or his/her condition is diagnosed as permanent and

---

117 O'Connell v. Interoceanic Mgmt. Corp., 90 F.3d 82, 83 (3d Cir. 1996).
118 O'Connell v. Interoceanic Mgmt. Corp., 90 F.3d 82, 83 (3d Cir. 1996).
119 O'Connell v. Interoceanic Mgmt. Corp., 90 F.3d 82, 83 (3d Cir. 1996).
120 O'Connell v. Interoceanic Mgmt. Corp., 90 F.3d 82, 84 (3d Cir. 1996).
121 Aggarao v. MOL Ship Mgmt. Co., Ltd., 675 F.3d 355, 378 (4th Cir. 2012).
122 Aggarao v. MOL Ship Mgmt. Co., Ltd., 675 F.3d 355, 378 (4th Cir. 2012).
123 Aggarao v. MOL Ship Mgmt. Co., Ltd., 675 F.3d 355, 378 (4th Cir. 2012).

incurable.[124] Interestingly, the Court went on to say that even in cases of permanent disability, *maintenance and cure* is required where palliative care would improve the seaman's condition.[125]

Fifth Circuit

Plaintiff Alario alleges that, while employed as a cook by OSV aboard the C–ESCORT, she fell and hit her arm and shoulder, leading to arm, neck, and shoulder pain.[126] She received orthopedic treatment for these injuries, including surgery and physical therapy, but continued to complain of pain.[127]

The Court declared that maximum cure is achieved when it appears probable that further treatment will result in no betterment of the seaman's condition, a determination that would be appropriate if the seaman's injury is incurable, or future treatment would merely relieve pain and suffering but not otherwise improve the seaman's physical condition.[128] Palliative treatment alone is insufficient to demonstrate an entitlement to continued *maintenance and cure.*[129]

Sixth Circuit

Plaintiff alleged that while he was handling the tow lines and traversing the deck of the tug *Louisiana*, he slipped and fell because an area of the deck did not have adequate not skid material causing Plaintiff to suffer serious and permanent disabling injuries to his lower back with radiculopathy into his lower extremities.[130]

In the decision, it was stated that the employer of an injured seaman must continue to pay *maintenance and cure* until the seaman reaches *MMI.*[131] *MMI* can be reached in three ways: a seaman may fully recover from his/her injuries, his/her injuries have been diagnosed as permanent, and/or the injured seaman has not fully recovered, but his/her functional ability

124 Aggarao v. MOL Ship Mgmt. Co., Ltd., 675 F.3d 355, 378, fn.24 (4th Cir. 2012).
125 Aggarao v. MOL Ship Mgmt. Co., Ltd., 675 F.3d 355, 378, fn. 24 (4th, Cir. 2012).
126 Alario v. Offshore Serv. Vessels, L.L.C., 477 F. App'x 186, 187 (5th Cir. 2012).
127 Alario v. Offshore Serv. Vessels, L.L.C., 477 F. App'x 186, 187 (5th Cir. 2012).
128 Alario v. Offshore Serv. Vessels, L.L.C., 477 F. App'x 186, 188 (5th Cir. 2012).
129 Alario v. Offshore Serv. Vessels, L.L.C., 477 F. App'x 186, 188 (5th Cir. 2012).
130 Nicholson v. Great Lakes Towing Co., 07-11134, 2008 WL 3200025 (E.D. Mich. Aug. 6, 2008).
131 Nicholson v. Great Lakes Towing Co., 07-11134, 2008 WL 3200025 (E.D. Mich. Aug. 6, 2008).

cannot be improved.[132] The Court clarified that if future treatment will merely relieve pain and suffering but not otherwise improve the seaman's physical condition, it is proper to declare that the point of maximum cure has been achieved; however, that is a medical and not judicial determination of permanency that terminates a right to *maintenance and cure*.[133]

The Court held that even in the case of a diagnosis of permanent impairment, when further treatment beyond that which is merely palliative can result in a permanent improvement short of a complete cure, this is enough to support an award of *maintenance and cure*.[134] Thus, a classification of palliative care is covered—care that is palliative but leads to partial cure. It appears that the Court is converging palliative and curative into a single system of medical care. Unfortunately, there is not a Six Circuit Appeals Decision on the topic.

Seventh Circuit

The District Court found in a summary judgment hearing that a plaintiff was entitled to cure because the medical treatment is clearly related to the work injury and aimed at resolving pain at the injury site so that the soft tissue has an opportunity to relax and heal.[135] Yet, the Court also cited law, which held that where it appears that the seaman's condition is incurable or that future treatment will merely relieve pain and suffering but not otherwise improve the seaman's physical condition, it is proper to declare that the point of maximum cure has been achieved.[136]

There were doctor reports and testimony that the nerve block treatments given to Plaintiff did not serve to relax the soft tissue, but instead merely served to help the pain and facilitate the rehabilitation; thus, the patient

---

132 Nicholson v. Great Lakes Towing Co., 07-11134, 2008 WL 3200025 (E.D. Mich. Aug. 6, 2008).

133 Nicholson v. Great Lakes Towing Co., 07-11134, 2008 WL 3200025 (E.D. Mich. Aug. 6, 2008).

134 Nicholson v. Great Lakes Towing Co., 07-11134, 2008 WL 3200025 (E.D. Mich. Aug. 6, 2008).

135 Frost v. Teco Barge Line, Inc., 04-CV-752 DRH, 2007 WL 178562 (S.D. Ill. Jan. 22, 2007).

136 Frost v. Teco Barge Line, Inc., 04-CV-752 DRH, 2007 WL 178562 (S.D. Ill. Jan. 22, 2007).

had reached *MMI*.[137] However, that very same expert did testify that the described palliative care caused functional improvement and improvement in her pain. He also testified that continued treatment would likely lead to increased improvement of Plaintiff's condition.[138]

The Court found that treatment appeared to continue to improve Plaintiff's condition and thus, she had not reached her *maximum medical improvement*. It is clear that this Court determined that palliative care served a dual role as both pain relief and function improvement. It did not cure the underlying condition, but it improved the symptoms. There has been no appeal to further clarify this position.

In a recent District Court case from the Sixth District, the plaintiff cited headaches and a wrist injury after *Ricky Boxing*, a slang term for masturbation, which originated in the United States Navy.[139] The Court found that the cure obligation is designed to provide a seaman, who is injured while in the service of his/her ship, with reimbursement for his/her medical expenses until he/she reaches *maximum medical improvement*.[140] The case was allowed to continue. There has been no further clarification on what is *MMI* in this circuit.

Eighth Circuit

On July 11, 2001, Plaintiff was serving as first mate aboard the M/V Mr. Tom, a vessel owned by defendant Jantran.[141] The vessel struck a bridge spanning the Arkansas River near mile mark 300.8 in the vicinity of Van Buren, Arkansas.[142] At or near the time of the allusion, Plaintiff fell approximately six feet from the deck on which he was working.[143] After picking himself up, Plaintiff went to the aid of another crew member, who had been knocked

---

137 Frost v. Teco Barge Line, Inc., 04-CV-752 DRH, 2007 WL 178562 (S.D. Ill. Jan. 22, 2007).

138 Frost v. Teco Barge Line, Inc., 04-CV-752 DRH, 2007 WL 178562 (S.D. Ill. Jan. 22, 2007).

139 McKinney v. Am. River Transp. Co., 12-CV-0885-MJR-SCW, 2013 WL 3270955 (S.D. Ill. June 27, 2013).

140 McKinney v. Am. River Transp. Co., 12-CV-0885-MJR-SCW, 2013 WL 3270955 (S.D. Ill. June 27, 2013).

141 McNeil v. Jantran, Inc., 258 F. Supp. 2d 926, 928-32 (W.D. Ark. 2003).

142 McNeil v. Jantran, Inc., 258 F. Supp. 2d 926, 928-32 (W.D. Ark. 2003).

143 McNeil v. Jantran, Inc., 258 F. Supp. 2d 926, 928-32 (W.D. Ark. 2003).

overboard and helped the man climb back onto the boat.[144] After a while, Plaintiff sat down and felt pain in his back and shoulder; he reported that he may have been injured in the allusion.[145] The Plaintiff was diagnosed with a torn rotator cuff in his shoulder and was recommended to have surgery for a lumbar disc herniation.[146] The Plaintiff had not been able to have the surgery due to financial constraints.[147]

As we have seen, the Court ruled that the ship-owner is obliged to pay *maintenance and cure* until the seaman has reached the point of maximum cure, that is, until the seaman is cured or his/her condition is diagnosed as permanent and incurable, which the Court determined was not the facts in this case; however, what maximum cure means remains undefined.[148]

Ninth Circuit

In an older Ninth Circuit, the Plaintiff suffered a dislocated shoulder as a result of a fall sustained in the course of his employment as a seaman-fisherman aboard the Lucky Star.[149] The Court found that at most, recovery should not be extended beyond the time when the maximum degree of improvement to his health was reached.[150] The Court could find no authority approving a longer period of recovery nor suggesting that a seaman permanently injured in the course of his/her employment should receive maintenance for life.[151]

More recently, the Court reaffirmed this decision in *Gypsum Carrier, Inc. v. Handelsman*.[152] Plaintiff was chief steward aboard the appellant's S.S. Ocean Carrier, and as the vessel was being prepared for sea, tackle, which two members of the crew were attempting to secure for the voyage, fell and struck the plaintiff.[153] When the voyage was completed, appellee sought medical care, which revealed a brain lesion.[154] It was found that cure cannot be awarded

144 McNeil v. Jantran, Inc., 258 F. Supp. 2d 926, 928-32 (W.D. Ark. 2003).
145 McNeil v. Jantran, Inc., 258 F. Supp. 2d 926, 928-32 (W.D. Ark. 2003).
146 McNeil v. Jantran, Inc., 258 F. Supp. 2d 926, 928-32 (W.D. Ark. 2003).
147 McNeil v. Jantran, Inc., 258 F. Supp. 2d 926, 928-32 (W.D. Ark. 2003).
148 McNeil v. Jantran, Inc., 258 F. Supp. 2d 926, 928-32 (W.D. Ark. 2003).
149 Luksich v. Misetich, 140 F.2d 812, 813-15 (9th Cir. 1944).
150 Luksich v. Misetich, 140 F.2d 812, 813-15 (9th Cir. 1944).
151 Luksich v. Misetich, 140 F.2d 812, 813-15 (9th Cir. 1944).
152 Gypsum Carrier, Inc. v. Handelsman, 307 F.2d 525, 527-37 (9th Cir. 1962).
153 Gypsum Carrier, Inc. v. Handelsman, 307 F.2d 525, 527-37 (9th Cir. 1962).
154 Gypsum Carrier, Inc. v. Handelsman, 307 F.2d 525, 527-37 (9th Cir. 1962).

beyond the time when maximum possible cure has been affected and the seaman's physical condition has become fixed beyond further improvement.[155] Again, this Court does not define what maximum possible cure consists of.

Tenth Circuit

The Tenth Circuit does not have a case regarding *MMI* in cure.

Eleventh Circuit

Zukowski was a sailor employed by the defendants' Gulf Caribe location.[156] On September 10, 2008, Zukowski injured his back while pulling a cable aboard Gulf Caribe's vessel, the M/V Caribe Pioneer.[157] The Plaintiff sought medical treatment and was diagnosed with low back pain and prescribed various medications, as well as a course of physical therapy.[158] The doctor declared him at *maximum medical improvement*.[159] As he returned to work, the lower back pain returned.[160] The Plaintiff returned to the doctor, and an MRI of the lumbar spine was ordered.[161] It was diagnosed that he was suffering from a lumbar strain with spasms and underlying disc herniations at L3–4 and L4–5, which were more probably than not, caused and/or made symptomatic by the September 10, 2008, accident at issue.[162]

The Court ruled that the obligation to pay *maintenance and cure* continues until such time as the seaman has reached the point of maximum cure.[163] However, no definition is provided, yet cure was ordered to continue.[164]

---

155 Gypsum Carrier, Inc. v. Handelsman, 307 F.2d 525, 527-37 (9th Cir. 1962).
156 Zukowski v. Foss Mar. Co., CIV.A. 11-0493-CG-M, 2013 WL 1966001 (S.D. Ala. May 10, 2013).
157 Zukowski v. Foss Mar. Co., CIV.A. 11-0493-CG-M, 2013 WL 1966001 (S.D. Ala. May 10, 2013).
158 Zukowski v. Foss Mar. Co., CIV.A. 11-0493-CG-M, 2013 WL 1966001 (S.D. Ala. May 10, 2013).
159 Zukowski v. Foss Mar. Co., CIV.A. 11-0493-CG-M, 2013 WL 1966001 (S.D. Ala. May 10, 2013).
160 Zukowski v. Foss Mar. Co., CIV.A. 11-0493-CG-M, 2013 WL 1966001 (S.D. Ala. May 10, 2013).
161 Zukowski v. Foss Mar. Co., CIV.A. 11-0493-CG-M, 2013 WL 1966001 (S.D. Ala. May 10, 2013).
162 Zukowski v. Foss Mar. Co., CIV.A. 11-0493-CG-M, 2013 WL 1966001 (S.D. Ala. May 10, 2013).
163 Zukowski v. Foss Mar. Co., CIV.A. 11-0493-CG-M, 2013 WL 1966001 (S.D. Ala. May 10, 2013).
164 Zukowski v. Foss Mar. Co., CIV.A. 11-0493-CG-M, 2013 WL 1966001 (S.D. Ala. May 10, 2013).

In the previously cited, *Costa Crociere, S.p.A. v. Rose*,[165] the Plaintiff had an incurable kidney condition that required regular dialysis treatment to keep him alive.[166] The Court ordered the defendant to pay for such treatments as being within the scope of *cure*.[167]

. In a recent Northern District of Florida case, a seaman contracted cancer and brought an action for *maintenance and cure*. It was determined that the Plaintiff initially had limited small cell lung cancer as distinguished from extensive small cell cancer; however, this metastasized into his brain.[168] The Court found that as of February 2004, the Plaintiff had an incurable permanent illness and that, although he had surprisingly survived to this point, any further treatment would be for the purpose of controlling his symptoms and reducing his pain and symptoms, thereby, improving his quality of life.[169]

The Court found that the "likelihood of future gains in his medical condition was virtually nonexistent." The Court also distinguished *Costa Crociere, S.p.A. v. Rose*,[170] the above case. In contrast to that case, the Plaintiff would not live indefinitely with the treatment even though he had done so thus far.[171] The doctors agreed that the treatment was palliative and not to better his physical condition.[172] There was no reasonable chance from a medical point of view that the Plaintiff could continue to function at a meaningful level with continued treatment.[173] "[T]he Court recognizes the

---

165 Costa Crociere, S.p.A. v. Rose, 939 F. Supp. 1538, 1996 A.M.C. 2797 (S.D. Fla. 1996).

166 Costa Crociere, S.p.A. v. Rose, 939 F. Supp. 1538, 1539, 1996 A.M.C. 2797 (S.D. Fla. 1996).

167 Costa Crociere, S.p.A. v. Rose, 939 F. Supp. 1538, 1541, 1996 A.M.C. 2797 (S.D. Fla. 1996).

168 Tern Ship holding Corp. v. Rockhill, 2006 A.M.C. 1708, 1709, 2006 WL 1788507 (N.D. Fla. 2006).

169 Tern Ship holding Corp. v. Rockhill, 2006 A.M.C. 1708, 1709, 2006 WL 1788507 (N.D. Fla. 2006).

170 Tern Ship holding Corp. v. Rockhill, 2006 A.M.C. 1708, 1710, 2006 WL 1788507 (N.D. Fla. 2006).

171 Tern Ship holding Corp. v. Rockhill, 2006 A.M.C. 1708, 17122006, 17 WL 1788507 (N.D. Fla. 2006).

172 Tern Ship holding Corp. v. Rockhill, 2006 A.M.C. 1708, 1712, 2006 WL 1788507 (N.D. Fla. 2006).

173 Tern Ship holding Corp. v. Rockhill, 2006 A.M.C. 1708, 1713, 2006 WL 1788507 (N.D. Fla. 2006).

'fuzzy boundary' that exists between improvement and palliation. The Court also recognizes that stopping treatment at this stage may decrease Rockhill's [plaintiff] lifespan. Nonetheless, keeping in mind that *maintenance and cure* is not the equivalent of long term disability insurance, the Court finds that the testimony from Rockhill's doctors demonstrate unequivocally that Rockhill's illness is permanent, incurable and not subject to 'betterment.'" Therefore, cure was terminated.

Throughout this survey of the Circuit's three classes of courts, they become obvious: those that are strict permanency, those that are converting with the evolution of medicine, and those that just follow. Unfortunately, few courts have actually defined the terms they are using as their rule *maximum medical improvement*. This may be because it is medically driven, factually driven, or simply because it is an allusion. There is never a maximum medical recovery because with medicine and science, there is no baseline and no end line, only possibilities.

V.   What is Curative Care?

cu ra tive: having healing or remedial properties[174]
cure: course of treatment to restore health[175]

The expression often employed in the various ordinances and in the decisions is that mariners are entitled to be cured of sickness and wounds received in service of the ship.[176] Seamen have an exposure to unusual labor or privations on the voyage that may induce maladies permanent or irremedial in their character; thus broken limbs or bodily debility resulting from services in the ship are very often the sailor's heritage for the residue of his/ her life....[177] The term *cure* was probably employed originally in the sense of taking charge or care of the disabled seaman and not in that of positive

---

174 Tabor's Medical Encyclopedia, 20th ed., F.A. Davis Company (2001).
175 Tabor's Medical Encyclopedia, 20th ed., F.A. Davis Company (2001).
176 The Law of Seamen § 26:23 (5th ed.).
177 The Law of Seamen § 26:23 (5th ed.).

healing.[178] Curative care includes care, nursing, medicines, medical care, traveling expenses, hospitalization, etc.[179]

The initial use of the term *cure* was to take charge or care of the disabled seaman, not to actually heal him/her. It was intended to provide these underprivileged wards the protection due to the hazards of their profession to know they would be cared for. There was not an original limit placed on this care. Cure does not mean to restore to perfect health, as is defined above; it means to have a course of treatment to restore one's health. There is no limit. If it is working to restore one's health, the underlying condition, symptoms, and related conditions, then it is under the definition of *cure*.

In medicine, nothing is segmented. There is not Pain. Fracture. Surgery. Infection. Etc. Each separate item is congealed into a treatment plan to CURE a patient. It is not a product of medicine that separates these items; it is a product of the courts that create our modern day seaman cure.

VI.   What is Palliative Care?

pall i a tive: An agent that alleviates or eases a painful or uncomfortable condition[180]

Palliative care is the interdisciplinary medical sub-specialty that focuses on relieving suffering and improving quality of life for patients with serious illness and their familiesl—it is offered simultaneously with other medical treatments.[181] Multiple studies have demonstrated the benefits of palliative

---

178 The Law of Seamen § 26:23 (5th ed.).
179 The Law of Seamen § 26:23 (5th ed.).
180 Tabor's Medical Encyclopedia, 20th ed., F.A. Davis Company (2001).
181 Laura P. Gelfman, M.D. & Diane E. Meier, M.D., Making the Case for Palliative Care: An Opportunity for Health Care Reform, 8 J. Health & Biomedical L. 57 (2012).

care for patients with serious illness in addressing these unmet needs.[182] More specifically, palliative care improves physical and psychological symptoms, caregiver wellbeing, and family satisfaction.[183] The care also prolongs survival[184] and reduces health care utilization and costs.[185] Additionally, studies have demonstrated the ability of palliative care to reduce costs by addressing

182 State-by-State Report Card, supra note 1, at 1; see Joan M. Teno et al., Family Perspectives on End-of-Life Care at the Last Place of Care, 291 JAMA 88, 88, 91-92 (2004); SUPPORT Principal Investigators, A Controlled Trial To Improve Care for Seriously Ill Hospitalized Patients: The Study To Understand Prognoses and Preferences for Outcomes and Risks of Treatments (SUPPORT), 274 JAMA 1591, 1592 (1995); Karl Lorenz et al., Evidence Report/Technology Assessment: End of Life Care and Outcomes: Summary 2-3 (2004), available at http://www.ahrq.gov/clinic/epcsums/eolsum.pdf.

183 David Casarett et al., Do Palliative Consultations Improve Patient Outcomes? 56 J. Am. Geriatric Soc'y 593, 597-98 (2008) (discussing results indicating palliative care can improve quality of end of life care); Laura P. Gelfman et al., Does Palliative Care Improve Quality? A Survey of Bereaved Family Members, 36 J. Pain & Symptom MGMT. 22, 25 (2008) (explaining that results show palliative care consultation services improve family-centered outcomes); Marit S. Jordhóy et al., Quality of Life in Palliative Cancer Care: Results From a Cluster Randomized Trial, 19 J. Clinical Oncology 3884, 3891 (2001) (finding palliative cancer care increased family satisfaction among other benefits).

184 Jennifer S. Temel et al., Early Palliative Care for Patients with Metastatic Non-Small-Cell Lung Cancer, 363 New Eng. J. Med. 733, 739 (2010) (explaining results show palliative care prolong survival of cancer patients).

185 Morrison et al., Cost Savings, supra note 10, at 1785 (stating "patients receiving palliative care consultation had significantly lower costs" than usual patients who did not); Joan D. Penrod et al., Hospital-Based Palliative Care Consultation: Effects on Hospital Cost, 13 J. Palliative Med. 973, 976 (2010) (finding "palliative care during hospitalizations was associated with significantly lower direct hospital costs."); R. Sean Morrison et al., Palliative Care Consultation Teams Cut Hospital Costs for Medicaid Beneficiaries, 30 Health Aff. 454, 457 (2011) [hereinafter Morrison et al., Palliative Care Consultation Teams] (finding overall results show "patients who received palliative care had significantly lower costs than patients who" did not).

goals of care and assisting patients and families to choose treatments that meet those goals.[186]

A randomized controlled trial of early palliative care for patients with advanced lung cancer demonstrated the benefits of a model for concurrent oncologic care with palliative care.[187] In this study, patients newly diagnosed with advanced non-small cell lung cancer who received palliative care simultaneous with standard oncologic care reported a better quality of life, had fewer depressive symptoms, and survived 2.7 months longer than those who received oncologic care alone.[188]

The patient's care, be it curative or palliative, is used cooperatively to maximize the result. A cavity is filled, but Novocain is used (palliative); a bone is set, but the area is under local anesthetic (palliative); a disk is herniated and needs surgery, but without the cortisone injection, the individual cannot walk (palliative); a person is under severe depression and needs therapy, but without the medication is a danger to himself/herself (palliative); a person needs a kidney transplant but has to have dialysis (palliative); etc. Medicine does not separate the treatment plan, only the courts do that.

---

186 Thomas J. Smith & J. Brian Cassel, Cost and Non-Clinical Outcomes of Palliative Care, 38 J. of Pain & Symptom MGMT. 32, 33 (2009) (finding palliative care services can generate substantial savings through cost avoidance); Anthony L. Back et al., Impact of Palliative Care Case Management on Resource Use By Patients Dying of Cancer at a Veterans Affairs Medical Center, 8 J. Palliative Med. 26, 30 (2005) (finding palliative care patients received case management desired in original plan); Morrison et al., Palliative Care Consultation Teams, supra note 14, at 460; Joan D. Penrod et al., Cost and Utilization Outcomes of Patients Receiving Hospital-Based Palliative Care Consultation, 9 J. Palliative Med. 855, 857 (2006) (finding "[p]alliative care patients were more likely to be on medical services and less likely" admitted to intensive care); Ahmed Elsayem et al., Palliative Care Inpatient Service In A Comprehensive Cancer Center: Clinical and Financial Outcomes, 22 J. Clinical Oncology 2008, 2011 (2004) (discussing how nurses are overwhelmed by expectations and demands of palliative care patients' families).

187 Jennifer S. Temel et al., Early Palliative Care for Patients with Metastatic Non-Small-Cell Lung Cancer, 363 New Eng. J. Med. 733, 739 (2010) (explaining results show palliative care prolong survival of cancer patients).

188 David Casarett et al., Do Palliative Consultations Improve Patient Outcomes? 56 J. Am. Geriatric Soc'y 593, 596 (2008) (discussing results indicating palliative care can improve quality of end of life care).

VII. Human Rights Analysis of Access to Pain Treatment and Palliative Care

The Court used international law to adopt the standard of *maintenance and cure* with the Draft Convention from the 1936 General Conference of the International Labor Organization at Geneva, which was ratified by the Senate and proclaimed by the President as effective for the United States on October 29, 1939: "The ship-owner shall be liable to defray the expense of medical care and maintenance until the sick or injured person has been cured or until the sickness or incapacity has been declared of a permanent character."[189] The Congress and the President adopted the international convention to set the current standard; however, has the law adapted as the standard evolved?

Pain treatment as a human right is relatively new. Early analysis of the issue and calls for pain treatment to be recognized as a human right came from medical professionals working in pain management and palliative care.[190] Subsequently, the *U.N. Special Rapporteur on The Right to the Highest Attainable Standard of Health*, Anand Grover, and the *Special Rapporteur on Torture and Other Cruel, Inhuman or Degrading Treatment or Punishment*, Manfred Nowak,

---

189 Farrell v. United States, 336 U.S. 511, 517, 1949 AMC 613, 617 (1949), (citing 54 Stat. 1693, art. 4, para. 1).

190 Joint Declaration and Statement of Commitment on Palliative Care and Pain Treatment as Human Rights, Int'l Hospice & Palliative Care Ass'n and World Wide Palliative Care Alliance, available at http:// www.hospicecare.com/resources/ pain_pallcare_hr/docs/jdsc.pdf; F. Brennan and M. J. Cousins, Pain Relief as a Human Right, IASP Pain Clinical Updates, Vol. XII, No. 5, March 2004, available at http:// www.hospicecare.com/resources/pdf-docs/pain_relief_as_a_human_right_pain_ clinical_updates_2004.pdf; Frank Brennan, Palliative Care as an International Human Right, 33 J. Pain & Symptom Mgmt. 494 (2007).

both recognized that a failure to address barriers to palliative care can be a violation of human rights. [191]

The failure to ensure access to controlled medicines for the relief of pain and suffering threatens fundamental rights to health and to protection against cruel, inhuman, and degrading treatment. International human rights' law requires that governments must provide essential medicines—which include, among others, opioid analgesics—as part of their minimum core obligations under the right to health.[192]

A. The Right to the Highest Attainable Standard of Health

The right to the highest attainable standard of health is found in the International Covenant on Economic, Social, and Cultural Rights (ICESCR) and several other human rights treaties.[193] State parties to ICESCR are obliged to "take steps...to the maximum of its available resources with a view to achieving progressively the full realization" of the right to health.[194]

However, as noted above, the Covenant on Economic, Social, and Cultural Rights (CESCR) (which interprets and monitors compliance with the ICESCR) has stated that there are certain "core obligations" which are

191 Joint Declaration and Statement of Commitment on Palliative Care and Pain Treatment as Human Rights, Int'l Hospice & Palliative Care Ass'n and World Wide Palliative Care Alliance, available at http:// www.hospicecare.com/resources/ pain_pallcare_hr/docs/jdsc.pdf; F. Brennan and M. J. Cousins, Pain Relief as a Human Right, IASP Pain Clinical Updates, Vol. XII, No. 5, March 2004, available at http:// www.hospicecare.com/resources/pdf-docs/pain_relief_as_a_human_right_pain_ clinical_updates_2004.pdf; Frank Brennan, Palliative Care as an International Human Right, 33 J. Pain & Symptom Mgmt. 494 (2007).

192 Letter to Chairperson of the Commission on Narcotic Drugs, United Nations Special Rapporteur on the Prevention of Torture and Cruel, Inhuman, or Degrading Treatment or Punishment & Special Rapporteur on Right of Everyone to the Highest Attainable Standard of Physical and Mental Health, U.N. Doc. G/SO 214 (52-21) (Dec. 10, 2008), available at http:// www.hrw.org/sites/default/files/related_material/12.10.2008%20Letter%C20to%C20CND%C20fromSpecial%Rapporteurs.pdf (last visited Nov. 6, 2010).

193 International Covenant on Civil and Political Rights, G.A. Res. 2200A (XXI), 21 U.N. GAOR Supp. No. 16, UN Doc. A/6316, art 2.1 (Dec. 16, 1966) [hereinafter ICCPR].

194 International Covenant on Civil and Political Rights, G.A. Res. 2200A (XXI), 21 U.N. GAOR Supp. No. 16, UN Doc. A/6316, art 2.1 (Dec. 16, 1966).

"non-derogable," meaning that "a State party cannot, under any circumstances whatsoever, justify its non-compliance."[195] These include provision of essential medicines, which, as defined by (World Health Organization) WHO, includes morphine.[196]

Other core obligations that are relevant to addressing the barriers discussed above include obligations to ensure the right of access to health facilities, goods, and services on a non-discriminatory basis.

B. Pain Treatment, Palliative Care, and the Right to be Free from Cruel, Inhuman, or Degrading Treatment

The prohibition of cruel, inhuman, or degrading treatment is found in the Convention Against Torture and Other Cruel, Inhuman or Degrading Treatment or Punishment (CAT) and other human rights instruments.[197] The Committee Against Torture, the treaty body that interprets the CAT, has stated that cruel, inhuman or degrading treatment or punishment "may differ [from torture] in the severity of pain and suffering and does not require proof of impermissible purposes."[198] In other words, governments may violate the CAT when they fail to take steps to prevent cruel, inhuman, or degrading treatment or punishment, regardless of whether any government official had malicious intent. The Committee Against Torture has stated

---

195 International Covenant on Civil and Political Rights, G.A. Res. 2200A (XXI), 21 U.N. GAOR Supp. No. 16, UN Doc. A/6316, art 2.1 (Dec. 16, 1966).

196 International Covenant on Civil and Political Rights, G.A. Res. 2200A (XXI), 21 U.N. GAOR Supp. No. 16, UN Doc. A/6316, art 2.1 (Dec. 16, 1966).

197 Convention Against Torture and Other Cruel, Inhuman or Degrading Treatment or Punishment, G.A. Res. 39/46, Annex 39, U.N. GAOR, Supp. No. 51, UN Doc. A/39/51, at 197 (Dec. 10, 1984); Universal Declaration of Human Rights, G.A. Res. 217A (III), U.N. GAOR, 3d Sess., U.N. Doc A/810 (Dec. 10, 1948); ICCPR, supra note 138, at 52; Inter-American Convention to Prevent and Punish Torture, entered into force Feb. 22, 1987, OAS Treaty Series No. 67, reprinted in 25 I.L.M. 519 (1987); European Convention for the Prevention of Torture and Inhuman or Degrading Treatment or Punishment, ETS 126 (1987); African [Banjul] Charter on Human and Peoples' Rights, adopted June 27, 1981, OAU Doc. CAB/LEG/67/3 rev. 5, 21 I.L.M. 58, art. 5 (1982), entered into force Oct. 21, 1986.

198 U.N. Comm. Against Torture, General Comment No. 2: Implementation of Article 2 by State Parties, P10, U.N. Doc. CAT/C/GV/2 (Jan. 24, 2008), available at http://www.unhcr.org/refworld/docid/47ac/78ce2.html.

that the CAT requires state parties to take "effective preventative measures" and "eliminate any legal or other obstacles that impede the eradication of torture and ill-treatment."[199]

The U.N. Special Rapporteur on Torture and Other Cruel, Inhuman and Degrading Treatment or Punishment stated in his February 2009 report to the Human Rights Council that "de facto denial of access to pain relief, when it causes severe pain and suffering, constitutes cruel, inhuman or degrading treatment or punishment."[200]

Human Rights Watch argues that not every case where a person suffers from severe untreated pain is cruel, inhuman, or degrading treatment or punishment.[201] Rather, the prohibition is only violated when the following conditions are met.

- The suffering is severe and meets the minimum threshold required under the prohibition against torture and cruel, inhuman, or degrading treatment or punishment;
- The state is, or should be, aware of the level and extent of the suffering;
- Treatment is available to remove or lessen the suffering, but no appropriate treatment was offered; and
- The state has no reasonable justification for the lack of availability and accessibility of pain treatment.[202]

Seamen under the historic doctrine of *maintenance and cure* are restricted

---

199 U.N. Comm. Against Torture, General Comment No. 2: Implementation of Article 2 by State Parties, P10, U.N. Doc. CAT/C/GV/2 (Jan. 24, 2008), available at http://www.unhcr.org/refworld/docid/47ac/78ce2.html.

200 Special Rapporteur on Torture and Other Cruel, Inhuman or Degrading Treatment or Punishment, Promotion and Protection of All Human Rights, Civil Political, Economic, Social and Cultural Rights, Including the Right to Develop, U.N. Doc. A/HRC/10/44, P72 (Jan. 14, 2009).

201 Special Rapporteur on Torture and Other Cruel, Inhuman or Degrading Treatment or Punishment, Promotion and Protection of All Human Rights, Civil Political, Economic, Social and Cultural Rights, Including the Right to Develop, U.N. Doc. A/HRC/10/44, P72 (Jan. 14, 2009).

202 Special Rapporteur on Torture and Other Cruel, Inhuman or Degrading Treatment or Punishment, Promotion and Protection of All Human Rights, Civil Political, Economic, Social and Cultural Rights, Including the Right to Develop, U.N. Doc. A/HRC/10/44, P72 (Jan. 14, 2009).

to live with the pain; they are not entitled to coverage for treatment. The world now recognizes that care for pain is a basic human right, yet the courts continue to live under an antiquated rule of thumb to oppress even in situations where the employer may have caused the injury. It appears to be that the courts progress as slowly to adapt to new science as the rule converts to accept new medical remedies.

VIII. Conclusion

Palliative care's emergence as a discreet medical discipline in the 1960s was designed to treat a fundamental and common medical condition—the experience of painl—which had been largely ignored by medicine and cast off as the responsibility of others. Human rights reject the idea that suffering from treatable pain is inevitable and that the provision of cheap, effective pain medicine must remain a matter of charity. Human rights' conventions obligate governments to identify health needs and to adopt national health policies that include detailed plans for realizing the right to health. A human rights' analysis places the onus of undertaking this reform effort upon the actors best able to implement systemic change—national governments.

Professor Randall Bridwell had it right when he said, "Maintenance and Cure is a seaman's remedy of ancient origin."[203] The remedy has not departed from its ancient origin to maintain pace with modern medicine or human rights. After thousands of years of maritime trade and exploration, hundreds of years of United States laws, decades of cases regarding *maximum medical improvement*, there is not one rule to provide adequate coverage for a U.S. seaman.

If a patient is enabled to lead a normal comfortable life due to such palliative treatment, certainly he/she has had his/her *condition* improved, even though no progress in eliminating the underlying injury or disease is currently feasible. Since it is impossible to imagine a disease with no symptoms at all,

---

203 Randall Bridwell, PRIMER ON MAINTENANCE AND CURE—THE MEANING OF THE WORDS MAXIMUM MEDICAL CURE, vol. 1 of ATLA Annual Convention Reference Materials, Association of Trial Lawyers of America, July, 2005.

elimination of all symptoms would be the equivalent of a complete cure.[204] However, some courts would determine that this medical treatment is not covered under the cure doctrine.

The U.S. District Courts have slowly started converting to allowing palliative care, and palliative care is now recognized as a human right. But truly, there is no conversion as the term *cure* has become an all-encompassing term to provide a complete treatment plan for a patient. The understanding of providing care to cure a patient has changed. There is no need for statutory change; there is need for simply an understanding of the modern medical definition. It is time for us to accept the 21ˢᵗ century characterization of *cure* and move off the ancient origin categorization.

---

204 Randall Bridwell, PRIMER ON MAINTENANCE AND CURE—THE MEAN-ING OF THE WORDS MAXIMUM MEDICAL CURE, vol. 1 of ATLA Annual Convention Reference Materials, Association of Trial Lawyers of America, July, 2005.

PART TWO:

Where Does the Tow Line Break?

When is a Tow a Salvage or a Salvage a Tow?

I. Introduction

Of course, as a vessel owner, issues never arise while your ship is on shore being repaired or in stowage. Problems occur on the water when you are just trying to get home after your run. You call for a tow, and the tow company comes out and presents you with a contract to sign. Many times, these contracts are for salvage, but all you wanted was a tow. Without assistance you are left adrift, so what is a vessel owner or captain to do?

According to Congress, a vessel owner cannot have his/her vessel obstruct navigable waterways. These obligations are set forth in what is popularly known as the *Wreck Act*.

The Rivers and Harbors Act, 33 U.S.C. §401-418, commonly referred to as the Wreck Act, 557

F.2d 438, 444 (5th Cir. 1977)[1] accomplishes this objective by imposing three (3) obligations on the owner of a vessel. First, the owner must immediately mark and maintain the wreck with a buoy or beacon. Second, if the wreck constitutes an obstruction to navigation, the owner must immediately remove the wreck. Finally, if the owner does not remove the vessel, the Wreck

Act authorizes the United States to commence removal and seek reimbursement from the owner.[2]

A duty has been placed on the vessel owner of a ship and salvage has become necessary.

Salvage can occur with both a sunken vessel and also one in peril from sinking. However, when is it a salvage or a towage? Clearly, no salvage award is due if salvage did not take place and before a salvage award is due; a salvage situation involving peril must exist. Because saving a vessel in peril from further destruction is a rather broad term, it is easy for an inexperienced boater or insurance carrier to be unable to clearly identify all salvage verse towage situations, especially those with a low degree of peril. The root cause of many salvage award disputes traces to this inability to distinguish

---

1 Univ. of Texas Med Branch v. United States, 557 F.2d 438, 444 (5th Cir. 1977).
2 http://www.hhlaw.com/News/Fact%20Sheet%20RJB%20Wreck%20Act%20
    longer%201110%20%28H0680316%29.PDF.

a low peril salvage situation from a much less costly towage operation. In these cases, it is often difficult to distinguish between the two. However, the distinction is critical.

A. What is Towage?

Towage differs from the carriage of goods in that under a towage situation, one vessel, which is self-propelled, generally tows one or more vessels, usually barges that are not self-propelled.[3] Simply put, towage is "[t]he supplying of power by a vessel…to draw another" vessel.[4] The key determination between towing and salvage is made at the moment help arrives. If no peril exists when help arrives, towage is the appropriate term for the propulsion or movement of the vessel in need of services, and towing rates apply. However, if a marine peril exists, even a slight peril at the moment help arrives, then, by legal definition, the operation is salvage, which entitles the salvor to claim a salvage award.

However, even simple towage can turn into a salvage operation if an unanticipated peril forces the salvor to perform a service "beyond the scope" of the towing agreement.[5] For example, suppose no peril existed at the time the tow line was passed to the stranded vessel and towing began. Then, on the way to the harbor, a storm approached, and the towed vessel broke free and required further rescue. Due to this unanticipated peril, the towage service turned into a salvage operation. As another example, given the same initial scenario, suppose on the way to harbor, the towed vessel began taking on water, and the bilge pumps did not work. This event also turned from simple towing

---

3 Mississippi Val. Barge Line Co. v. T. L. James & Co., 244 F.2d 263, 1957 A.M.C. 1647 (5th Cir. 1957).
4 Stevens v. The WHITE CITY, 285 U.S. 195, 200 (1932).
5 Waterman S.S. Corp. v. Shipowners and Merchants Towboat Co., 199 F.2d 600, 601, 1952 AMC 1988 (9th Cir. 1952).

into a salvage situation. However, the converse is also true. If a salvage situation is present but then the peril evaporates, then the subsequent action may be a towage.

To further the confusion, many towing memberships offer services for towing a vessel that is soft aground. For example, Sea Tow offers members various benefits, including free soft ungroundings.[6] Sea Tow defines a free soft ungrounding situation as

Sea Tow will provide free ungrounding assistance to covered vessels when all five of the following conditions apply. Namely that the vessel is in a stable, safe condition, is not in dangerous surf or inside a dangerous surf line, is surrounded by water on all sides, has some movement (i.e. rocking), and can be refloated upon initial arrival or at the next high tide in 15 minutes or less by one Sea Tow boat. [7]

Under this towing membership, soft aground represents a situation where no peril exists and, therefore, hourly towage rates apply. However, this membership also distinguishes between soft aground and hard aground.[8] A vessel hard aground or stranded is in a perilous situation that requires salvage and is usually covered by a vessel's hull or salvage insurance policy.[9] Whether the vessel faces a peril or is in danger is both fact and situation specific and not easily determined, especially for low order salvage situations, despite typical language to the contrary. Even the language of the tow agreement or insurance contract may not be dispositive of the issue of tow or salvage as this issue is determined by general maritime law. For example,

---

6 http://www.seatow.com/membership.
7 http://www.seatow.com/membership/memberguide.pdf.
8 http://www.seatow.com/membership/memberguide.pdf.
9 http://www.boatus.com/insurance.

the arbitrator deciding whether the situation involved towage or salvage between Mahoney Marine Services, Inc. and a 28' Boston Whaler named ELLIE ROSE found that the nature of the services provided cannot be determined by resort to the Parol documentation of either the Sea Tow membership materials, or the representations regarding coverage provided by BoatUS[.] Rather, we will look to maritime law to make the determination. . . . If the grounded vessel faced a *peril*, then she could be the subject of salvage. If there was no peril, then there could be no salvage.[10]

Therefore, the threshold issue for the salvage of recreational vessels is to determine if a marine peril, however slight, existed at the time assistance was summoned and arrived. If a peril did exist, the assistance provided is likely subject to a salvage award and not covered under a towing membership.

Towage and salvage each operate under different rules and produces potentially very different outcomes. The definition and ultimate determination between towage and salvage is not an issue to be decided by the parties; rather the terms are defined by the general maritime law of salvage.[11]

Towage and salvage are frequently confused because salvage often includes the physical act of towing a distressed vessel out of danger or back to shore for repairs. The main difference is that salvage always requires an *unanticipated peril*[12] at the time of rescue, and towing is a propulsion service rendered with-

---

10 2002 AMC at 2842-43.

11 G. Gilmore and C. Black, The Law of Admiralty, ch. VII (2d ed. 1975); McConnochie v. Kerr, 9 Fed. 50, 53 (S.D.N.Y. 1881); Am. Home Assurance Co. v. L & L Marine Serv., Inc., 688 F. Supp 502, 1989 AMC 684 (E.D. Mo. 1988); Kuhr, 1986 AMC 2299.

12 3 A. Norris, Benedict on Admiralty § 5-13 (7th ed. 1983).

out such peril. Towing services are usually compensated at an hourly rate or a quantum meruit basis, whereas salvage services entitle a salvor to a salvage award, which is a percentage of the post-casualty value of the vessel.[13] Salvage is based on the principle of risk and reward. Saving a vessel from additional or total destruction, while risking the safety of the salvors' crew and equipment, entitles the salvor to share in this savings from loss.

The language of towage memberships, very popular among recreational vessel owners, often adds to the confusion. Less experienced vessel owners often think the tow membership, which operates in a similar way to *road service* memberships, also covers salvage operations that involve towing.[14] Sometimes, the mistake between towage and salvage is a costly one. For instance, even a one percent salvage award on a $1.5 million yacht ($15,000) is significantly different than a towage fee of $450 for a three-hour tow at $150 per hour. Other times, little monetary difference may exist between a low order salvage award for an inexpensive vessel and a towage fee. Since compensation for assistance could vary greatly between the two, knowing whether the aid is towage or salvage is of prime importance to vessel owners and their insurance carriers.

II. Salvage—Pure and Contract

Three elements are necessary to a valid salvage claim:
1. A marine peril.
2. Service voluntarily rendered when not required as an existing duty or from a special contract.

---

13 3 A. Norris, Benedict on Admiralty § 5-13 (7th ed. 1983).
14 3 A. Norris, Benedict on Admiralty § 5-13 (7th ed. 1983).

3. Success in whole or in part, or that the service rendered con-
tributed to such success. [15]

General maritime law distinguishes between pure salvage and contract salvage. In a pure salvage situation, the salvor is a volunteer, and the "compensation is dependent on success."[16] This is commonly known as the *no cure-no pay principle.* If the volunteer is unsuccessful in saving the vessel, the owner does not owe the would-be salvors anything for their efforts. In contract salvage, the parties usually enter into an agreement prior to starting the salvage operation, and the salvor will expect payment regardless of the level of success of the salvage operation. The distinction is important because even an oral salvage contract will prevent a salvor from recovering payment based upon pure voluntary salvage and will instead enforce the negotiated terms of the agreement.[17]

For example, although a vessel owner might be able to negotiate a lower price for services using contract salvage, the unanticipated peril of the situation prevents such negotiations taking place. Since recreational vessels usually face an unanticipated need for salvage services, an initial understanding of pure salvage is of primary importance in reducing the frequency of refusals to pay claims with merit and instances of overcharging.

1. Pure Salvage

As previously mentioned, the three elements of a valid pure salvage claim are (1) a marine peril placing the property at risk of loss; (2) the service must

---

15 The Law of Seamen § 9:8 (5th ed.), citing The "Sabine", 101 U.S. 384, 25 L. Ed. 982 (1879); see also Larue v. United Fruit Co., 1950 A.M.C. 161 (D.Md.1949), affd, 181 F.2d 895, 1950 A.M.C. 1312 (4th Cir. 1950), regarding lack of peril or distress; West Coast Shipping Brokers Corp., M/V "Cebu I" v. Ferry "Chuchequero", 582 F.2d 959 (5th Cir. 1978).

16 The ELFRIDA, 172 U.S. 186, 192 (1989).

17 Flagship Marine Servs., Inc. v. Belcher Towing Co., 966 F.2d 602, 606, 1992 AMC 2901 (11th Cir. 1992).

be voluntarily rendered; and (3) the salvage efforts must be successful, in whole or in part.[18]

a. Marine Peril

A marine peril is a situation that might expose the vessel to loss or destruction and that existed at the time assistance was rendered.[19] The peril need not "be actual or imminent; it is sufficient if, at the time assistance was rendered, the vessel was stranded so that it was subject to the potential danger of damage or destruction."[20]

This potential danger may be "either present or to be reasonably apprehended."[21] For example, a distress call from a vessel indicated a level of apprehension sufficient for a finding of a marine peril, even though the facts later indicated otherwise.[22] If the vessel has the situation under control and does not request assistance, there is no peril.[23] An approaching storm, stormy conditions, rising or ebbing tide, fast moving currents, taking on water, sinking, loss of propulsion, incapacitation of the master or crew, stranding, or fire, are all examples of common marine perils faced by recreational vessel owners.

b. Service Voluntarily Rendered

The determination of whether an act was voluntary turns on whether the salvor had a pre-existing legal *obligation* to assist.[24] A pre-existing contract or other *binding engagement* for salvage

---

18 The SABINE, 101 U.S. 384, 384 (1879).

19 Conolly v. S.S. KARINA II, 302 F. Supp. 675, 679, 1969 AMC 319 (E.D.N.Y. 1969).

20 McNabb v. O.S. BOWFIN, 565 F. Supp. 22, 23, 1984 AMC 177 (W.D. Wash. 1983).

21 McConnochie v. Kerr, 9 F. 50, 53 (S.D.N.Y. 1881).

22 Coastal Towing & Salvage, Inc. v. MV SEA ROBIN, No. 3632, Soc'y of Mar. Arbitrators, Inc. (June 29, 2000) (Siciliano, Arb.).

23 Neptune Maritime Co. of Monrovia v. ESSI CAMILLA, 714 F.2d 132, 1984 AMC 2983 (4th Cir. 1983).

24 Sun Oil Co., 342 F. Supp. 976, 981, 1972 AMC 2258 (S.D.N.Y. 1972), aff'd 474 F.2d 1048, 1973 AMC 572 (2d Cir. 1973).

services negates the voluntary act.[25] However, if the contractor performs acts beyond those required by contract or engagement, those acts can be considered voluntary.[26] Additionally, the motive of the salvor is immaterial, and a professional salvor working for "monetary gain, humanitarian purposes or merely error" is still a volunteer salvor.[27] It is important to remember that "the burden of proving a salvage contract to disprove . . . voluntariness lies with the respondent."[28] Voluntariness is often tied to the discussion of the duty owed by a pre-existing towing or salvage agreement.[29] For example, a salvor that signs an agreement to raise a sunken barge for $10,000 cannot later assert that their efforts were purely voluntary and request a salvage award of $40,000 based on an award of 10% of the $400,000 value of the barge. The pre-existing salvage contract prohibits this later claim of voluntariness.

Another exception is for salvors who are statutorily obligated to render assistance, such as members of the Coast Guard, and police and fire departments. They typically cannot present a salvage claim because their service is not considered *voluntary*.[30]

c. Effort Must be Successful

Historically, "[s]uccess is essential to the claim" of a salvage award, [31] and the services of the salvor must also have "con-

---

25 Flagship Marine Servs., Inc., 966 F.2d at 605 (quoting The CAMANCHE, 75 U.S. 448, 477 (1869)).

26 Sobonis v. Steam Tanker NAT'l DEFENDER, 298 F. Supp 631, 637-38, 1969 AMC 1219 (S.D.N.Y. 1969). See also The CAMANCHE, 75 U.S. 448, 2003 AMC 2979 (1869); Smith v. Union Oil Co. of Cal., 274 F. Supp 248, 251, 1967 AMC 1097 (N.D. Cal. 1966).

27 B.V. BUREAU WIJSMULLER v. United States, 702 F.2d 333, 1983 AMC 1471 (2d Cir. 1983).

28 Clifford v. M/V ISLANDER, 751 F.2d 1 at 5, n. 1, 1985 AMC 1855 (1st Cir. 1984).

29 Clifford v. M/V ISLANDER, 751 F.2d 1 at 3, 1985 AMC 1855 (1st Cir. 1984).

30 http://www.offshorerisk.com/definitions/salvage.html.

31 The BLACKWALL, 77 U.S. 1 at 12 (1869).

tributed to such success." [32] This means that there is no reward for trying and no salvage award is due if the vessel is a total loss. The policy reason underlying the requirement of success is that in voluntary salvage, the reward is carved out of the property saved from loss. This no cure-no pay principle distinguishes voluntary salvage from contract salvage in that

under voluntary salvage, if the salvor is successful in saving property, the salvor is "paid a salvage award in an amount to be later determined; if unsuccessful, [salvor] would receive no payment."[33] However, in contract salvage, the service is performed using best efforts, often without the requirement of success. Even though no financial liability to the salvor may attach for an unsuccessful salvage attempt, the vessel owner may still be "liable for wreck removal expenses or civil fines or criminal penalties for environmental damage."[34]

If these three requirements of (1) peril, (2) voluntariness, and (3) success are met, then a salvage award is appropriate. Courts, arbitrators, and even the parties to a dispute weigh a number of factors in determining the actual amount of the salvage award, which is often expressed as a percentage of the salved value of the vessel. In 1869, in The BLACKWALL, the Court listed

---

32 Reynolds Leasing Corp. v. Tug PATRICE MCALLISTER, 572 F. Supp 1131 at 1134, 1984 AMC 1303 (S.D.N.Y. 1983).

33 Donald A. Kerr, The Past and Future of "No Cure-No Pay," 23 J. Mar. L. & Com. 411, 411-17 (1992); Martin J. Norris, The Law of Salvage (1958); 3A Benedict on Admiralty, § 1-129; Gilmore and Black, The Law of Admiralty, § 8-1.

34 Thomas J. Schoenbaum, Admiralty and Maritime Law, § 14-1 n.25 (Hornbook Series) (4th ed. 2001). ("The 1989 International Convention on Salvage, Article 14 allows 'special compensation' for the salvor who has 'prevented or minimized damage to the environment' even if no property is saved. The special compensation is equal to the salvor's out-of-pocket expenses plus, in exceptional cases, up to 100% of the expenses incurred.") (citations omitted).

what are now viewed as the traditional criteria for fixing the award.[35] Those criteria are

(1) The labor expended by the salvors in rendering the salvage service.

(2) The promptitude, skill, and energy displayed in rendering the service and saving the property.

(3) The value of the property employed by the salvors in rendering the service and the danger to which such property was exposed.

(4) The risk incurred by the salvors in securing the property from the impending peril.

(5) The value of the property saved.

(6) [T]he degree of danger from which the property was rescued.[36]

In 1989, the International Convention on Salvage, Article 13[37], updated this list, adding such factors as preventing or minimizing damage to the environment. The Convention criteria typically do not have applicability in the recreational vessel context except through agreement.

For example, the MARSALV[38] agreement lists the Convention criteria, rather than The BLACKWALL criteria, as the factors

35 Trico Marine Operators, Inc. v. Dow Chemical Co., 809 F. Supp. 440, 1993 AMC 1042 (E.D. La. 1992) (adding the salvor's skill and effort to protect the environment as a criteria in fixing the award); Ocean Servs. Towing and Salvage, Inc. v. Brown, 810 F. Supp. 1258, 1993 AMC 2701 (S.D. Fla.1993).

36 The BLACKWALL, 77 U.S. 1 at 14 (1869).

37 International Convention on Salvage, 1989 art. 13, Apr. 28, 1989, S. Treaty Doc. No. 102-12, 1953 U.N.T.S. 165, reprinted in 6 Benedict, Benedict on Admiralty, Doc. 4-2A at 4-13 (Frank L. Wiswall, Jr. ed., 7th ed. Rev. 2007). The Convention criteria are similar to The BLACKWALL factors and include (1) the salved value of the vessel and other property; (2) the skill and efforts of the salvors in preventing or minimizing damage to the environment; (3) the measure of success obtained by the salvor; (4) the nature and degree of the damage; (5) the skill and efforts of the salvor in saving the vessel, other property, and life; (6) the time expended and expenses incurred by the salvors, noting that efficient salvors should not be penalized; (7) the risk of liability and other risks by the salvors and their equipment; (8) the promptness of the services; (9) the availability and use of vessels or other equipment during the salvage operations; and (10) the state of readiness and efficiency of the salvor's equipment and the value of the equipment.

38 http:// www.smany.org/sma/salvrule.html.

for determining the salvage award. For pure salvage claims of recreational vessels in U.S. waters, absent an agreement to the contrary, courts and arbitrators will apply The BLACKWALL factors in determining the size of the award.

2. Contract Salvage

In pure salvage, there is no pre-existing agreement. Courts will "closely scrutinize" efforts to create an agreement while the vessel is in extremis.[39] In such instances, the courts may set aside such a salvage agreement if "corruptly entered into, or made under fraudulent representations, a clear mistake or suppression of important facts,"[40] or if the salvor made misrepresentations amounting to fraud.[41] However, if an agreement, either oral or written, was entered into after fair bargaining, even under perilous conditions, courts will typically uphold the terms.[42]

Contract salvage is salvage conducted under a pre-negotiated contract. The contract can state very specific terms, such as a daily rate, or can designate the salvor by name, and the item to be salved. However, in an *in extremis* situation where there is not time to negotiate or choose from a selection of salvors, a contract for salvage services is usually not presented or signed until after the salvage operation is complete. These are pure salvage operations. The term is no *cure—no pay*, and the contract for salvage services serves as a receipt for the services rendered.

For example, in the commercial context, an agreement for con-

---

39 The ELFRIDA, 172 U.S. 186 at 196 (1989).

40 The ELFRIDA, 172 U.S. 186 at 192 (1989).

41 Black Gold Marine, Inc. v. Jackson Marine Co., 759 F.2d 466, 470, 1986 AMC 137 (5th Cir. 1985).

42 Southernmost Marine Servs., 250 F. Supp. 2d 1367; Smit Americas, Inc. v. M/V MANTINIA, 259 F. Supp. 2d 118, 2003 AMC 1096 (D.P.R. 2003).

tract salvage services, like any other agreement, is usually negotiated or signed, or both prior to the start of the salvage operation. Two popular standard salvage agreements are Lloyd's Open Form 2000[43] (LOF) and a MARSALV[44] agreement (Society of Maritime Arbitrators).[45] Contract salvage agreements can retain flexible terms like no cure—no pay or can lock in specific terms, like daily rates. Contract salvage is a result of negotiation and drafting of the specific terms of the agreement.

For example, even when "signed prior to the commencement of the salvage operation, the LOF no cure—no pay arrangement allows the named salvor to conduct salvage operations without first negotiating rates."[46] At the completion of the salvage, the salvor submits the claim to the vessel owner.[47] If the claim is denied, the salvor will ask the "arbitration committee of Lloyds in London to grant the salvage award."[48] While the open form is still used, the United States passed the 1989 Salvage Act, which no longer requires a barrister in London to arbitrate the dispute when two American flagged ships are parties to the contract.[49]

Alternatively, the parties could negotiate specific terms, such

---

43 For a printable version of the LOF 2000, visit the Lloyd's of London website (for the United States) at:http://www.lloyds.com/LloydsWorldwide/Lloyds_Agents/Salvage_Arbitration_Branch/Lloyds_Open_Form_LOF.htm.
44 In an effort to provide assistance to recreational vessel owners, in 1996 the Society of Maritime Arbitrators at New York (SMA) created and published a U.S. Open Form Salvage Agreement, known as MARSALV. A downloadable version of the form is available at http://www.smany.org/sma/salvform.html (last visited on Mar. 26, 2007).
45 http://www.smany.org.
46 Peter D. Clark, US Open-Form Salvage Agreement Gives Shipping Sector New Options, Journal of Commerce, June 14, 1996, at 4B.
47 Peter D. Clark, US Open-Form Salvage Agreement Gives Shipping Sector New Options, Journal of Commerce, June 14, 1996, at 4B.
48 Peter D. Clark, US Open-Form Salvage Agreement Gives Shipping Sector New Options, Journal of Commerce, June 14, 1996, at 4B.
49 http://www.offshorerisk.com/definitions/salvage.html.

as time, materials, and hourly or per diem rates for salvage services.[50] For example, a salvee could contract with a salvor to *use best endeavors* to raise a sunken barge. The agreement might specify a contract rate of $1500 per day plus cost of equipment use.

The maritime industry favors form contracts like the LOF to create a uniformity of understanding between vessel owners or operators and would-be salvors. In a situation requiring immediate action, there is not time to negotiate terms. For this reason, the salvage of commercial vessels relies heavily on form agreements where the parties often simply check boxes to signify their intent. These form agreements and their terms are very familiar to commercial vessel operators and represent a standard or uniform way to conduct business. Due to this common understanding, all parties understand the basic terms under which a salvage operation will occur, even in an emergency.

Contrarily, most recreational vessel owners do not negotiate salvage terms prior to the start of a salvage operation due to the immediacy of the situation. Additionally, most recreational vessel owners are not repeat players in the maritime salvage industry and, therefore, do not understand the nature of the services rendered. On the eastern seaboard, the MARSALV form agreement is commonly used for the salvage of recreational vessels. The MARSALV agreement, with the no cure-no pay box already checked, is usually presented for signature by the salvor after the salvage operation is complete. Obviously, the salvor would not present such a form after the fact if the operation were unsuccessful. Signing this agreement after the fact does not turn the operation into contract salvage but merely acts as an acknowledgement that services were provided and the terms were no cure-no pay. The MARSALV agreement indicates that

---

50 LOF 2000, Clauses C and D.

the Salvage Convention factors listed on the back of the form will determine the amount of the award. Despite the presence of an agreement, the operation was pure salvage and the form serves as the receipt for services rendered. Additionally, these after-the-fact form agreements usually call for arbitration as the method of dispute resolution. The arbitration clauses usually designate the salvor's choice of location for the proceedings and the requirement that the unsuccessful party pays the attorneys' fees.

As discussed, most contested salvage operations involving recreational vessels will not involve contract salvage but will involve pure salvage or no cure—no pay agreements signed after the fact. If a salvage situation exists at the time services were rendered and the salvage was successful, a salvage award is due and will be determined by use of The BLACKWALL factors. Under certain conditions, the Salvage Convention factors may apply but only by agreement. Either set of factors should yield approximately the same award amount.

III.   Towage Versus Salvage

A frequently heard argument is services rendered by a salvor, which brings in a disabled vessel at the end of a hawser were *simple towage* is one frequently heard. Often, insurance companies make such arguments because while they are liable to pay a claim for salvage, in many cases, the insurance companies are not liable for claims for towage, and payment of such claims is the owner's responsibility. However, the admiralty courts of the United States have addressed the difference between *simple towage* and salvage services on numerous occasions and have made it abundantly clear that, in most such situations, the services rendered are salvage.[51] Indeed, one leading admiralty

---

51 Martin J. Norris, The Law of Salvage (1958); 3A Benedict on Admiralty, §§ 1-129; Donald A. Kerr, *The Past and Future of "No Cure-No Pay,"* 23 J. Mar. Law & Com. 411, 411-17; Gilmore and Black, The Law of Admiralty, § 8-1 and accompanying notes (2d ed. 1975).

treatise has described the act of rescuing a ship at sea by towing her to a place of safety as the *prototypical* act of salvage.[52] This does not necessarily mean that the salvor will be entitled to a huge reward for such services.[53]

As previously discussed, a salvage service implies that there was some degree of danger or some need of extraordinary assistance to the vessel, which characterizes a salvage service. Although a marine peril to the salved property is a necessary ingredient of a valid salvage claim, the peril required in a salvage service does not need to be one that is necessarily imminent or an absolute danger. It is sufficient if the property is in danger, either presently or reasonably to be apprehended.[54]

Simple towage, on the other hand, is a service that is based on the employment of one vessel to expedite the voyage of another when nothing more is required than the acceleration of her progress. Simple towage is regarded as having taken place when a tow is called for or taken by a *sound* vessel as a mere means of saving time or for considerations of convenience.[55] The hallmark of *towage* is the absence of peril. The motivation for the towing service is convenience not safety. An example would be where a sailboat, proceeding under sail in light airs without difficulty, requests towing assistance from a power vessel to expedite the vessel's return to her mooring in order to allow the passengers to meet an appointment.

In many cases of salvage, there is no generic difference between the physical acts of towage and salvage, where towage may be a salvage service when it is rendered to property actually in danger or where danger is reasonably to be apprehended. Some courts have designated the term as either *salvage towage* or as extraordinary *towage* where salvage service has been recognized. A typical case would arise when a powered vessel has run out

---

52 Gilmore and Black, The Law of Admiralty, § 8-2 and accompanying notes (2d ed. 1975).
53 The ANGIE & FLORENCE, 77 F. Supp. 404 (D. Mass. 1948).
54 3A Benedict on Admiralty, §§ 1-185.
55 Scott v. The CLARA E. BERGEN, 21 F. Cas. 816 (D.S.C. 1882) (No. 12,526a).

of fuel or is disabled and adrift at sea, but the only assistance required is a tow to a safe mooring.[56] In such cases, the level of salvage services would be extremely low when the service is rendered in harbor or close to shore in calm weather and when numerous other vessels or towboats were available to render the same service.[57]

Because of the relatively low order of salvage in such cases, coupled with the ready availability of numerous other companies to render such services on fixed price hourly rates, it is the almost universal practice of salvors to provide such services on a fixed price basis or hourly rate. However, the services remain salvage services albeit rendered on a fixed price basis. The distinction is important because if the good weather and calm seas are replaced with high seas and an approaching hurricane, if the locale is moved many miles offshore where no other assistance is available, and if the entire context of the services and their value changes radically.

Context is very important in determining both the nature of services and the amount of compensation. Another issue of *context*, which often leads to confusion with regard to the nature of the services involved, is that of the recreational vessel, which is aground.

IV. Peril in Groundings

One of the most litigated areas of salvage verses towage is that of groundings. Groundings in shallow water pose additional questions with regard to the existence of a *marine peril*. As previously stated, the admiralty courts of the United States have universally held that a vessel, which is aground, is presumed to be in a condition of peril exposed as she is to wind, weather, and waves.[58] However, some parties have difficulty in understanding this

---

56 Baker v. Hemenway, 2 F. Cas. 463 (D. Mass. 1876) (No. 770); *see also* The REBECCA SHEPHERD, 148 F. 727 (D. Me. 1906); Blake v. Baltimore & Carolina C.S.S. Co., 211 F. 116 (5th Cir. 1914).
57 AMERICAN PRODUCER, 1972 AMC 1647 (1972); J.M. Guffey Petroleum Co. v. Borison, 211 F. 594 (5th Cir. 1914).
58 De Aldamiz v. Th. Skogland & Sons, 17 F.2d 873 (5th Cir. 1927).

concept inasmuch as they feel that if a vessel is aground, she is not in any danger of sinking. The uninitiated do not appreciate the dangers and perils inherent in a grounding situation.

First, the underwater body or hull of a vessel is designed by a naval architect to be supported by the hydrostatic forces of the water. When vessels are not supported by such hydrostatic forces, as when the vessel is placed in dry dock, great care must be taken to ensure that the hull of the vessel is properly supported at places designated for support by the naval architect. If supporting stresses are not placed at pre-designed locations, the hull can fracture or cause the vessel to break her keel. This is especially true of larger yachts and so-called *mega-yachts*, while smaller, trailer-size vessels are much more capable of sustaining a *soft* grounding without any hull damage.

Hull stress peril is especially significant in the case of a large (45' or larger) vessel in a grounding situation. In a typical grounding, the bow of the vessel is hard aground. As the vessel attempts to back off the grounding, the propeller washes the bottom material away from underneath the hull between the propellers and the bow. When the vessel's efforts to free herself with her propellers are unsuccessful, the vessel then settles onto the propellers, struts, afterkeel, and rudders. Frequently, the efforts to free the vessel result in a condition where the bow and the stern are aground with a depression under the center of the hull as a result of the prop wash. Such a condition is extremely dangerous to a vessel and may result in the vessel sagging and breaking her back. Experienced salvors are aware of this possibility and move quickly to place air bags under the hull in order to provide support.

Similarly, in many grounding situations, although the vessel does not possess sufficient reserve buoyancy to float itself off the strand, there can be enough buoyancy that the vessel, when acted upon by wind and waves, will momentarily be lifted completely or partially off the strand and then come back into contact with the bottom as the influence of the swell or wind withdraws from the vessel. This condition is commonly referred to as *pounding*, and it is a significant danger to any vessel in a grounding situation. Under such conditions, the hull of the vessel may be brought into violent contact with portions of the reef, rocks, or hardpan shoal. Pounding conditions are especially common toward the stern, including propellers and rudders, since this is usually the last portion of the vessel to ground and is usually in deeper water than the bow.

Pounding conditions in the vicinity of a vessel's stern are especially dangerous regardless of the size of the vessel. Propellers, which pound across the bottom, can be bent to the point where they cannot be repaired. Pounding stresses on propellers can bend fragile propeller shafts and damage expensive stern tubes. Pounding forces can also cause significant bending and damage to rudders and struts. In some cases, pounding can also drive propeller struts and rudders up through the bottom of the vessel, resulting in flooding of the interior hull and/or release of bilge water, fuel and other contaminants, resulting in marine pollution. In the case of gasoline vessels, driving propeller struts or rudders into fuel tanks can result in fire and explosion. Pounding, therefore, is a significant marine peril, which is inherent in any grounding situation. It has been said that a vessel that is pounding is in great peril, and successful deliverance from such a situation commends the salvors for a liberal salvage reward.[59]

Even if the vessel does not pound under normal or moderate weather conditions, most vessels will pound when tropical thunderstorms, squalls, and weather fronts move through the area. In the tropics particularly, it is well known that benign, calm, and sunny conditions can quickly deteriorate in a matter of hours into violent winds and seas as the result of a passing tropical thunderstorm. From the end of April until the beginning of November, severe tropical thunderstorms are an almost daily occurrence. As lines of thunderstorms or thunder cells pass through the area, winds will suddenly increase to 30 to 40 mph and quickly generate seas of four to six feet even

---

59 The CRASTER HALL, 213 F. 436 (5th Cir. 1914).

in shallow bay areas. The threat of such storms has been found by the Fifth Circuit to be sufficient peril to justify a salvage award.[60]

Vessels, which are grounded in shallow water in such circumstances, face not only the peril of pounding but, unless the vessels are properly secured and monitored, the fierce winds and wind-driven seas have been known to drive them off the strand and ashore on other reefs in an uncontrolled manner, resulting in significant additional damage. Similarly, a vessel aground under such conditions is also exposed to a high degree of peril as a result of the lightning, which often accompanies such storms. A grounded vessel under such circumstances, which receives a lightning strike will, at a minimum, suffer severe damage to her electronics and electrical system and, in many cases, undergo a resultant fire.

It must be remembered that the marine peril to vessels under such circumstances increases with the passage of time. Passage of time not only increases the probability of additional damage through severe weather, wind, waves, or lightning but also increases the duration of the period during which other natural forces are at work on the vessel. In bays and inlets, there are many currents, which are affected both by tide, weather, and wind. These currents set up hydraulic forces on the vessel, which can result in damage, or ,which can significantly impair recovery of the vessel. In some cases, hydraulic currents will deposit bottom material and siltation against the hull of the vessel creating a suction effect, which makes it increasingly difficult to free the vessel from the bottom. Again, this threat is directly proportional to the size of the vessel and can be a very real problem in the case of larger yachts. Unless prompt action is taken to remove the vessel, future recovery operations may require that fuel, bilge water, water, and other consumables be pumped off the vessel and that the vessel be stripped of electronics, furnishings, and other equipment in order to lighten it. Such operations are not only time consuming and expensive but also significantly increase the

---

60 Ft. Myers Shell & Dredging Co. v. BARGE NBC 512, 404 F.2d 137 at 139 (5th Cir. 1968).

possibility of marine pollution and damage to the vessel and its contents. Hydraulic currents have also been known to scour bottom material from partial areas beneath the hull, thus setting up an increased probability of stress fractures to the hull or sagging. In areas of soft sand bottoms, there is a likelihood of the vessel working herself into the bottom and becoming embedded in the sand. In such a case, if the vessel is not removed promptly, the stranding becomes permanent and the vessel breaks up or sinks.[61]

Aside from the danger inherent to the vessel in a grounding situation, there is also inherent danger to the people involved in attempting to remove the vessel from the strand. Undeniably, a certain amount of danger is inherent in any salvage operation. Since braided nylon lines are used to pull and tow grounded vessels, the strain placed upon these lines creates a significant risk of injury to salvage crews should the line part or a hull fitting on the salvaged vessel give way. The larger the vessel being pulled, the greater the strain. When a nylon line under strain parts, the resulting whiplash effect is capable of taking off limbs and has been known to kill salvage crew members. Should cleats or hull fittings on the salvaged vessel give way, they become missiles, which have killed and maimed crew members on the towing vessel. Because of the extremely shallow water around the vessel, the salvage vessels involved are in constant danger of going aground and causing damage to their own hulls, propellers, and rudders. Additionally, when operating in shallow water, the possibility of ingesting bottom material causing damage to engines and pumps is also a constant threat to salvage vessels.

From the foregoing, it should be obvious to even the most lubberly that the concept of a *simple grounding* of which the uninformed speak with such ease is far from *simple.* Varying degrees of peril to both the vessel and the salvor are almost always present. There are, however, some circumstances when a vessel aground is not in peril and the services involved in removing her from the grounding are, in fact, towage rather than salvage.

---

61 Atlantic Towing Co. v. The CALICHE, 47 F. Supp. 610 (D. Ga. 1942).

Vessels can and do intentionally safely ground themselves on soft bottoms for a variety of reasons. This is particularly true of smaller recreational vessels whose hulls and running gear are not unduly stressed by the forces of such a situation. Similarly, when the vessel is undamaged, aground on a soft bottom, and capable of freeing herself without assistance at the next tide, the service of towing her off before the tide to save strain on the vessel's engines or to avoid the necessity of the persons on board getting out and pushing may be more of a convenience than a necessity.[62]

Each such case must be decided on its own facts. The issue is whether the services were necessitated by the peril or provided as a matter of convenience. Generally, the better practice, and one followed by many pleasure boat salvors in such situations is the *one boat, one hour* concept, which is treated as a convenience tow and billed on a fixed rate—hourly basis. In other words, if they can get the vessel off using one boat within an hour, it is a *convenience* to the owner and not treated as salvage. It must be remembered, however, that when the vessel is hard aground, pounding on a reef, disabled, seriously damaged, or otherwise in appreciable peril, the concept does not apply regardless of the number of vessels or the amount of time involved. In each case, the presence of peril and the degree of that peril must be determined based on the circumstances applicable to that case. There are *few rules of thumb* or inviolate principles that can be applied to every case.

V. A Case Review of Other Potential Towage Versus Salvage Situations

A. Evanow v. M/V Neptune, 163 F.3d 1108, 1111-19 (9th Cir. 1998):

> One evening, the vessel Neptune encountered a major storm and sought refuge in the Crescent City harbor. While in the harbor, the Neptune became disabled and grounded on a sandy

---

62 La Rue v. United Fruit Co., 181 F.2d 895 (4th Cir. 1950).

shoal. The crew of the Neptune secured the barge alongside the disabled tug.

That night the storm, which was the worst in the Crescent City area in years, caused gusts up to ninety knots and swells inside the harbor to reach six to eight feet. These conditions pounded the barge against the port side of the tug. Because of the diesel fuel and oil aboard the Neptune, as well as hydraulic fluid in the landing craft unit, the Coast Guard Pacific Pollution Strike Team assessed the threat of pollution as *substantial*, and a tow was called in to retrieve the barge.

The question presented was whether a contract is one for towage or for salvage. The Court enumerated that this distinction has several consequences.

"If the fee is not agreed to, salvage service commands a larger award. 1 Martin J. Norris, *The Law of Seamen* § 9:45 (4th ed. 1985) (*Norris*). Under a salvage contract, not only is the vessel liable for payment, but the cargo is as well. 3A Martin J. Norris, *Benedict on Admiralty* § 186 (7th ed. 1993) (*Benedict*). A salvage contract also creates a *preferred* maritime lien, which has a higher priority than the maritime lien created by a contract. *Compare* 46 U.S.C. § 31301(5) *with* § 31342(a). Finally, the crew of the salving vessel has additional rights under a salvage contract. *Norris* at § 9:45."

The Court examined the character of the service rendered to determine whether a contract is one for salvage.[63] The Court found a marked and clear distinction between a towage and a salvage service. When a tug is called or taken by a sound vessel as a mere means of saving time or from considerations of

---

63 The Camanche, 75 U.S. (8 Wall.) 448, 477, 19 L.Ed. 397 (1869).

convenience, the service is classed as towage; but if the vessel is disabled and in need of assistance, it is a salvage service.

It was determined that the existence of a marine peril distinguishes a salvage contract from one for towage.[64] Such a peril exists "when a vessel is exposed to any actual or apprehended danger which might result in her destruction." *Faneuil Advisors, Inc. v. O/S Sea Hawk,* 50 F.3d 88, 92 (1st Cir.1995). Whether a marine peril exists is a question of fact reviewed for clear error. *Clifford v. M/V Islander,* 751 F.2d 1, 5 (1st Cir.1984). In this case it was determined that this was indeed a salvage action.

B. The Flottbek, 118 F. 954, 960-65 (9th Cir. 1902):

The Flottbek was a vessel caught in a rough storm about a quarter mile to a half mile from the rocks. While the peril was in dispute, the fact that the vessel was unable to pull out of the predicament on its own accord was not. Thus, it anchored and called for help.

In cases of simple towage, only a reasonable compensation is allowed, as upon a quantum meruit. In case of salvage, the award is upon a broader and more liberal scale, as we have before stated. In McConnochie v. Kerr (D.C.) 9 Fed. 50, 53, Judge Brown said: "A salvage service is a service which is voluntarily rendered to a vessel needing assistance, and is designed to relieve her from some distress or danger either present or to be reasonably apprehended. A towage service is one which is rendered for the mere purpose of expediting her voyage without reference to any circumstances of danger." The Court found that the crew felt that they were in enough peril to call for assistance and to drop their anchors for an expedited departure. Therefore, this was a salvage.

---

64 The Flottbek, 118 F. 954, 960 (9th Cir.1902).

C. The Catalina, 105 F. 633 (5th Cir. 1900):

The Catalina suffered a broken shaft and lost the ability to steer the vessel. They flagged down the Olympia, and a hawser of the Catalina was carried aboard by the crew of the Catalina, made fast on the Olympia, and the towage service commenced. The weather was calm and pleasant, the sea also, and the towage service went on without incident until about 12:45 p.m. of the 13th of January, when, near South Pass, the Olympia stopped to take on pilots, and then, starting abruptly, the hawser parted. Thereupon the Catalina furnished another hawser, delivered it aboard the Olympia, and the towing proceeded until about 2 p.m., when the Catalina was left in a condition of safety at South Pass, and the Olympia resumed her voyage; having been detained by the services rendered to the Catalina from 22 to 24 hours. The Lower Court found

> This cause having been submitted on the evidence, and after arguments of counsel, the court finds: The court thinks this is clearly a case of salvage. The steamer had
>
> broken her shaft and was without sufficient sails to make steering way; and in the month of January, in the Gulf of Mexico, in that condition, she was in need of assistance. She was in distress. She so signaled, and received the necessary aid. The late Judge Billings, in the case of The Delhonde, very properly says that a vessel in the Gulf of Mexico with a broken shaft or propeller is at the mercy of the elements because the Gulf of Mexico is a dangerous water. It is true that both of the vessels in this case were in ballast and without passengers and that there was no evidence of immediate or imminent peril. There was little or no immediate danger to the officers or crew of either of the vessels.

The Appeals Court found that there was no salvage, as there was no peril.

> Salvage, in its simple character, is the service, which volunteer adventurers spontaneously render to the owners in the recovery of property from loss or damage at sea, under the responsibility of making restitution and with a lien for their reward (Macl Shipp. 608). Salvage is the compensation due to persons by

whose voluntary assistance a ship or its lading has been saved to the owner from impending perils or recovered after actual loss. Ben. Adm. Sec. 300. Salvage consists of an adequate compensation for the actual outlay of labor and expense used in the enterprise and of the reward as bounty allowed from motives of public policy as a means of encouraging extraordinary exertions in the saving of life and property in peril at sea.

D. Mississippi Valley Barge Line Co. v. Indian Towing Co., 232 F.2d 750, 751-55 (5th Cir. 1956):

A barge was adrift in a calm sea with running swells and a southwest wind of 18 to 20 mph. As the Cherokee was rolling 15 to 20 degrees in the swells, the tug pulled beside the barge in order to get a mate on board, thus commencing the tow and delivering the barge at a Pensacola dock three hours later.

A derelict barge, like a derelict person, may be exposed to many perils, the least of which is foundering on an obvious shoal. Salvage at sea may and often does call for the performance of exciting acts of great bravery to rescue lives or property from the jaws of a near and certain doom. But it need not for the aim of salvage is to save and to aid before it is a do-or-die wager with high risks, high stakes, and high rewards and assures the greatest likelihood of recovery at the least peril. Maritime salvage is not reserved for hero alone. Its generous but judicious liberality is to encourage mariners instinctively to respond to need—be it great or small, drab or spectacular, certain in the knowledge that the scale of The Blackwall, 10 Wall. 1, 77 U.S. 1, 19 L.Ed. 870, provides the means to find a balance. Is a barge at drift in peril a salvage? The Court thought so.

E. The Joseph F. Clinton, 250 F. 977, 978-80 (2d Cir. 1918):

The tow is contracted to take on a barge, which it was clearly the tug's duty under the contract of towage to get the barge, Clinton, to a place of safety, if reasonably nearby and to be reached without danger to the rest of the tow,

Henrico. As the barge begins to take on water, and the tower repairs the tow in order to deliver the goods under contract, is it still a tow or a salvage?

There is a principle that a tug is bound by the contract of towage not to abandon both tow and contract when the former gets into trouble until the reasonable resources of good seamanship are exhausted. The tug's engagement is usually, as here, to take the tow from one place to another in a skillful manner (The Thomas Purcell, Jr., 92 Fed. 406, 34 C.C.A. 419), and when danger arises, the tow cannot be abandoned until all reasonable efforts for its preservation have been exhausted (The Carbonero, 122 Fed. 753, 58 C.C.A. 553; The Geo. Hughes, 183 Fed. 211, 105 C.C.A. 643), and the burden of showing such efforts is on the tug (Re Cahill, 124 Fed. 63, 59 C.C.A. 519).

For services outside the contemplation of the parties in making the contract for towage, remuneration may be given, and if they amount to salvage, a salvage award is due. The City of Haverhill (D.C.) 66 Fed. 159. What is salvage, as distinguished from mere towage, has been sometimes discussed (The Viola, 55 Fed. 829, 5 C.C.A. 283; United States v. Morgan, 99 Fed. 570, 39 C.C.A. 653) without, we think, advancing beyond the test for salvage laid down by Brown, J. (The Plymouth Rock (D.C.) 12 Fed. 634; McConnochie v. Kerr (D.C.) 9 Fed. 50); that is a successful effort to rescue from an actual or apprehended danger.[1]

As applied to a boat in tow, it is said, and truly, that promptly to deviate into a harbor of refuge is to guard against danger; and it is also true that volunteer towage is often a salvor's effort, but the contract of towage, while not imposing the duty of deviation, established a relation, which made a moderate charge for deviating sufficient. After reaching the destination, the two would have sunk at her mooring had it not been for the prompt and efficient labors of the Henrico's engineers and the use of the tug's syphon. That rescue from imminent danger was beyond both the towage agreement and reasonable expectation except as a salvage service.

F.   La Rue v. United Fruit Co., 181 F.2d 895, 896-99 (4th Cir. 1950):

A storm arose and the vessel, The San Jose, has pushed up soft aground. It was scheduled to disembark with a load of cargo but had to wait until high tide. The crew unloaded and reloaded another vessel; in the meantime, The San Jose was freed from its muddy a grounding.

The Court found that the services rendered to the San Jose were towage and not salvage.

A concise statement of the distinction between towage and salvage is cited from The Emanuel Stavroudis, D.C., 23 F.2d 214, 216, 1927 A.M.C. 1313, 1317:

> A salvage service is a service, which is voluntarily rendered to a vessel in need of assistance and is designated to relieve her from distress or danger, either present or to be reasonably apprehended; and salvage is the reward or compensation allowed by the maritime law for service rendered in saving maritime property, at risk or in distress, by those under no legal obligation to render it, which results in benefit to the property, if eventually saved. The Blackwell, 10 Wall. 1, 77 U.S. 1, 19 L.Ed. 870; The Pleasure Bay, D.C., 226 F. 55; The Neshaminy, 3 Cir., 228 F. 285. Salvage service is to be distinguished from towage service in that the latter is a service, which is rendered for the mere purpose of expediting a vessel's voyage without reference to any circumstances of danger although the service in each case may be and frequently is rendered in the same way.

To the same effect see The Mercer, 2 Cir., 297 F. 981, 984. In most cases, which allowed salvage for the rescue of a stranded vessel, the ship was unable to free itself and even if not in imminent danger, would have been in peril in case of storm. Thus, in DeAldamiz v. Th. Skogland & Sons, 5 Cir., 17 F.2d 873, at page 874, the Court said, "There was real danger that the ship would become a total loss. It is idle to argue that a ship aground in shallow water on a sea beach, exposed to wind and wave in the hurricane season, is in a safe place."

In the Leonie O. Louise, 5 Cir., 4 F.2d 699, at page 700, it was stated, "Although the danger was not imminent, it was reasonably to be apprehended, and there was pressing necessity for prompt action to return the schooner to the water. She was out of commerce and useless in her then situation—to all intents and purposes a total loss as a vessel unless floated."

In The Freedom, 1932 A.M.C. 933 at page 935, the Court said, "It is not necessary that there be danger immediately impending, but if the vessel is stranded so that it is subject to the potential danger of damage or destruction, she may well be a subject of salvage services."

In The Sahara, D.C., 246 F. 141, 142, where the Court found that "the ship's engines might have gotten her off" and "during all the time the weather was good, and the ship was in no imminent danger." A salvage award was granted, but the Court went on to say, 246 F. at page 142, that "the coast, however, is very dangerous, and no ship can wisely take chances with it." See also Baker v. Hemenway, 2 Fed. Cas. page 463, No. 770, where a stranded vessel could have freed herself, but a salvage award was allowed because it was doubtful whether she could have gotten off before high water, at which time, she would have been placed in a dangerous situation.

In Bond v. A. H. Bull S.S. Co., D.C., 13 F.2d 893, 894, 1926 A.M.C. 1120, a vessel was stranded and unable to get off under her own power. Under a contract of towage, which stipulated that the service was not salvage, the ship was freed by a tug. Though the Court stated that 'the ship cannot deprive the crew of their salvage rights,' the crew of the tug was not allowed any salvage award. In Stone v. Tug Pejepscot, 1939 A.M.C. 316, a tug and barge went aground. The weather was good and the vessels were in no danger. Attempts to pull the tug off were successful and the barge finally managed to free itself. The Court held that the service to the grounded vessels was high towage and not salvage.

In the instant case there was substantial evidence to support the conclusion of the District Court that the San Jose was not in danger, either imminent or reasonably to be apprehended. There was evidence that the

San Jose was in a protected harbor, anchored so as to prevent her from being blown farther aground, and that she could have gotten off the mud bank unaided. Therefore, this was merely an act of towage.

G. Magnolia Petroleum Co. v. Nat'l Oil Transp. Co., 286 F. 40 (5th Cir. 1923)

The Barryton used coal for fuel, and while she was at Aransas Pass, Tex., her master on November 9th notified the charterer that he could not go any farther without coal. The charterer replied that it would furnish coal at Tampico and ordered the master to proceed to that place. In obedience to this order, the Barryton arrived on November 11th at Tampico, where great difficulty was encountered in procuring a supply of coal. On November 16th, the charterer telegraphed the owner's agent that the Barryton was unable to sail on account of shortage of fuel and that it was sending 100 tons from Galveston.

Thereupon the captain of the Bolikow entered into negotiations with the master of the Greer for a tow of the Bolikow to Tampico. The master of the Greer demanded $20,000. The

captain of the Bolikow refused to pay that amount but stated he would pay anything within reason. Finally, the master of the Greer stated that he would perform the service for the sum of $15,000 and that he was going to leave if the captain of the Bolikow did not agree to pay it. Under these circumstances, the captain of the Bolikow signed an agreement to pay $15,000 to the owners of the Greer for towing the Bolikow to Tampico. The Bolikow was then made fast to Barge No. 7 and was towed by the Greer without incident back to Tampico. The weather was fine and the sea smooth from the time the Bolikow was anchored at sea until she was towed into port.

The Court supported the District Court in refusing to enforce the contract for salvage. The refusal of the master of the Greer to render assistance, and his threat to leave the Bolikow unless his exorbitant demand was acceded to, amounted to moral compulsion, and the contract, which he procured by the methods adopted, is not protected or made binding and valid by the rule laid down in The Elfrida, 172 U.S. 186, 19 Sup.Ct. 146, 43 L.Ed. 413.

The only element of salvage present in this case was the apparent danger to the Bolikow and her crew. The Bolikow, because of her inability to trim cargo for lack of fresh water and the consequent uselessness of her pumps, would have been in serious danger in case of heavy weather or a rough sea. The helpless condition of the Bolikow raised the assistance rendered from a towage to a salvage service. But the salvage service was of a low order, and the amount awarded, therefore, by the District Judge is, in our opinion, too liberal. The utmost time contended for is from 10:30 a.m. of November 25th to 2:30 p.m. of the next day, or a period of 28 hours, and includes 3 hours before the Bolikow was taken in tow.

The greatest allowance for towage, which could be justified, would be $700. Double the towage rate under the facts of this case would be full compensation. The Catalina, 105 Fed. 633, 44 C.C.A. 638; The Colonel Moore (C.C.A.) 263 Fed. 868; The Jean L. Somerville (C.C.A.) 286 Fed. 35 (decided December 19, 1922). The time lost by the Greer did not exceed half a day and was of the value of about $300. We are of opinion, therefore, that an award of $1,700 is amply sufficient. Thus, while this was salvage, the Court clearly did not take kindly to the extortion attempted by the rescuing party.

H. The Kennebec, 231 F. 423, 424-27 (5th Cir. 1916):

The steamship Kennebec grounded at the mouth of the Brazos River near the jetties about 40 miles from Galveston. S. E. Paul, the agent of the owner of the vessel from Brazos Port, a place on shore nearby, had a conversation over the long-distance telephone with Mr. Stoneburner, an officer of the owner of the steam tug, Senator Bailey at Galveston, with reference to getting that tug to render the assistance required to get the Kennebec afloat. The result of that conversation was that Mr. Stoneburner, for his company, the libellant, agreed to furnish the services of the tug and equipment for $250 per day from the time she left Galveston until she returned. Following the making of that agreement, the tug on the same day went to the mouth of the Brazos, reaching there after dark, and the next morning it pulled the Kennebec from where it was aground.

If the contract made by Mr. Stoneburner and Mr. Paul was a binding one and the service mentioned was rendered in pursuance of it, though it was a salvage service, the only compensation recoverable for it is the one which was stipulated for $250 per day, which was awarded by the decree appealed from. A valid contract by one party to pay at all events and by the other to receive a fixed compensation for a salvage service is as conclusive as any other valid contract. The Elfrida, 172 U.S. 186, 19 Sup.Ct. 146, 43 L.Ed. 413; Elphicke v. White Line Towing Company, 106 Fed. 945, 46 C.C.A. 56. Therefore, this was a contracted salvage at a fixed price and the final word.

I. Blake v. Baltimore & C. S. S. Co. of Baltimore City, 211 F. 116 (5th Cir. 1914): The vessel owners call in a mayday as they are practically aground and pounding on the shoal lumps in the vicinity; a tow was sent out to help. However, whatever may have been the Davenport's condition the night before or when her first call for assistance was sent out, at the time the Weems arrived the Davenport was afloat, and, although in a dangerous position, needed nothing but towage services to take her out of danger into safe waters.

Thus, the Court found that the services actually rendered by reason of the call for assistance, the dangerous waters navigated, and the skillful pilotage required were extraordinary towage services, and not salvage as the conditions had changed over time.

VI.   Conclusion

The importance of whether it is a tow or salvage is not important on the front end, as the work must be done either to save the vessel or to transport to the vessel, but on the back end where the compensation is measured. The compensation can be contracted for or *pure* as described above.

As far as towage is concerned, ***Art. 4 of the* Brussels Convention**

on Salvage 1910 provides as follows: "A tug has no right to remuneration for assistance to or salvage of the vessel she is towing or of the vessel's cargo, except where she has rendered exceptional services which cannot be considered as rendered in fulfilment of the contract of towage."

Similarly, **Article 17 of the 1989 Salvage Convention** provides that "No payment is due under the provisions of this Convention unless the services rendered exceed what can be reasonably considered as due performance of a contract entered into before the danger arose."

The distinction between salvage and towage is an important one to the crew of the salving ship because the crew has no interest or rights in a contract for towage, but if the owners of the respective vessels contract for towage, when in fact the services are salvage services, the crew of the salving ship is entitled to salvage and can look either to the salved vessel[65], or if the owner of the salving ship—that is the salving crew's employer—has received it to the money paid under the contract for its share of a salvage award.[66] Purely put there is no maritime lien upon a tow for the payment of the price fixed by the towage contract, whereas a salver has a maritime lien over property salved, which could include a tower, if the duties were above those contracted for.

The salvor, who has earned the right to a salvage award through successful, voluntary salvage services to a vessel in peril has a high-priority possessory, preferred maritime lien on the vessel.[67] A salvor in possession of a vessel is not bound to surrender it on demand to the owner until reasonable security has been provided for his claim. On the other hand, the salvor must move with all deliberate speed to either arrange for the posting of security or bring an action *en rem* against the vessel to foreclose his lien. However, it is improper for the salvor to deny the owner or his agents' access

---

65 The Olockson, 281 F. 690 (C.C.A. 5th Cir. 1922); Evanow v. M/V Neptune, 163 F.3d 1108 (9th Cir. 1998); Bergher v. General Petroleum Co., 242 F. 967 (N.D. Cal. 1917); Rauch v. Gulf Refining Co., 129 F. Supp. 843 (E.D. La. 1955); Squires v. The Ionian Leader, 100 F. Supp. 829 (D.N.J. 1951).

66 Force and Norris, The Law of Seamen § 9:47 (5th ed.).

67 46 U.S.C. § 31301(5)(F) (1993); The FAIRFIELD, 30 F. 700 (D. Ga. 1887).

to his vessel or property to inspect or preserve it.[68] Thus, the general rule is that the salvor may retain possession of a vessel until either the owner posts adequate security, or it is established that he will not. The salvor must in the former case release the vessel to the owner or, in the latter case, turn the vessel over to the U.S. Marshal and proceed to foreclose his lien. When the salvor is not in possession of the vessel, such as when he tows a vessel with its crew still aboard off a strand and it then can proceed on its own, there is little that the salvor can do when the vessel throws off the towline and departs. The salvor must rely on his lien and seek enforcement by an action against the vessel or its owner.[69] Thus, the distinction between a tow and a salvage not only affects the amount of payment it may also affect whether you have priority to receive payment. At the end of the day, the real difference between towage and salvage is how big a hole in the water your vessel has created to throw money in.

68 ALCAZAR, 227 F. 633 (D.N.Y. 1915).
69 Albion Lumber Co. v. Inter-Ocean Transp. Co., 240 F. 1017 (D. Cal. 1914).

PART THREE

The End of the American Small Port:
A Prospectus on the End of Small Ports in the United States

As the pendulum lifts one, it leaves the other to fall.

I. Introduction

On December 10, 1912, a meeting of public port officials from throughout the United States convened in New York City to "exchange ideas relative to port organizations, to promote the exchange of information and the development of uniform methods of administration, and possibly to provide for some permanent organization between the principal port authorities,"[1] thus the American Association of Port Authorities was founded. It was organized to promote the American ports and also to coordinate their efforts, but over the course of 100 years, it appears that the American port landscape has drastically shifted. The bread and butter of American commerce, the American small port, have been reduced in favor of the big, do-it-all port. The treatment of these ports by U.S. maritime policy is much like the end of the mom-and-pop stores for large department/grocery/hardware stores.

Many of the ports that have been left to wade in their own silt have been the American small ports, like the Port of Georgetown, South Carolina. Once historically significant but no longer able to handle the large ships nor equipped to handle containers, it has closed permanently. These ports have been left in the wake of modernization by the shippers, carriers, and their port authority. Many of these ports will close and devastate their local economy; however, salvation may be available. The salvation for small ports will not be in their history but in their future. The ability to adapt to the modern world of giant ports is much like David with his slingshot taking aim at one specific spot on the giant.

A. Maritime Commerce Over the Last 100 years

1. Panama Canal

In 1914, the Panama Canal opened to commercial shipping

---

1 Aaron Ellis, *Ports Association Formed 100 Years Ago Today*, December 10, 2012, at http://www.aapa-ports.org/Press/PRdetail.cfm?itemnumber=18847.

traffic.[2] The opening of the canal created a new world for global trade and forever altered shipping routes for United States ports. Now, 100 years later by the end of 2014, the Panama Canal is scheduled to have completed its greatest expansion, more than doubling its capacity and allowing it to handle the world's most massive ships.[3] Currently, the maximum capacity of a ship crossing the Panama Canal is 4,800 TEUs (TEU is one standard shipping container).[4] The improvements currently underway would allow for much bigger ships: 50 percent wider, 25 percent longer, and with a volume of more than 12,000 TEUs.[5] These vessels draft at a significantly lower depth and need the ability to draft at minimum from 39.5 feet to 50 feet.[6]

Seventeen ports across the United States are being studied for dredging by the U.S. Army Corps of Engineers, including Baltimore, Charleston, Jacksonville, Miami, Baltimore, and Savannah.[7] Each of these ports is a massive, centralized port that is designed to handle the post-Panamex ships that have become the focus of maritime commerce in the modern world. Long forgotten are the break bulk ships and ports that service such rarities. With a current port required channel depth of a minimum 40 feet to handle the largest ships currently coming through the canal, many small ports are unable to accommodate such large ships. However, a loaded 8,000 TEU vessel (i.e., a

---

2 Ryan Holeywell, *Panama Canal Expansion Has U.S. Ports Rushing,* July 2012, at http:// www.governing.com/panama-canal-expansion-has-ports-rushing.html.

3 Ryan Holeywell, *Panama Canal Expansion Has U.S. Ports Rushing,* July 2012, at http:// www.governing.com/panama-canal-expansion-has-ports-rushing.html.

4 Ryan Holeywell, *Panama Canal Expansion Has U.S. Ports Rushing,* July 2012, at http:// www.governing.com/panama-canal-expansion-has-ports-rushing.html.

5 Ryan Holeywell, *Panama Canal Expansion Has U.S. Ports Rushing,* July 2012, at http:// www.governing.com/panama-canal-expansion-has-ports-rushing.html.

6 Ryan Holeywell, *Panama Canal Expansion Has U.S. Ports Rushing,* July 2012, at http:// www.governing.com/panama-canal-expansion-has-ports-rushing.html.

7 Ryan Holeywell, *Panama Canal Expansion Has U.S. Ports Rushing,* July 2012, at http:// www.governing.com/panama-canal-expansion-has-ports-rushing.html.

Post-Panamex vessel) sits 46 to 47 feet deep in saltwater and a foot deeper in freshwater.[8]

This deeper draft requirement necessitates a channel depth of nearly 50 feet, which many East and Gulf Coast ports currently lack. A 2010 U.S. Army Corps of Engineers study determined that insufficient navigation channel depths restrict nearly 30% of port vessel calls, thus necessitating the need for large ports to dredge in order to incorporate larger vessels; however, this need eliminates the funding available for smaller ports.[9] This lack of funding available to maintain America's small ports has led many small ports that are unable to accommodate the larger vessels, to fall into disrepair due to lack of maintenance and eventually become fully obsolete due to their inability to be accessed.

2. *Containerization*

The current need to expand the Panama Canal originated in 1956 with the advent of containerization. Malcom McLean first invented the method of containerization to affect the efficiency and costs of shipping cargo from his trucking line, McLean Trucking.[10] In 1961, before the container was in international use, ocean freight costs accounted for 12 percent of the value of U.S. exports and 10 percent of the value of U.S. imports. According to the staff of the Joint Economic Committee of Congress, "these costs are more significant in many cases than governmental trade barriers," noting that the average U.S. import tariff

---

8 Jeffery Spivak, *The Battle of the Ports*, American Planning Association, May/June 2011, at http://aapa.files.cms-plus.com/Battle%20of%20the%20Ports%20-%20 Planning%20mag%20-%20May_June%202011.pdf.

9 Jeffery Spivak, *The Battle of the Ports*, American Planning Association, May/June 2011, at http://aapa.files.cms-plus.com/Battle%20of%20the%20Ports%20-%20 Planning%20mag%20-%20May_June%202011.pdf.

10 Brian Cudahy, *The Containership Revolution: Malcom McLean's 1956 Innovation Goes Global*, TR News, October 2006, at http://onlinepubs.trb.org/onlinepubs/trnews/trnews246.pdf.

was 7 percent.[11] This process was so expensive that in many cases, selling internationally it was not worthwhile due to the costs of shipping. The container dramatically affected these costs.

The elimination of piece-by-piece freight handling brought lower expenses for long shore labor, insurance, pier rental, and the like. Containers were quickly adopted for land transportation, and the reduction in loading time and transshipment cost lowered rates for goods that moved entirely by land. As ship lines built huge vessels designed to handle containers, ocean freight rates plummeted. As container shipping became intermodal, with a seamless shifting of containers among ships, trucks, and trains, goods could move in a never-ending stream from Asian factories directly to the stockrooms of retail stores in North America or Europe, making the overall cost of transporting goods little more than a footnote in a company's cost analysis.[12]

Global containerized trade, 2001 to 2011 (forecast), in million TEU global containerized trade has grown at a compound annual rate of 12 percent from 2001 to 2005. The forecast growth rate for the period 2005 to 2011 was 6.5 percent. In 2011, global containerized trade is forecast to reach 134 million TEU, 2.3 times as much as the 58 million TEU recorded in 2001. The data above represents maritime trade in fully loaded containers, not port throughout, or the movement of full and empty containers.[13] The container trade continues to grow, and as of 2013, represented nearly 90% of maritime commerce into the

---

11 Joint Economic Committee, U.S. Congress, *Discriminatory Ocean Freight Rates and the Balance of Payments,* Washington, D.C., 1964.
12 Marc Levinson, *Shipping Containers and the Economy,* TR News, October 2006, at http://onlinepubs.trb.org/onlinepubs/trnews/trnews246.pdf.
13 Marc Levinson, *Shipping Containers and the Economy,* TR News, October 2006, at http://onlinepubs.trb.org/onlinepubs/trnews/trnews246.pdf.

United States.[14] The growth of these container ships is only a
stepping stone.[15]

As seen in Table 1 and reflected in the value of its imports and
exports, the United States has experienced an explosion in the
growth of its involvement in international trade as trade barriers
have been reduced and containerization has grown. Also noted
in Table 1 is the growing significance of the international trade
in goods for the economy of the United States; by the year 2000,
the total value of imports and exports was equivalent to twenty
percent of the total Gross Domestic Product (GDP).

Table 1. U.S. International Trade in Goods (Billions of Dollars)[16]

Year	Export Value	Import Value	Total Value of Trade	U.S. GDP	Total value of International Trade as Per Cent of U.S. GDP
1960	19.7	14.8	34.5		
1965	26.6	21.5	48.1		
1970	42.5	39.9	82.4	1,039.7	7.93%
1975	107.1	98.2	205.3	1,635.2	12.56%
1980	224.3	249.8	474.1	2,795.6	16.96%
1985	215.9	338.1	554.0	4,213.0	13.15%

---

14 Rose George, *Ninety Percent of Everything*, Metropolitan Books, 2013.
15 Gavin van Marle, *Small ports feel the heat from big box ships as cascade effect begins*, The Load Star, July 1, 2013 at http://theloadstar.co.uk/small-ports-feel-the-heat-from-big-box-ships-as-cascade-effect-begins/.
16 Calculated from data from U.S. Department of Commerce, International Trade Administration, "U.S. Aggregate Foreign Trade Data" at www.ita.doc.gov/td/industry/otea/usfth/tabcon.html.

Year	Export Value	Import Value	Total Value of Trade	U.S. GDP	Total value of International Trade as Per Cent of U.S. GDP
1990	389.3	498.3	887.6	5,803.2	15.3%
1995	575.2	749.4	1,324.6	7,400.5	17.90%
2000	772.2	1,224.4	1,996.6	9,962.7	20.00%

The importance, value, and tonnage will continue to grow as the ships continue to grow. Steamship company Maersk's research concluded that while an 18,000TEU vessel is expected to incur total costs per day at sea of $197,198.00, a 22,000TEU vessel would run-up costs of $220,892.00 per day, and a 24,000TEU ship would incur costs of $229,693.00 per day. However, the cost per slot goes down—with an 18,000TEU vessel incurring a cost of $10.96 per TEU, per day at sea—while a 22,000TEU vessel would cost $10.04 per TEU per day at sea, and a 24,000TEU ship calculated to cost $9.57 per TEU per day at sea. In contrast, a 12,500TEU ship is currently calculated to cost $12.43 per TEU per day at sea. [17]

While these huge vessels carry almost three times as many shipping containers as the freighters currently passing through the canal are capable of carrying, and the containers unloaded from just one giant ocean Post-Panamex vessel fill up the equivalent of more than 20 trains or 3,000 semi-trailer trucks,[18] the revolution begun by Malcom McLean is still growing. Globalization of the past fifty years has resulted in a 90-fold increase in

---

17 Gavin van Marle, *Small ports feel the heat from big box ships as cascade effect begins,* The Load Star, July 1, 2013 at http://theloadstar.co.uk/small-ports-feel-the-heat-from-big-box-ships-as-cascade-effect-begins.
18 Ryan Holeywell, *Panama Canal Expansion Has U.S. Ports Rushing,* July 2012, at http://www.governing.com/panama-canal-expansion-has-ports-rushing.html.

the value of foreign trade,[19] thus with the advent of these massive vessels to reduce the cost of transport, there is no end in sight, but the ports that can handle these ships are limited.

According to the Maritime Administration, in 1997 only four of the ten major U.S. container ports that collectively loaded and unloaded almost eighty percent of container traffic had channel and berthing areas deep enough in draft for fully laden mega-containerships.[21] (See Table 2.)

Table 2. Water Depth for Selected U.S. Container Ports[20]

Port	Channel Depth	Berth Depth	Container Port Ranking
Boston	40	45	23
New York/New Jersey	40	35-45	3
Philadelphia	40	40	21
Baltimore	50	36-42	13
Hampton Roads	50	36-45	7
Wilmington (NC)	40	40	22
Charleston	42	40	4
Savannah	42	42	11

---

19 The combined value of goods exported and imported grew from $35,408 million in 1960 to $3,243,042 in 2009 of which approximate 30% was with Canada and Mexico. The amount moving by sea changed little due impart to the increase in the volume of bulk commodities, especially oil, that moves by sea. "U.S. Trade in Goods and Services - Balance of Payments (BOP) Basis,: U.S. Census Bureau, Foreign Trade Division, http://www.census.gov/foreign-trade/statistics/historical/gands.pdf.

20 U.S. Department of Transportation, Maritime Administration, A Report to Congress on the Status of the Public Ports of the United States, 1996-1997, at www.marad.dot.gov/publications/public_portshtm.htm, p. 50.

Port	Channel Depth	Berth Depth	Container Port Ranking
Jacksonville	38	38	16
Everglades	47	37-44	12
Miami	42	42	8
Gulfport	36	36	18
New Orleans	36 & 45	35	14
Houston	40	38-40	9
Honolulu	45	40	26
Long Beach	76	35-50	1
Los Angeles	45	45	2
Oakland	42	35-42	6
Portland (OR)	40	40	15
Tacoma	40-50	40-50	10
Seattle	75	40-50	5

The future is bright for ports that can handle containerization; however, the focus on the larger container vessels has led to the decrease in funding for the smaller ports unable to accommodate such deep drafting needs. This policy has led to the destruction of lesser-known ports in communities that have relied upon the port for their economic needs.

B. American Small Ports - "Emerging Harbors"

1. The Port of Georgetown, South Carolina

Georgetown is the third oldest city in South Carolina located on the Winyah Bay, the confluence of the Great Pee Dee, Wac-camaw, and Sampit rivers.[21]

Georgetown was founded in 1729 and became an official port of entry in 1732.[22]

Prior to this, all foreign exports and imports had to pass through Charleston. Duties and the added freight had to be paid there.[23] With the designation of Georgetown as a port of entry, the area's merchants and planters could deal directly with all ports bypassing Charleston.[24]

Georgetown was the second largest seaport in South Carolina, behind the Port of Charleston.[25] The Port of Charleston is ranked fifth in the United States based upon the value on its imported cargo.[26] Thus, relegating Georgetown to little sister status, although in 2000, the Port of Georgetown was handling 1.8 million tons of material.[27] However, that number declined to 265,000 pounds in 2008.[28] At the time of closure, the port was handling 550,000 pounds a year despite its limitations.[29]

The Georgetown Channel was last dredged in 2004 to its permitted depth of 29 ft.; however, no maintenance dredging was ever completed resulting in the current depth of 19 ft.[30] In fiscal

---

21 County of Georgetown Website, http://www.cogsc.com/history/history.cfm

22 County of Georgetown Website, http://www.cogsc.com/history/history.cfm

23 County of Georgetown Website, http://www.cogsc.com/history/history.cfm

24 County of Georgetown Website, http://www.cogsc.com/history/history.cfm.

25 Yates Snowden & Harry Gardner Cutler, *History of South Carolina,* The Lewis Publishing Company, 1920.

26 John Frittelli, *Harbor Maintenance Trust Fund Expenditures,* Congressional Research Service, January 25, 2010.

27 Alliance for Economic Development for Georgetown County, *Dredging needed for Georgetown Port, 2010.*

28 Alliance for Economic Development for Georgetown County, *Dredging needed for Georgetown Port, 2010.*

29 Alliance for Economic Development for Georgetown County, *Dredging needed for Georgetown Port, 2010.*

30 Timothy M. Tilley, P.E./CPE, *Port Advisory Committee: Overview of Georgetown Port and Harbor Maintenance Trust Fund,* March 3, 2011.

year 2000, the Georgetown Port handled 1.8 million tons of shipments; unfortunately, in 2010, the Georgetown Port only handled 5 or 6 ships and 107,000 tons of cargo.[31]

The slow steady decline in Georgetown tonnage until its closure can potentially be blamed on a number of factors; however, the United States' own maritime policy shares responsibility in the decline of this American port.

2. America's Small Ports and Harbors Are Suffering

With over 85 percent of our nation's containerized freight flowing through 10 ports,[32] it is understandable that the vast majority of attention is paid to a select few. However, this funding strategy creates a problem for American small ports. This is not a problem for just the Port of Georgetown, SC, but it is severely affecting communities across the United States. In the Pacific Northwest at the Port of Ilwaco, the two-mile channel leading into the Columbia River has been silting in and currently sits at a foot deep at low tide.[33] The U.S. Army Corps of Engineers told officials in Port Orford that its budget for maintaining small harbors—those handling less than 1 million tons of cargo a year—was cut in half this year and is not expected to improve next year or anytime soon.[34] The lack of consistent maritime policy regarding dredging our nation's waterways is

---

31 Timothy M. Tilley, P.E./CPE, *Port Advisory Committee: Overview of Georgetown Port and Harbor Maintenance Trust Fund*, March 3, 2011.

32 US Maritime Administration, *America's Ports and Intermodal Transportation System*, January 2009, at http://www.glmri.org/downloads/Ports&IntermodalTransport.pdf, p. 21.

33 Andre Stepankowsky, *Small Ports in Peril: Federal Cuts mean less dredging*, TDN.com, 2012, at http://tdn.com/news/local/small-ports-in-peril-federal-cuts-mean-less-dredging/article_b41da214-264a-11e2-b09b-001a4bcf887a.html.

34 Andre Stepankowsky, *Small Ports in Peril: Federal Cuts mean less dredging*, TDN.com, 2012, at http://tdn.com/news/local/small-ports-in-peril-federal-cuts-mean-less-dredging/article_b41da214-264a-11e2-b09b-001a4bcf887a.html.

quickly becoming a commercial pandemic, which can only be described as a fiscal boondoggle for this nation.

As the U.S. Maritime Administration recognized almost every one of the nation's top 50 ports handling foreign commerce requires regular maintenance dredging,[35] so do the nation's small ports at a substantially lower cost. While the Port of Charleston will require $13 million to complete its study and over $300 million to actually dredge the harbor,[36] the Port of Georgetown (45 minutes North) will only cost $13 million to dredge, including the already completed study.[37]

Thus, not to be overlooked, the U.S. small and medium size ports play a vital role in the nation's port system. These ports serve specific market niches and have developed special handling techniques for specific commodities, such as fresh `produce, frozen meats, and building materials that are containerized and/or palletized. They can also be the sole source of commodities for isolated communities. Also, these ports provide redundancy and resiliency for emergency preparedness.[38]

C. American Dredging Policy

Since 1789, the federal government has authorized navigation channel improvement projects; the General Survey Act of 1824 established the U.S.

---

35 US Maritime Administration, *America's Ports and Intermodal Transportation System*, January 2009, at http://www.glmri.org/downloads/Ports&IntermodalTransport.pdf, p. 21.

36 Peter Leach, *Charleston Dredging Project Beating Expectations, 2012, at* http://www.joc.com/international-trade-news/infrastructure-news/charleston-dredging-project-beating-expectations_20120711.html.

37 Timothy M. Tilley, P.E./CPE, *Port Advisory Committee: Overview of Georgetown Port and Harbor Maintenance Trust Fund*, March 3, 2011.

38 US Maritime Administration, *America's Ports and Intermodal Transportation System*, January 2009, at http://www.glmri.org/downloads/Ports&IntermodalTransport.pdf, p. 21.

Army Corps of Engineers' role as the agency responsible for the navigation system.[39] Since then, ports have worked in partnership with the Corps of Engineers to maintain waterside access to port facilities.[40] Over 300 million cubic yards of dredged material are removed from navigation channels each year.[41] Another 100 million cubic yards are dredged from berths and private terminals.[42] The total, 400 million cubic yards of dredged material, equals a four-lane highway, 20 feet deep, stretching from New York City to Los Angeles.[43]

Over 90 percent of the nation's top 50 ports in foreign waterborne commerce require regular maintenance dredging.[44] Together these ports move nearly 93 percent of all U.S. waterborne commerce in a given year and receive a large percentage of the Harbor Maintenance Trust Funding.[45] The funding projects of these large ports require massive payouts that leave little funding available for the projects of small ports, which generally require a small percentage of the funding necessary for a large port project.

1. The Harbor Maintenance Trust Fund

In 1986, the Harbor Maintenance Trust Fund was created to provide funds for the U.S. Army Corps of Engineers to use in maintaining operations of U.S. Ports.[46]

The Harbor Maintenance Tax (HMT) currently obligates ex-

---

39 American Association of Port Authorities at http://www.aapa-ports.org/Industry/content.cfm?ItemNumber=1032.

40 American Association of Port Authorities at http://www.aapa-ports.org/Industry/content.cfm?ItemNumber=1032.

41 American Association of Port Authorities at http://www.aapa-ports.org/Industry/content.cfm?ItemNumber=1032.

42 American Association of Port Authorities at http://www.aapa-ports.org/Industry/content.cfm?ItemNumber=1032.

43 American Association of Port Authorities at http://www.aapa-ports.org/Industry/content.cfm?ItemNumber=1032.

44 US Maritime Administration, *America's Ports and Intermodal Transportation System*, January 2009, at http://www.glmri.org/downloads/Ports&IntermodalTransport.pdf.

45 US Maritime Administration, *America's Ports and Intermodal Transportation System*, January 2009, at http://www.glmri.org/downloads/Ports&IntermodalTransport.pdf.

46 26 U.S.C. § 9505 (1994).

porters, importers, and domestic shippers,[47] to pay 0.125 percent of the value of the commercial cargo they ship through the Nation's ports.[48] The HMT was imposed at the time of loading for exports and unloading for other shipments.[49] It is collected by the Customs Service and deposited in the Harbor Maintenance Trust Fund, from which Congress may appropriate amounts to pay for harbor maintenance and development projects and related expenses.[50] However, the U.S. Supreme Court faced the question of whether this *fee* was constitutional under the Export Clause of the Constitution, which states, "No Tax or Duty shall be laid on Articles exported from any State."[51] It had been previously held that the Export Clause categorically bars Congress from imposing any tax on exports.[52] The Clause, however, does not rule out a *user fee*, provided that the fee lacks the attributes of a generally applicable tax or duty and is instead a charge designed as compensation for Government supplied services, facilities, or benefits.[53] The Court held that the fee, which is imposed on an ad valorem basis, was not a fair approximation of services, facilities, or benefits furnished to the exporters and, therefore, do not qualify as a permissible user fee but as an unconstitutional tax.[54] This Export Clause exception was found to also apply to the carriage of passengers on cruise ships.[55]

Even with the noted judicial exceptions, the Harbor Mainte-

---

47 26 U.S.C. § 4461(c)(1) (1994).
48 26 U.S.C .§ 4461(a) (1994).
49 26 U.S.C. § 4461(c)(2) (1994).
50 United States v. U.S. Shoe Corp., 523 U.S. 360, 118 S. Ct. 1290, 1291, 140 L. Ed. 2d 453 (1998).
51 U.S. Const., Art. I, § 9, cl. 5.
52 United States v. International Business Machines Corp., 517 U.S. 843, 116 S.Ct. 1793, 135 L.Ed.2d 124 (1996).
53 Pace v. Burgess, 92 U.S. 372, 375-376, 23 L.Ed. 657 (1876).
54 United States v. U.S. Shoe Corp., 523 U.S. 360, 362-63, 118 S. Ct. 1290, 1292, 140 L. Ed. 2d 453 (1998).
55 Carnival Cruise Lines, Inc. v. United States, 200 F.3d 1361 (Fed. Cir. 2000).

nance Trust fund is not lacking. According to the Department of Transportation, U.S. port facilities annually service the movement of more than 2 billion tons of domestic and international cargo, 3.3 billion barrels of oil, 134 million ferry passengers, and over 5 million cruise ship passengers.[56] The Department of Transportation estimates that waterborne cargo contributes more than $742 billion to the U.S. gross domestic product and provides employment for more than 13 million people.[57] It has been estimated that by 2020, American overseas trade will more than double, further increasing dependence on the maritime transportation system.[58] All of these imports generate funds to be used in adherence with the Harbor Maintenance Trust Fund.

According to the Harbor Maintenance Trust Fund Act of 1996, the expenditures from Harbor Maintenance Trust Fund can be used
(1) to carry out section 210 of the Water Resources Development Act of 1986 (as in effect on the date of the enactment of the Water Resources Development Act of 1996), (2) for payments of rebates of tolls or charges pursuant to section 13(b) of the Act of May 13, 1954 (as in effect on April 1, 1987), and (3) for the payment of all expenses of administration incurred by the Department of the Treasury, the Army Corps of Engineers, and the Department of Commerce related to the administration of subchapter A of chapter 36 (relating to harbor maintenance tax), but not in excess of $5,000,000 for any fiscal year. [59]
Section 210(a) (2) of the Water Resources Development Act of 1986 reads (2) up to 100 percent of the eligible operations and

---

56 Department of Transportation, *An Assessment of the U.S. Marine Transportation System: A Report to Congress* (1999), at www.dot.gov/mts/report.
57 Department of Transportation, *An Assessment of the U.S. Marine Transportation System: A Report to Congress* (1999), at www.dot.gov/mts/report.
58 Department of Transportation, *An Assessment of the U.S. Marine Transportation System: A Report to Congress* (1999), at www.dot.gov/mts/report.
59 26 USC § 9505(C) (1994).

maintenance costs assigned to commercial navigation of all harbors and inland harbors within the United States.[60]

Currently, the Harbor Maintenance trust fund generates roughly $1 billion per year with equal expenditures; however, the current balance including interest is roughly $8 billion.[61] In the administration of the tax, there is no attempt to identify particular port usage and allocate funds accordingly. In other words, the HMT generates a national pool of funds, which is distributed without regard to which ports used triggered collection of the tax. However, the tax is meant to be a port user-charge and comparing where the tax is assessed and where the revenues are spent raises a number of policy issues especially considering Article I, section 9 of the United States Constitution:

Article I, Section 9
No Preference shall be given by any Regulation of Commerce or Revenue to the Ports of one State over those of another; nor shall Vessels bound to or from one State be obliged to enter, clear, or pay Duties in another.[62]

However, the Port Preference Clause has not barred Congress from authorizing specific navigational projects, including dredging, that incidentally benefit a particular port or group of ports while exercising its power to regulate interstate commerce as shown in Table 3.[63]

---

60 33 U.S.C. § 2306 (1994).
61 United States Army Corps of Engineers, *Annual reports to Congress on the HMTF*, Federal Budget Appendix for FY08-FY10.
62 U.S. Const., Art. I, § 9.
63 Lawrence Juda & Richard Burroughs, Dredging Navigational Channels in A Changing Scientific and Regulatory Environment, 35 J. Mar. L. & Com. 171, 184-85 (2004).

Table 3. USACE HMTF Expenditures by State/Territory 64 (FY1999-FY2008)

State/Territory	Total Expenditures, FY1999-FY2008	% of Total
LA	$1,337,545,344	19.5%
TX	$528,914,950	7.7%
FL	$463,824,357	6.8%
CA	$454,587,858	6.6%
MI	$368,793,819	5.4%
WA	$360,905,495	5.3%
NY	$335,275,282	4.9%
OR	$315,371,259	4.6%
AL	$308,013,423	4.5%
PA	$203,939,882	3.0%
NC	$203,995,135	3.0%
VA	$199,879,311	2.9%
MD	$196,123,467	2.9%
DE	$175,487,487	2.6%
SC	$169,894,554	2.5%
GA	$165,198,241	2.4%
OH	$158,648,355	2.3%

---

64 Based on 2007 data. U.S. army Corps of Engineers, Waterborne Commerce Statistics.

The table indicates each state's receipt from the HMTF. When this data is compared to the below list of ports with highest import cargo value (thus paying the highest tax) it is understandable why many state port authorities are calling foul.

Table 4. Top 10 Ports by Value of Imported Cargo[65] (2005, in millions of dollars)

Rank	Port	ImportValue	% of Total
1	Los Angeles, CA	$116,489	13.7%
2	New York, NY	$104,366	12.2%
3	Long Beach, CA	$103,801	12.2%
4	Houston, TX	$52,306	6.1%
5	Charleston, SC	$36,487	4.3%
6	Tacoma, WA	$28,743	3.4%
7	Hampton Roads, VA	$27,540	3.2%
8	Seattle, WA	$27,519	3.2%
9	Baltimore, MD	$27,048	3.2%
10	Oakland, CA	$23,880	2.8%

The distribution of the funding is drastically tilted in the favor of a few states, such as Louisiana. With 19.5% of all funds available, they do not rank in the top ten in generating contributory taxes for the Harbor Maintenance Trust Fund. Meanwhile, California generates 28.7% of all tax in the Harbor Maintenance Trust Fund but only receives 6.6% of funding. The most significant

---

65 Rexford Sherman, *2005 Port Analysis*, Association of American Port Authorities, at www.aapa-ports.org.

data to extrapolate from the above tables is that when the funds are made available to a state port authority, the limited funding constrains their use to the large port projects, leaving very little if anything to the small ports who typically are fully reliant and unable to fund their port in solitude based on the impact of containerization.

2. The Future Dredging of the U.S. Small Ports

Until 1986, the federal government paid the full costs of dredging necessary for the construction, maintenance, or deepening of navigational channels leading into ports; the costs of dredging berthing areas for ships, on the other hand, were left to the ports.[66] The Water Resources Development Act (WRDA) of 1986,[67] however, introduced cost sharing for construction projects with local sponsors paying between ten and fifty percent, based on the depth of navigation channels.

As channels were dredged deeper, the local share of cost increased.[68] The cost of maintenance dredging was left completely to the federal government except where the channel's depth exceeded forty-five feet; in such a case, the local sponsor was responsible for half of the cost of dredging.[69]

There is a current surplus of $8.0 billion in the Harbor Main-

---

66 Planning and Management Consultants, Ltd., *The National Dredging Needs Study of Ports and Harbors-Implications to Cost-Sharing of Federal Deep Draft Navigation Projects Due to Changes in the Maritime Industry*, submitted to U.S. Army Corps of Engineers at iv, 2 (2000).

67 Pub. L. 99-662, 100 Stat. 4082 (1986).

68 See 33 U.S.C. § 2211. According to this section, non-federal interests, during the construction period are to pay the following costs associated with general navigation features: 10% of construction costs of project portion with depth of less than 20 feet, 25% of costs for the portion deeper than 20 feet but no more than 45 feet, and 50% of costs for the portion deeper than 45 feet. Non-federal interests are also to pay 10% of the general navigation features cost over a period not to exceed 30 years.

69 Pub. L. 99-662, § 101(b) (1986).

tenance Trust Fund.[70] The U.S. Congress has the authority to appropriate funds from the Harbor Maintenance Trust Fund to the U.S. Army Corps of Engineers for intended purposes of harbor maintenance, but the fund has instead repeatedly been mismanaged and underutilized.

Legislative attempts to correct this trend have been proposed but not enacted. Senators Levin and Hutchison introduced S.3213 in 2010 to require the full use of the HMTF for the intended purpose.[71] In 2010, Congressman Boustany-LA introduced a companion bill H.R. 4844 to require the full use of the HMTF for the intended purpose.[72] On January 5, 2011, Congressman Boustany-La introduced H.R.104 to require the full use of the HMTF for the intended purpose.[73] The bill has been referred to Transportation & Infrastructure Committee.[74]

In the 113th CONGRESS, 1st Session, U.S. Rep. Shuster and other representatives introduced HR 3080, Water Resources Reform and Development Act of 2013.[75] This proposed legislation calls for an expanded use of the Harbor Maintenance Trust Fund.[76] The Act calls for a staggered increase in the use of the Harbor Maintenance Trust Fund tax as shown.

(1) For fiscal year 2014, 65 percent of the total amount of harbor maintenance taxes received in fiscal year 2013.

---

70 HRES 236, May 23, 2013.

71 Timothy M. Tilley, P.E./CPE, *Port Advisory Committee: Overview of Georgetown Port and Harbor Maintenance Trust Fund*, March 3, 2011.

72 Timothy M. Tilley, P.E./CPE, *Port Advisory Committee: Overview of Georgetown Port and Harbor Maintenance Trust Fund*, March 3, 2011.

73 Timothy M. Tilley, P.E./CPE, *Port Advisory Committee: Overview of Georgetown Port and Harbor Maintenance Trust Fund*, March 3, 2011.

74 Timothy M. Tilley, P.E./CPE, *Port Advisory Committee: Overview of Georgetown Port and Harbor Maintenance Trust Fund*, March 3, 2011.

75 HR 3080, September 11, 2013.

76 HR 3080, September 11, 2013.

(2) For fiscal year 2015, 67 percent of the total amount of harbor maintenance taxes received in fiscal year 2014.

(3) For fiscal year 2016, 69 percent of the total amount of harbor maintenance taxes received in fiscal year 2015.

(4) For fiscal year 2017, 71 percent of the total amount of harbor maintenance taxes received in fiscal year 2016.

(5) For fiscal year 2018, 73 percent of the total amount of harbor maintenance taxes received in fiscal year 2017.

(6) For fiscal year 2019, 75 percent of the total amount of harbor maintenance taxes received in fiscal year 2018.

(7) For fiscal year 2020 and each fiscal year thereafter, 80 percent of total amount of harbor maintenance taxes received in the previous fiscal year.

The Act further defines "eligible harbors and inland harbors" as a harbor or inland harbor that, historically, as determined by the Secretary, (A) generates an amount of harbor maintenance taxes; that exceeds (B) the value of maintenance dredging work carried out for the harbor or inland harbor using amounts from the Harbor Maintenance Trust Fund.[77]

Further, the Act allows for the *expanded uses* of the Harbor Maintenance Trust Fund to include[78]

(A) The maintenance dredging of a berth in a harbor that is accessible to a Federal navigation project and that benefits commercial navigation at the harbor.

(B) The maintenance dredging and disposal of legacy-contaminated sediment and sediment unsuitable for open water disposal, if such dredging and disposal benefits commercial navigation at the harbor; and such sediment is located in and affects the

---

77 HR 3080, September 11, 2013.
78 HR 3080, September 11, 2013.

maintenance of a Federal navigation project or is located in a berth that is accessible to a Federal navigation project.

The word *historically* provides hope to many small ports that have seen their tonnage decrease due to the negligent care of the Army Corps of Engineers in dredging activity. Reportedly, the Army Corps of Engineers' policy is that they will not consider port maintenance for ports less than 1.0 million tons per year.[79] Consequently, many small ports like the Georgetown Port have a chicken and egg scenario; whereas, the port cannot get the permitted depth dredged unless the volume is above the 1.0 million threshold, and the port cannot obtain enough tonnage unless the depth is adequately dredged.

The key term in HR 3080 for small ports like Georgetown is *historically*. When looking at the history of the many small ports when properly maintained, they were able to operate effectively and efficiently at well over 1,000,000 tons. It allows these ports to escape the *chicken and egg* situation.

D. Securing funding for the American Small Port

Although, HR 3080 makes American Small Ports eligible to receive funding to perform the desperately needed dredging, the question of whether the necessary funds will be allotted remains to be seen. Will the limited funds still be funneled to the larger ports, although the small ports future rest in the hands of the legislative budget?

1. *The Port of Charleston, SC*

Fifty feet is what the Port of Charleston, SC, wants to maintain.

---

79 Timothy M. Tilley, P.E./CPE , Port Advisory Committee: Overview of Georgetown Port and Harbor Maintenance Trust Fund, March 3, 2011.

There are two primary drivers of this number; the first being that the Post-Panamex ships will require this new depth.

According to Jim Newsome, the former Director of the South Carolina Port Authority, "We have based our growth and investment plans on the reality that fifty feet is the required depth of a true post-Panamex harbor. Charleston is the deepest harbor in the region today and will remain the deepest in the future, positioning our port as the Southeast's hub for exporting activity."[80] However, the fifty foot depth operation and maintenance requires a cost-sharing provision as outlined in Table 5.

Table 5. Cost-Share Requirements for Corps Harbor Projects[81]
Operation and Maintenance and Construction Federal Share and (Source of Funds)

Harbor Depth	Operation & Maintenance	Construction
< 20 feet	100% (HMTF)	80% (General Treasury)
20-45 feet	100% (HMTF)	65% (General Treasury)
> 45 feet	50% (HMTF)	40% (General Treasury)

The Army Corps stated the cost to complete the study for the Port of Charleston, SC, to be $13 million while the actual dredging/construction costs to be $300 million.[82] Based on the table, the Port Authority of South Carolina was left with the responsibility

80 Tyrone Richardson, *Charleston Lawmakers Question 2016 Completion for dredging Savannah,* http://www.postandcourier.com/article/20130607/PC05/130609422/charleston-lawmakers-question-2016-completion-for-dredging-savannah-x2019-s-port, June 7, 2013.
81 33 U.S.C. § 2211 (1994).
82 Liz Segrist, *Army Corps drills samples to figure dredging costs,* http://www.charlestonbusiness.com/news/48794-army-corps-drills-samples-to-figure-dredging-costs, September 9, 2013.

to locate $180 million to complete its dredging construction, while the U.S. General Treasury would contribute $120 million. However, the State of South Carolina is weary of the federal government's ability/willingness to pay the allotted full $300 million to fund the dredging without outside contribution from any source.[83]

The second primary reason for the Port of Charleston's dredging to fifty feet and the budgeted $300 million is to maintain "our port as the Southeast's hub for exporting activity."[84] Savannah, G.A., is the Port of Charleston's biggest competitor, and Georgia's port officials have said a 30-mile-plus stretch of the Savannah River will be deepened from 42 feet to 47 feet by as early as 2016.[85] However, the State of South Carolina sued to block the $652 million project based on environmental concerns.[86] This tactic by the State of South Carolina appears to be working; it is a minimum of a six-year construction timeline.[87] "I'd say [Charleston] is at even footing with Savannah now with the exception that we have natural advantages Savannah does not,"

---

83 South Carolina Port Authority, *Harbor Deepening,* http://www.port-of-charleston.com/Cargo/ReadytoGrow/harbordeepening.asp.

84 Tyrone Richardson, *Charleston Lawmakers Question 2016 Completion for dredging Savannah,* http://www.postandcourier.com/article/20130607/PC05/130609422/charleston-lawmakers-question-2016-completion-for-dredging-savannah-x2019-s-port, June 7, 2013.

85 Tyrone Richardson, *Charleston Lawmakers Question 2016 Completion for dredging Savannah,* http://www.postandcourier.com/article/20130607/PC05/130609422/charleston-lawmakers-question-2016-completion-for-dredging-savannah-x2019-s-port, June 7, 2013.

86 Tyrone Richardson, *Charleston Lawmakers Question 2016 Completion for dredging Savannah,* http://www.postandcourier.com/article/20130607/PC05/130609422/charleston-lawmakers-question-2016-completion-for-dredging-savannah-x2019-s-port, June 7, 2013.

87 Tyrone Richardson, *Charleston Lawmakers Question 2016 Completion for dredging Savannah,* http://www.postandcourier.com/article/20130607/PC05/130609422/charleston-lawmakers-question-2016-completion-for-dredging-savannah-x2019-s-port, June 7, 2013.

said Rep. Jim Merrill of Charleston. "They still have environmental issues to be addressed and triggers to take the next step."[88]

A 2019 completion for the Savannah deepening would put it on roughly the same schedule as the Charleston Harbor project; however, the Port of Georgetown, SC, has been shuttered just north of this dispute.

2. The Port of Georgetown, S.C,

Georgetown, SC, as previously described, sits on the Winyah Bay and acted as a break bulk port for shipment of dry goods, such as forest products and cement.[89] Primarily, the Georgetown Port was utilized for export purposes. The Port has suffered a chronic decline in tonnage as their harbor has slowly silted in. Tonnage has dropped from 1.8 million tons in Fiscal Year 2000 to roughly 150,000 tons in 2009.[90] This drop in tonnage occurs as the silt continues to rise. The Georgetown Channel was last dredged in 2004 to a depth of 29 ft. but currently rests between 17 and 19 feet in certain locations.[91] The lack of maintenance dredging (100% HMTF responsibility according to Table 4) has necessitated construction dredging back to its permitted depth of 29 ft.[92]

As the permitted depth is 29 ft., 65% of the dredging/construction funding is expected to be provided by the US Treasury;

---

88 Tyrone Richardson, *Charleston Lawmakers Question 2016 Completion for dredging Savannah,* http://www.postandcourier.com/article/20130607/PC05/130609422/charleston-lawmakers-question-2016-completion-for-dredging-savannah-x2019-s-port, June 7, 2013.

89 Timothy M. Tilley, P.E./CPE, *Port Advisory Committee: Overview of Georgetown Port and Harbor Maintenance Trust Fund,* March 3, 2011.

90 Timothy M. Tilley, P.E./CPE, *Port Advisory Committee: Overview of Georgetown Port and Harbor Maintenance Trust Fund,* March 3, 2011.

91 Timothy M. Tilley, P.E./CPE, *Port Advisory Committee: Overview of Georgetown Port and Harbor Maintenance Trust Fund,* March 3, 2011.

92 Timothy M. Tilley, P.E./CPE, *Port Advisory Committee: Overview of Georgetown Port and Harbor Maintenance Trust Fund,* March 3, 2011.

however, since 2004, the Port of Georgetown has gone with no funding, not even the $4 to $6 million needed annually to maintain the harbor.[93] The dredging impact study was completed in 2011 for $400,000; however, no further action has taken place to start the dredging project.[94] According to the Army Corps of Engineers, the actual dredging is expected to costs $33 million and take three years.[95]

The South Carolina State Legislature did authorize $18.5 million in bonds to the Port of Georgetown but noted that these funds would only be made available should the remainder of the need be found elsewhere.[96] Yet again a small port is left to wallow in their own silt, or in this case, pluff mud until its closure.

3. *Comparison*

A simple comparison between the Port of Charleston, SC, and the Port of Georgetown, SC, shows that the costs of completion for the Port of Georgetown to be less than a tenth of the Port of Charleston and nearly half the time of completion. Further, while the state is willing to provide $300 million for construction and $13 million to study construction to a large port like the Port of Charleston, small ports like Georgetown, SC, go neglected by those responsible for their maintenance and care. Recently, the Fiscal Year 2013 Work Plan was released by the Office of Management and Budget and included $20.4 million

93 Lindsey Theis, *Back to square one for Georgetown Port Dredging funding,* http://www.caro-linalive.com/news/story.aspx?id=823269#.UkmX-T9mFqM, November 8, 2012.

94 Gina Vasselli and James Rosen, *Charleston Gets funding while Georgetown waits,* http://www.myrtlebeachonline.com/2011/05/18/2164678/experts-to-begin-studying-sc-port.html, May 18, 2011.

95 Gina Vasselli and James Rosen, *Charleston Gets funding while Georgetown waits,* http://www.myrtlebeachonline.com/2011/05/18/2164678/experts-to-begin-studying-sc-port.html, May 18, 2011.

96 Lindsey Theis, *Back to square one for Georgetown Port Dredging funding,* http://www.caro-linalive.com/news/story.aspx?id=823269#.UkmX-T9mFqM, November 8, 2012.

for the US Army Corps of Engineers, Charleston District to perform a beach renourishment at Folly Beach while the Harbor of
Georgetown, South Carolina, received no support.[97] At the same
time, President Obama is touting the big harbors and ignoring
the needs of the small harbors stating, "If we don't deepen our
ports all along the gulf in places like Charleston, South Carolina, Savannah, Georgia, and Jacksonville, Florida. If we don't
do that, those ships are going to go someplace else. We'll lose
jobs. Businesses won't locate here."[98] While small ports may
not be as well-known, they provide a necessity to the maritime
infrastructure of the United States and must be maintained to
protect the commerce of larger ports as will be explained later.

E. The Need of the American Small Ports to American Maritime Policy

While many large ports receive funding for their construction projects, the
small ports and their adjoining communities continue to suffer. The econ-
omies of these communities routinely rely on these ports and the jobs they
create; however, the backbone of the American maritime history lays in the
small ports. Without the support of the American small ports, the American
maritime industry becomes exposed.

1. Economy of Small Town Port Communities

When the Port of Georgetown does not operate, the community
suffers as shown in the table, "Table 2. Georgetown County
Labor Market Data, 2009 (Jan-Nov).

---

97 Press Release, *USA: Folly Beach Gets Funding for Renourishment,* http://www.dredging-today.com/2013/06/26/usa-folly-beach-gets-funding-for-renourishment, June 26, 2013.

98 Live 5 News, *Obama plugs deepening Charleston Harbor on Jay Leno,* http://www.live5news.com/story/23072563/obama-plugs-deeper-sc-harbor-on-jay-leno, August 7, 2013.

Table 2. Georgetown County Labor Market Data, 2009 (Jan-Nov)

Labor Force	Employed	Unemployed	Unemployment Rate
30,330	26,537	3,793	12.5%

However, with a properly maintained and operating port, the Community of Georgetown unemployment rate reduces immediately by 1% with the additional, direct jobs created.

With an Additional 251 Jobs:

Employed	Unemployed	Unemployment Rate
26,788	3,542	11.7%

Dredging to the proper depth for the Port of Georgetown, just like the many other small ports hit hardest by the recession, has the potential to reverse the downward trends of recent years. If the Port was able to attract additional business to the region, the local economy benefits not just from the jobs and income of the port but from the activities related to the port. While large ports generally rest in large communities with a diversified tax base, the American small port is reliant on the limited resources they possess.[100] Should the Georgetown Harbor be dredged to its permited limit allowing 3 million tons, the impact could be tremendous with over 251 new jobs and nearly $35 million newly-generated revenue as the chart indicates.

---

99 Dr. Don Schunk, *The Port of Georgetown: Potential Economic Impacts of Port Resurgence*, February 2010.

100 Bandon Western World, *Kitzhaber: Small ports to be dredged*, http://theworldlink.com/bandon/news/kitzhaber-small-ports-to-be-dredged/article_f916ba4e-20aa-11e3-9b15-0019bb2963f4.html, September 19, 2013.

Figure 7. Estimated Total Effects of a 3,000,000 Ton Increase

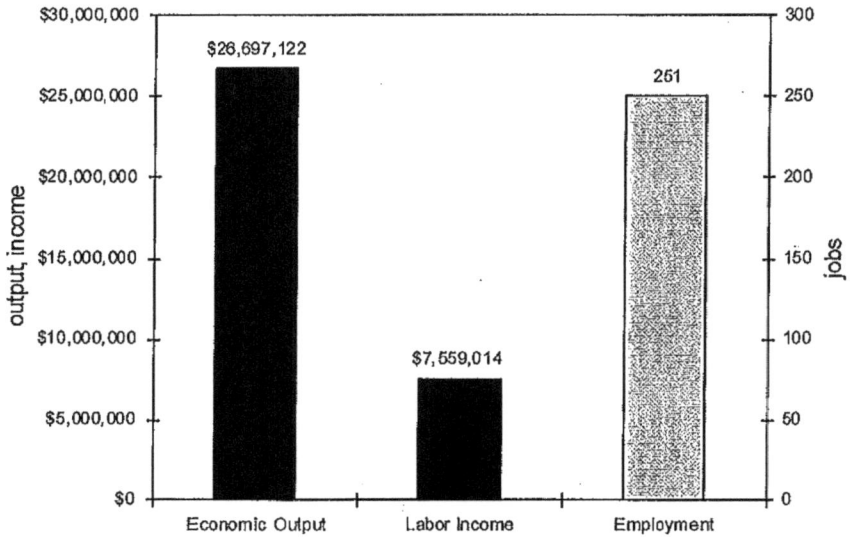

This is the same for many small ports across the United States. A 2013 economic impact study analyzing the small Port of Bandon, Oregon, illustrates the positive economic effects small ports have on their communities. The study concluded that maintaining adequate depths at Bandon was vital to the viability and growth of 54 local businesses directly employing 441 people with an additional 177 jobs also dependent on the same economic activity.[102] In only one year, this modest-sized coastal port directly and indirectly added more than $27.4 million in value to the regional economy in 2012, while returning nearly $8 million in state, local, and federal taxes.[103]

---

101 Dr. Don Schunk, *The Port of Georgetown: Potential Economic Impacts of Port Resurgence,* February 2010.

102 Bandon Western World, *Kitzhaber: Small ports to be dredged,* http://theworldlink.com/bandon/news/kitzhaber-small-ports-to-be-dredged/article_f916ba4e-20aa-11e3-9b15-0019bb2963f4.html, September 19, 2013.

103 Bandon Western World, *Kitzhaber: Small ports to be dredged,* http://theworldlink.com/bandon/news/kitzhaber-small-ports-to-be-dredged/article_f916ba4e-20aa-11e3-9b15-0019bb2963f4.html, September 19, 2013.

"As you work to fund our nation's navigation infrastructure, we ask that you take into consideration the needs of small coastal including Great Lakes, waterways," Senator Cantwell wrote in a letter, "Our nations' small ports and harbors serve as the lifeblood of their communities and greatly contribute to the nation's economic vitality....Without adequate funding, the navigation channels leading to these ports will silt in, and the jetties protecting these communities will crumble."[104]

2. *Emergency*

The nation's small ports serve or should be designated to serve as contingency in the unfortunate incident that some of America's larger ports are targeted by terrorism, man-made disaster, or by a natural disaster.

3. *Natural Disaster*

On August 29, 2005, Hurricane Katrina destroyed one-third of the Port of New Orleans.[105] In 2003, New Orleans ranked fifth among U.S. ports in tons of cargo handled, and 12th in total foreign trade.[106] Before Katrina hit on August 29, the port was getting 36 to 40 ship calls a week.[107] Five months after the hurricane, of January 2006, the count was only 18 to 20 per

104 Maria Cantwell, *Cantwell, Senators Urge Support for Dredging of Small Ports Including Swinomish Channel, Port of Ilwaco*, http://www.cantwell.senate.gov/public/index.cfm/press-releases?ID=a0f7b14e-7b07-4617-8306-c2dd7422bf7e, March 22, 2012.

105 Alan Sayre, *New Orleans port is getting over Katrina*, http://www.nytimes.com/2006/01/03/business/worldbusiness/03iht-port.html?_r=0, January 3, 2006.

106 American Association of Port Authorities, www.aapa-ports.org/.

107 Alan Sayre, *New Orleans port is getting over Katrina*, http://www.nytimes.com/2006/01/03/business/worldbusiness/03iht-port.html?_r=0, January 3, 2006.

week.[108] The goal was to hit 70 percent of the pre-Katrina calls into the Port of New Orleans by March or April 2006.[109]

Most ports rest on the water (unless it is an inland port) and, therefore, face the consequences that come with that positioning. If New Orleans, one of U.S. busiest ports, can be severely limited, so can any other port. What is the contingency plan when the larger ports are unable to handle 100%, 50%, or 25% of the scheduled calls due to a natural disaster?

4. Man Made Disaster

On March 24, 1989, shortly after midnight, the oil tanker *Exxon Valdez* struck Bligh Reef in Prince William Sound, Alaska, spilling more than 11 million gallons of crude oil.[110] The spill was the largest in U.S. history until the Deep-water Horizon disaster. Since the incident occurred in open U.S. navigable waters, the U.S. Coast Guard's On-Scene Coordinator had authority for all activities related to the cleanup effort.[111] His first action was to immediately close the Port of Valdez to all traffic.[112] No ships in or out of the Port of Valdez, a life line to the people of many remote areas of Alaska, was closed. No food in or out of the Port. No clothing in or out of the port. Nothing in or out of the port.

In response, the Oil Pollution Act of 1990 (OPA 90) was passed requiring the development of Area Contingency Plans (ACP) for

108 Alan Sayre, *New Orleans port is getting over Katrina,* http://www.nytimes. com/2006/01/03/business/worldbusiness/03iht-port.html?_r=0, January 3, 2006.

109 Alan Sayre, *New Orleans port is getting over Katrina,* http://www.nytimes. com/2006/01/03/business/worldbusiness/03iht-port.html?_r=0, January 3, 2006

110 United States Environmental Protection Agency, Exxon Valdez, http://www.epa. gov/oswero e1/content/learning/exxon.htm.

111 United States Environmental Protection Agency, Exxon Valdez, http://www.epa. gov/oswero e1/content/learning/exxon.htm.

112 United States Environmental Protection Agency, Exxon Valdez, http://www.epa. gov/oswero e1/content/learning/exxon.htm.

each port area.[113] The first requirement for nearly every ACP is the directive of containment.[114] Containment will generally necessitate the closure of the port to all ships for an extended period of time until the man-made disaster, whether it is oil, chemicals, or other material is eradicated. Why are the American small ports not incorporated into the contingency plan when the larger ports are unable to handle 100%, 50%, or 25% of the scheduled calls due to a man-made disaster?

5. *Terrorism*

In October 2000, 17 U.S sailors were killed when an Al Qaeda suicide squad was able to ram its explosives-laden boat into the side of Navy destroyer USS Cole while it was harbored in the Yemeni port of Aden.[115] In November 2008, militants used speedboats to bypass security in the Indian port of Mumbai where they carried out attacks on landmark buildings, killing more than 160 people.[116]

Eighty-Five (85) percent of our Nation's containerized freight is flowing through 10 ports.[117] On September 11, 2001, two planes destroyed the World Trade Center in New York City in an attempt to disrupt U.S. commerce and lives.[118] The terror threat to

113 Charleston Area Committee, *Charleston Area Contingency Plan,* http://ocean.floridam-arine.org/acp/chacp/Documents/ACP/Charleston_ACP_Jan_2011_Revision.pdf, January 2011, p. 5.
114 Charleston Area Committee, *Charleston Area Contingency Plan,* http://ocean.floridam-arine.org/acp/chacp/Documents/ACP/Charleston_ACP_Jan_2011_Revision.pdf, January 2011, p. 85.
115 Barry Neild, *The small vessel threat,* http://www.globalpost.com/dispatch/america/110207/US-ports-terrorism, February 9, 2011.
116 Barry Neild, *The small vessel threat,* http://www.globalpost.com/dispatch/america/110207/US-ports-terrorism, February 9, 2011.
117 US Maritime Administration, *America's Ports and Intermodal Transportation System,* http://www.glmri.org/downloads/Ports&IntermodalTransport.pdf, January 2009, p. 21.
118 *World Trade Center History,* http://www.911memorial.org/world-trade-center-history.

America continues today, and an attack on America's commerce could not be greater than a targeted attack on American ports.

Meanwhile, millions of cargo containers are unloaded from ships each year at American seaports, providing countless opportunities for terrorists to smuggle and unleash a nuclear bomb or weapon of mass destruction on our shores.[119] At current staffing and funding levels, U.S. Coast Guard personnel and Customs agents can thoroughly inspect only about 5 percent of the 9 million shipping containers that arrive at U.S. ports every year.[120] It is estimated that an attack on an American port could cause tens of thousands of deaths and cripple global trade with losses ranging from $45 billion to more than $1 trillion, according to estimates by the RAND Corporation and the Congressional Research Service.[121] The American small ports should be the contingency plan when the larger ports are unable to handle 100%, 50%, or 25% of the scheduled calls due to a terror caused disaster.

6. National Security

American small ports play a vital role in meeting the needs of the American defense and military readiness. The Merchant Marine is the fleet of privately owned ships, which carries imports and exports during peacetime and becomes a naval auxiliary during wartime to deliver troops and war material,[122] a vital role that our seaman serve to protect the United States.

---

119 Jerrold L. Nadler, Edward J. Markey, & Bennie G. Thompson, *Cargo, the Terrorists' Trojan Horse*, http://www.nytimes.com/2012/06/27/opinion/the-dangerous-delay-on-port-security.html, June 26, 2012.

120 http://www.cfr.org/border-and-port-security/targets-terrorism-ports/p10215.

121 http://www.nytimes.com/2012/06/27/opinion/the-dangerous-delay-on-port-security.html.

122 Merchant Marine Website, http://www.usmm.org/faq.html.

According to the Merchant Marine Act of 1936, "It is necessary for the national defense…that the United States shall have a merchant marine of the best equipped and most suitable types of vessels sufficient to carry the greater portion of its commerce and serve as a naval or military auxiliary in time of war or national emergency…."[123] The Merchant Marine has served the United States during World War II, the Korean, Vietnam, Persian Gulf and Iraq wars.[124] The military relied on the U.S. merchant fleet to transport much-needed ammunition and supplies in support of the logistics chain for each branch of the military.[125] A soldier cannot fight without food and weapons, which is the role of the Merchant Marine. As the table demonstrates that mariners served with honor and distinction during World War II:[126]

Service	Number serving	War Dead	Percent	Ratio
Merchant Marine	**243,000***	**9,497****	**3.90%**	**1 in 26**
Marines	669,108	19,733	2.94%	1 in 34
Army	11,268,000	234,874	2.08%	1 in 48
Navy	4,183,466	36,958	0.88%	1 in 114
Coast Guard	242,093	574	0.24%	1 in 421
Total	16,576,667	295,790	1.78%	1 in 56

* Number varies by source and ranges from 215,000 to 285,000.
**Total killed at sea, POW killed, buried in ABMC cemeteries, plus died from wounds ashore

As noted earlier, Transportation and Infrastructure Committee Chairman Bill Shuster (R-Pennsylvania) proposed legislation to improve the state of our waterways' infrastructure. According to the Chairman, "[i]mproving the efficiency of our locks and

---

123 Merchant Marine Website, http://www.usmm.org/faq.html.
124 Merchant Marine Website, http://www.usmm.org/faq.html.
125 Denise Krepp, *Haphazard Policies Threaten Future of U.S. Merchant Marine*, http://www.maritime-executive.com/article/Haphazard-Policies-Threaten-Future-of-US-Merchant-Marine—2013-03-26/, March 26, 2013.
126 War Shipping Administration Press Release 2514, January 1, 1946, http://www.usmm.org/faq.html.

dams, inland waterways, ports, and waterborne transportation is essential to maintain and improve U.S. competitiveness in the global economy."[127] These improvements, however, can't be made if U.S. crews and vessels are not available to transport goods along America's vast waterways system.

The majority of practical Merchant Marine experience comes from American small ports where small to medium-size vessels call home.[128] Large ports service large ships, which merchant mariners will not typically handle within their day-to-day duties. However, the U.S. Merchant Marine fleet is gradually being whittled away by the elimination of cargo preference, the loss of experienced mariners, and the loss of available vessels.[129]

The closure of American small ports, whether intentional or through natural occurrences, continues to dwindle the available crews and ships to serve in the logistical role demanded by our armed forces. The U.S. mariners who transport this cargo are vital to our national security if it is to avoid this grim prognosis.[130] The only ones who will win from disjointed policies that gut the U.S. merchant fleet are foreign carriers.[131] These carriers are poised to take over the responsibility of transporting our military's guns and supplies, which is the role of the American Merchant Marine.[132] The closure of American small ports will

127 Denise Krepp, *Haphazard Policies Threaten Future of U.S. Merchant Marine,* http://www.maritime-executive.com/article/Haphazard-Policies-Threaten-Future-of-US-Merchant-Marine—2013-03-26/, March 26, 2013.

128 Denise Krepp, *The End of the U.S. Merchant Marine?,* http://www.maritime-executive.com/article/The-End-of-the-US-Merchant-Marine-2013-03-12/, March 12, 2013.

129 Denise Krepp, *The End of the U.S. Merchant Marine?,* http://www.maritime-executive.com/article/The-End-of-the-US-Merchant-Marine-2013-03-12/, March 12, 2013.

130 Denise Krepp, *The End of the U.S. Merchant Marine?,* http://www.maritime-executive.com/article/The-End-of-the-US-Merchant-Marine-2013-03-12/, March 12, 2013.

131 Denise Krepp, *The End of the U.S. Merchant Marine?,* http://www.maritime-executive.com/article/The-End-of-the-US-Merchant-Marine-2013-03-12/, March 12, 2013.

132 Denise Krepp, *The End of the U.S. Merchant Marine?,* http://www.maritime-executive.com/article/The-End-of-the-US-Merchant-Marine-2013-03-12/, March 12, 2013.

only lead to the inevitable dependence upon foreign nations to support the United States military, thus we fall to their mercy and prime those nations to take control of the sea.

F. Saving the American Small Port

Small ports across the United States continue to struggle to survive. With over 90% of cargo being transported by container and this number expected to grow Post-Panamex,[133] many small ports would not be able to handle these larger ships even if their channels were dredged. That leaves the questions of "do we need small ports?" and "how will the American small port survive?"

1. Emergency Readiness

Earlier the question was asked, "What will the U.S. maritime policy be when terrorism, man-made disasters, or natural disasters close a large port?" The answer should be to have in place a contingency plan of distributing the ship calls amongst ports that can facilitate the needs of the carrier and cargo.

The Maritime Administration's (MARAD's) mission is to strengthen and improve the U.S. maritime transportation system including infrastructure, industry, and labor to meet the nation's economic and security needs.[134] There is nothing more important to preventing the collapse of the U.S. economy than supporting the commercial shipping industry.

A review of the majority of Area Contingency Plans, including Charleston's Contingency Plan, does not provide a contingency to continue the shipping commerce in case of a disaster at one

---

133 Rose George, *Ninety Percent of Everything*, Metropolitan Books, 2013.
134 U.S. Maritime Administration, http://www.seapowermagazine.org/pdf_files/almanac/marad.pdf.

of our top ports.[135] The reason for this may be the competitive nature of the shipping business or the inherent distrust between states of the union, but whatever the reason in the interest of the American economy, MARAD must invest time to facilitate a workable plan to preempt the chaos created (such as with Katrina) by disaster.

Instead of constantly being reactionary, maritime policy must be established to continue the import and export of necessary cargo. The American small ports are a tool that must be utilized due to their logistical prowess. The American small port is advantageous for multiple reasons including, but not limited to, the likely proximity to the larger port, the unlikely event of man-made disasters, or terror affecting their harbor, and the ability to resume operations quickly after a natural disaster with proper attention. The small port should be the strategic support for the continuation of American Commercial Shipping in case of such national emergency.

2. Port Specialization (niche)

America's small communities survive due to the specific abilities of their citizens. They maximize their resources and exploit that potential; the same must be done with their ports. John Carver, Executive Vice President, Ports Airports and Global Infrastructure Group, Jones Lang LaSalle stated, "Containerized cargo represents the most coveted—and the most profitable—use for the U.S. maritime industry. It also requires the greatest upfront investment in both channel and pier-side improvements. Further, container terminals are of most value to the carrier lines and their customers when they are built to a critical mass of volume

---

135 Charleston Area Committee, *Charleston Area Contingency Plan*, http://ocean.floridamarine.org/acp/chacp/Documents/ACP/Charleston_ACP_Jan_2011_Revision.pdf, January 2011.

and can accommodate the larger vessels in their fleets. However, there are many other viable non-container maritime uses for the smaller ports to cater to in order to find their niche and capture market share. These can include break-bulk operations, heavy equipment, automobiles, raw materials, cold supply chain, and dedicated single-use terminals."[136]

Every small port must evaluate what its niche or specialization is. They must select a service that differentiates them from the larger, more sophisticated port.[137] The luxury most small ports hold is that they can make quick decisions and have beautiful locations. Many of these locations would be perfect to incorporate a mix of tourism and industry, such as bringing in a river cruise to facilitate tourism, which can draft as low as 80 cm.[138]

3.   *Using the American Small Port to Refresh the Merchant Marine*

On March 12, 2013, Denise Krepp, the former Chief Counsel at the U.S. Maritime Administration and Special Counsel to the General Counsel at the U.S. Department of Transportation, predicted that "the Merchant Marine will be dead in 10 years."[139] That is an alarming predication coming from a former attorney with MARAD. As previously described, she predicts that the lack of good maritime policy and the lack of willingness by the legislature to address the issue will continue to lead to the demise of our primary naval auxiliary and our primary military supplier in time of war.[140]

---

136 John Carver, *Smaller Ports Find Their Niche,* http://www.areadevelopment.com/answers/logisticsInfrastructure/smaller-ports-find-niche32992.shtml/.

137 Jim Newsome, SC Port Authority Interview, September 16, 2013.

138 *Viking Fontane,* http://www.vikingrivercruises.com/cruiseships/europe/viking-fontane/shipinfo.aspx.

139 Denise Krepp, *The End of the U.S. Merchant Marine?,* http://www.maritime-executive.com/article/The-End-of-the-US-Merchant-Marine-2013-03-12/, March 12, 2013.

140 http://www.maritime-executive.com/article/The-End-of-the-US-Merchant-Marine-2013-03-12/.

The Objectives and Purpose of the Merchant Marine Act of 1920 are encapsulated in TITLE 46, CHAPTER 24, SECTION 861. Purpose and Policy of United States:

> It is necessary for the national defense and for the proper growth of its foreign and domestic commerce that the United States shall have a merchant marine of the best equipped and most suitable types of vessels sufficient to carry the greater portion of its commerce and serve as a naval or military auxiliary in time of war or national emergency, ultimately to be owned and operated privately by citizens of the United States; and it is declared to be the policy of the United States to do whatever may be necessary to develop and encourage the maintenance of such a merchant marine and, insofar as may not be inconsistent with the express provisions of this Act, the Secretary of Transportation shall, in the disposition of vessels and shipping property as hereinafter provided, in the making of rules and regulations, and in the administration of the shipping laws keep always in view this purpose and object as the primary end to be attained.[141]

However, is this still the U.S. policy? The President of the United States stated in 2008 that "America needs a strong and vibrant U.S.-Flag Merchant Marine. That is why you can continue to count on me to support the Jones Act (which also includes the Passenger Vessel Services Act) and the continued exclusion of maritime services in international trade agreements."[142] So, what policy has been introduced to save the U.S. Merchant Marine? According to The AFL-CIO Maritime Trades Department, nothing has been done and states "the Obama Administration is asleep at the Helm."[143]

There is no citable plan/policy in place to resurrect the U.S. merchant

---

141 46 U.S.C. 24 § 861(1994).
142 Barack Obama letter to Michael Sacco and SIU, August 28, 2008.
143 Polly Parks, *Obama Administration Asleep at the Helm,* http://www.maritimeprofessional. com/Blogs/Vessel-and-Marine-Structure-Recycling/November-2011/Obama-Administration-Asleep-at-the-Helm.aspx, November 17, 2011.

marine/naval auxiliary. In a world of terrorism, our maritime fleet continues to suffer. The Navy League of the United States released a maritime policy statement indicating a need for a "Maritime Security Act that provides the foundation to support the U.S. commercial fleet in international trade and an economically viable U.S.-flag Merchant Marine for national defense and economic security. That includes a strong strategic sealift Merchant Reserve component in the U.S. Navy to ensure that critical Mariner skills and experience are retained to support Navy and strategic sealift transportation."[144]

American small ports can play a critical role in the vessel requirement and crew training of the Strategic Sealift/merchant marine; many of the vessels employed at these harbors can and have served valiantly in Iraq and Afghanistan.[145] They are crewed by experienced seaman who need minimal training and perform heroic tasks bravely and diligently daily. The small port seamen operate vessels that require knowledge that many large ports pleasure boaters and container ship operators do not possess. The American small port should be the training ground for the new generation of Merchant Mariners.

G. Conclusion

The United States and her military need small ports to be prepared commercially and militarily. The value of the American small port cannot be underscored in its place with the economy of the U.S. in order to promote the continued growth of American Commerce. The American small port continues to suffer but cannot be overlooked as a vital component to train competent seamen and provide necessary logistical support in the time of war.

A contingency plan must be formed as a part of the American maritime

---

144 Navy League, *Navy League calls for support for Merchant Marine and Navy auxiliary*, http://www.marinelog.com/index.php?option=com_content&view=article&id=2172:2012mar00233&catid=1:latest-news, March 23, 2012.

145 Navy League, *Navy League calls for support for Merchant Marine and Navy auxiliary*, http://www.marinelog.com/index.php?option=com_content&view=article&id=2172:2012mar00233&catid=1:latest-news, March 23, 2012.

policy that exemplifies the vast resources of these small ports. The economic, cultural, and defensive value of these ports remains unheralded, yet unaltered in their place in history. The book remains unwritten as to their future; however, their importance cannot be trumpeted enough.

As other nations continue to assume dominance over the high seas, the U.S. must adopt a maritime policy that promotes the growth of America's large ports, but supports American small ports both as a vital contributor to commerce and defense. Without the American small port, the U.S. ability to compete militarily and commercially will continue to dwindle and so will America's ability to lead.

PART FOUR:

Carolina Gold

The New Crop to Put South Carolina Back into Prominence

I.   Introduction

The economy of South Carolina was built in the minds of a few who had the foresight to implement a crop that may or may not grow in the marshy area of the low country of the coast. Emanating from Africa and Indonesia, Carolina Gold Rice, a long grain was the basis of the colonial and antebellum economy of the Carolina region and Georgia. Considered the grandfather of long grain rice in the Americas, became a commercial staple grain in the coastal lands of Charles Towne in the Carolina Territory in 1685.[1]

Carolina Gold grew in prominence and demand on the backs of those who worked on the farms. It brought prominence to the Carolinas, wealth to many families, and work to even more. It was not the perfect crop as it had its issues and led to many disagreements, but its implication on historic South Carolina and America cannot be disputed. Likewise, the new crop to be harvested on the farms in the United States and specifically South Carolina will have major implications on the future of many people.

Like Carolina Gold, offshore energy is ripe for the picking in the Atlantic Ocean territory of the United States of America. In 2008, the South Carolina General Assembly established the South Carolina Natural Gas Exploration Feasibility Study Committee to examine the potential of wind and natural gas exploration off the coast of South Carolina.[2] The Committee recommended that the state consider the development of an offshore natural gas industry, but only when the Bureau of Energy Management executes a five year plan that includes natural gas exploration off the South Carolina coast (South Carolina Natural Gas Exploration Feasibility Study Committee, 2009).[3] Further, of the offshore renewable energy sources (wind, ocean current, and wave), wind has the greatest potential for development in the South Atlantic Planning Area within the next several years. Ocean current and wave energy technologies are being explored in other regions

---

1 http://www.slowfoodusa.org/ark-item/carolina-gold-rice (last visited April 29, 2014).
2 http://www.data.boem.gov/PI/PDFImages/ESPIS/5/5296.pdf (last visited April 29, 2014).
3 http://www.data.boem.gov/PI/PDFImages/ESPIS/5/5296.pdf (last visited April 29, 2014).

where their resource potential is greater. Wind maps for South Carolina, North Carolina, and Georgia show that there are areas with sufficient wind speed, water depth, and distance to shore for potential offshore wind energy development in these three states.

Wind energy becomes feasible with annual average wind speeds greater than seven meters/second at 90 meters (m) above the surface.[4] There are initiatives in South Carolina, North Carolina, and Georgia to develop offshore wind. In March 2009, a project was launched by the Palmetto Wind Research Project, a collaborative project of Santee Cooper (a public utility), Coastal Carolina University, and the South Carolina Energy Office to study the possibilities of generating wind energy off the South Carolina coast.[5] As of May 2011, this project had completed preliminary wind mapping (the strongest, closest to shore winds are in the northern part of the state), deployment of coastal anemometers (measures wind speed) and six offshore buoys along two transects, high level environmental checks, a preliminary design of an offshore meteorological tower off the mouth of Winyah Bay, and a conceptual design for a demonstration-scale offshore wind farm of up to 20 wind turbines 6.5–8 km off the mouth of Winyah Bay.[6] The demonstration wind farm is planned to produce 40 megawatts (MW) of electricity.[7] In May 2011, BOEM announced the establishment of a task force with the federal, state, local, and tribal governments in South Carolina to facilitate intergovernmental communications regarding OCS renewable energy activities.

According to the National Renewable Energy Lab (NREL), **Virginia, North Carolina, South Carolina, and Georgia have 82% of the East Coast resource in shallow water and more than 12 miles offshore** and 45% of the total East Coast offshore wind resource.[8] Offshore

---

4 http://www.data.boem.gov/PI/PDFImages/ESPIS/5/5296.pdf (last visited April 29, 2014).

5 http://www.data.boem.gov/PI/PDFImages/ESPIS/5/5296.pdf (last visited April 29, 2014).

6 http://www.data.boem.gov/PI/PDFImages/ESPIS/5/5296.pdf (last visited April 29, 2014).

7 http://www.data.boem.gov/PI/PDFImages/ESPIS/5/5296.pdf (last visited April 29, 2014).

8 http://www.secoastalwind.org/~secoast/images/fact_sheets/JBanks_OSWP12_poster.pdf (last visited April 29, 2014).

wind and biomass represent the two largest scale renewable energy options for the Southeastern U.S.

Table 1: [9]

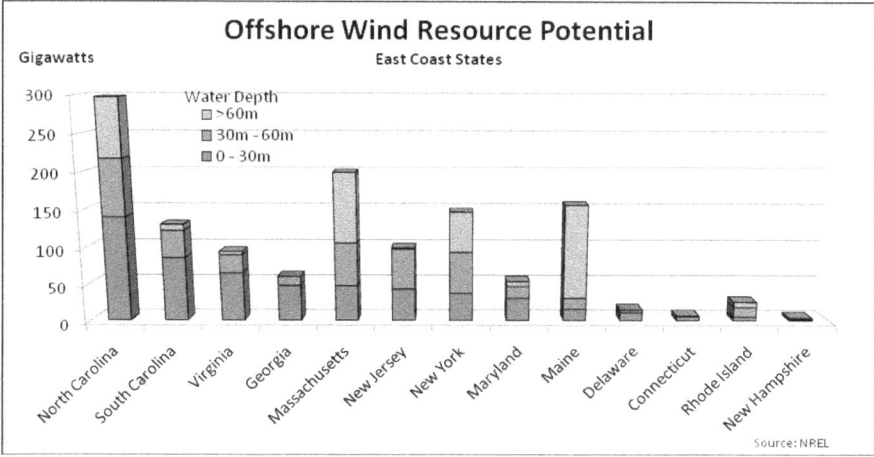

Based on this potential, South Carolina Act 318 of 2008 created a committee to review, study, and make recommendations regarding the feasibility of windmill farms in the state including, but not limited to, whether South Carolina is a suitable site for wind production on land or in offshore areas, the economic and environmental impact to the state, and the cost of wind farm installation and operation in the state.[10] In response on May 29, 2013, H. 4166 was introduced in the South Carolina House and on February 16, 2014, S. 1011 was introduced in the South Carolina Senate to introduce Offshore Wind as a viable energy source in the State of South Carolina.[11] These bills are only the beginning in a long arduous process involving state and federal permitting/leasing, regulations, and legal implications for offshore wind energy. We will explore this process for implementing offshore energy in South Carolina, as offshore oil and gas have been discussed by many authors in many journals, we will look at offshore alternative energy (wind), however

9 www.secoastalwind.org/~secoast/images/fact_sheets/JBanks_OSWP12_poster.pdf (last visited April 29, 2014).

10 http://www.energy.sc.gov/renewable/wind (last visited April 29, 2014).

11 http://www.energy.sc.gov/files/view/S1011Windcostrecovery.pdf and http://www.energy.sc.gov/files/view/ H4166.pdf (last visited April 29, 2014).

many of the regulations/laws are shared concern concerning offshore energy sources in the United States and specifically in South Carolina.

II. Current Status of Wind Energy in the United States

The projects in the planning and permitting stage include the Cape Wind project, to be located off the coast of Cape Cod in Massachusetts,[12] and the Bluewater Wind project, to be located approximately eleven miles off the coast of Delaware.[13] The Cape Wind project in particular has encountered considerable local opposition from some quarters: fishermen, sailors, some environmentalists, boaters, and others.[14] However, despite the opposition, Cape Wind has received the permits necessary to commence the project.[15]

When completed, Cape Wind will consist of approximately 130 wind turbine generators[16] capable of producing approximately 454 megawatts ("MW") of energy.[17] The 3.6 MW wind turbine generators will be located approximately 0.3 to 0.5 miles apart and the total array spread over twen-

---

12 http:// www.mms.gov/offshore/AlternativeEnergy/PDFs/FEIS/Cape%20Wind% C20Energy%C20Project%FEIS.pdf (last visited April 29, 2014).

13 http:// www.capewind.org/ (last visited April 29, 2014).

14 Peter B. Brace, Nantucket Shows Signs of Split on Cape Wind, Cape Cod Today, Mar. 12, 2008, http://www.capecodtoday.com (search for "Nantucket shows signs of split," then follow article link); Mike Seccombe, Fishing Concerns Dominate Cape Wind Hearings, Vineyard Gazette Online, Mar. 14, 2008, http://www.mvgazette. com/article.php?15714; Mike Seccombe, Two Sides Debate Cape Wind Plan, Vineyard Gazette Online, Sept. 25, 2007, http:// www.mvgazette.com/article. php?912. Despite concerns about harm to birds from some quarters, the National Audubon Society determined that studies show minimal threat to birds. Assessing the Threat to Birds, Online News Hour, Nov. 16, 2005, http://www.pbs.org/news-hour/indepth_coverage/science/wind_ power/threattobirds.html (last visited April 29, 2014).

15 Minerals Management Service, U.S. Dep't of the Interior, Cape Wind Energy Project Final Environmental Impact Statement at http:// www.mms.gov/offshore/Alter-nativeEnergy/PDFs/FEIS/ Cape%20Wind%C20Energy%C20Project%FEIS.pdf (last visited April 29, 2014).

16 http:// www.capewind.org/article24.htm (last visited April 29, 2014).

17 Minerals Management Service, U.S. Dep't of the Interior, Cape Wind Energy Project Final Environmental Impact Statement at http:// www.mms.gov/offshore/Alter-nativeEnergy/PDFs/FEIS/ Cape%20Wind%C20Energy%C20Project%FEIS.pdf (last visited April 29, 2014).

ty-four square miles.[18] Although the towers will extend only 257.5 feet above the water surface, each wind tower blade will reach 440 feet above the water.[19] This wind facility will be located in federal waters in Nantucket Sound, sheltered on the north by Cape Cod, to the west by Martha's Vineyard, to the south by Nantucket Island, and to the east by the Great Sound Shoal.[20] One reason Nantucket Sound was chosen as the location of this project is that it is relatively sheltered from significant Atlantic Ocean wave action and extreme storm waves.[21] Its closest distance to shore will be 4.7 miles, and its furthest will be approximately 11 miles.[22] This means a number of turbines will be visible from some points on the shores of Cape Cod and Martha's Vineyard but not from Nantucket. The cost of construction for this project is estimated to be as high as $2 billion.[23]

In 2006, Bluewater Wind LLC ("Bluewater Wind")[24] proposed a similar project, estimated to cost $1.6 billion,[25] to be located in federal waters, at

---

18 Mineral Management Service, U.S. Dep't of the Interior, Cape Wind Energy Project Draft Environmental Impact Statement 1-4 (2004) [hereinafter Cape Wind Draft EIS], at http:// www.nae.usace.army.mil/projects/ma/ccwf/ section1.pdf (last visited April 29, 2014).

19 Minerals Management Service, U.S. Dep't of the Interior, Cape Wind Energy Project Final Environmental Impact Statement at http:// www.mms.gov/offshore/Alter-nativeEnergy/PDFs/FEIS/ Cape%20Wind%C20Energy%C20Project%FEIS.pdf (last visited April 29, 2014).

20 Mineral Management Service, U.S. Dep't of the Interior, Cape Wind Energy Project Draft Environmental Impact Statement 1-4 (2004) [hereinafter Cape Wind Draft EIS], at http:// www.nae.usace.army.mil/projects/ma/ccwf/ section1.pdf (last visited April 29, 2014).

21 Walter Brooks, Long Island Offshore Wind Farm Scuttled; Cape Wind Predicted This Outcome 4 Years Ago, Cape Cod Today, Aug. 24, 2007, http:// www.cape-codtoday.com/blogs/index.php/2007/08/24/long_island_offshore_wind_farm_scuttled?blog=109 (last visited April 29, 2014).

22 Mineral Management Service, U.S. Dep't of the Interior, Cape Wind Energy Project Draft Environmental Impact Statement 1-4 (2004) [hereinafter Cape Wind Draft EIS], at http:// www.nae.usace.army.mil/projects/ma/ccwf/ section1.pdf (last visited April 29, 2014).

23 http://www.mms.gov/offshore/PDFs/CWFiles/68.pdf (last visited April 29, 2014).

24 Babcock & Brown Buys Bluewater Wind Power Firm, Reuters, Sept. 30, 2007, http:// www.reuters.com/article/innovationNews/idUSSYD29636020070930 (last visited April 29, 2014).

25 Bluewater to Work with Delaware on Wind Farm, Reuters, Nov. 12, 2007, http:// uk.reuters.com/article/environmentNews/idUKN0823936520071112 (last visited April 29, 2014).

least eleven miles off the coast of Delaware in the Atlantic Ocean.[26] At this distance, the turbines would be barely visible from the Delaware coastline.[27] The future of this project is uncertain. The original project proposed the installation of more than 100 wind turbine generators capable of producing approximately 450 MW of electricity;[28] however, the June 2008 power purchase agreement between Bluewater Wind and an onshore receiving utility company will only support the construction of fifty-five to seventy wind turbines.[29] If Bluewater Wind decides to build more than seventy turbines, it will have to find another purchaser for the generated power.[30] Another factor is the uncertain financial future of Bluewater Wind itself. In February 2009, Babcock & Brown, the Australia-based company that owns virtually all of Bluewater Wind, announced plans to liquidate its assets in order to satisfy creditor claims.[31] This means that Bluewater Wind will need to find new financial backing for the Delaware project.[32]

A major difference between the Cape Wind project and the Bluewater Wind project is that the Bluewater Wind project is the first one proposed for open ocean waters; for that reason, it will confront significant location and construction challenges. Sea conditions in an ocean location may be one reason for the September 2007 official cancellation of a similar project proposed by the Long Island Power Authority ("LIPA") to be sited off the

---

26 http://www.bluewaterwind.com/delaware.htm (last visited April 29, 2014).

27 http://www.bluewaterwind.com/delaware.htm (last visited April 29, 2014).

28 http://www.bluewaterwind.com/delaware.htm (last visited April 29, 2014).

29 Jeff Montgomery, Bluewater Wind Owner's Financial Woes Threaten Offshore Project, The News Journal, Feb. 9, 2009, at A1, available at http:// www.windaction. org/news/19887 (last visited April 29, 2014).

30 Jeff Montgomery, Bluewater Wind Owner's Financial Woes Threaten Offshore Project, The News Journal, Feb. 9, 2009, at A1, available at http:// www.windaction. org/news/19887 (last visited April 29, 2014).

31 Jeff Montgomery, Bluewater Wind Owner's Financial Woes Threaten Offshore Project, The News Journal, Feb. 9, 2009, at A1, available at http:// www.windaction. org/news/19887 (last visited April 29, 2014).

32 Aaron Nathans, Bluewater Wind Project OK for Now; Plenty of Time to Line Up Financing, Experts Say, The News Journal, Mar. 18, 2009, at A7, available at http:// www.wind-watch.org/news/2009/03/18/bluewater-wind-project-ok-for-now-plenty-of-time-to-line-up-financing-experts-say/ (last visited April 29, 2014).

South Shore of Long Island.[33] In 2003, when Cape Wind evaluated that site, the president of Cape Wind wrote a letter to LIPA stating "that the anticipated sea conditions in the Target Area pose unacceptable conditions. Both the significant wave and extreme storm wave are nearly three times that associated with current state-of-the-art offshore wind projects."[34] The official LIPA reason for cancellation was the high cost of construction.[35] The original projected cost in 2003 was $200 million but eventually ballooned to $811 million by the time LIPA decided to cancel the project.[36]

Other states, such as New Jersey and Rhode Island, are also pursuing wind energy development off their coasts. New Jersey has adopted a renewable energy incentive program[37] and an offshore wind rebate program for the installation of meteorological towers,[38] in addition to awarding a $4 million grant to Garden State Offshore Energy for a 345.6 MW offshore wind facility tentatively to be located sixteen miles southeast of Atlantic City.[39] In Rhode Island, interest in wind energy development in coastal and offshore waters will likely rise as the state seeks to achieve its renewable energy portfolio stan-

33 Renewable Energy Long Island, Long Island Wind Park Description, http:// www. lioffshorewindenergy.org/index.php?module=pagemaster&PAGE_user_op=view_page&PAGE_id=24. (Last visited April 29, 2014).

34 Renewable Energy Long Island, Long Island Wind Park Description, http:// www. lioffshorewindenergy.org/index.php?module=pagemaster&PAGE_user_op=view_page&PAGE_id=24 (last visited April 29, 2014).

35 Bruce Lambert, LIPA Chairman Advises a 'No' on Offshore Windmills, N.Y. Times, Aug. 24, 2007, available at http:// www.nytimes.com/2007/08/24/nyregion/24lipa.html?scp=1&sq=lipa%20chairman% 20advises&st=cse (last visited April 29, 2014).

36 Bruce Lambert, LIPA Chairman Advises a 'No' on Offshore Windmills, N.Y. Times, Aug. 24, 2007, available at http:// www.nytimes.com/2007/08/24/nyregion/24lipa.html?scp=1&sq=lipa%20chairman% 20advises&st=cse (last visited April 29, 2014).

37 Office of Clean Energy, N.J. Board of Public Utilities, Renewable Energy Incentive Programs, http://www.njcleanenergy.com/renewable-energy/programs/renewable-energy-incentive-program (last visited April 29, 2014).

38 New In the Matter of the Offshore Wind Rebate Program for the Installation of Meteorological Towers, Docket No. EO08110971 (N.J. Board of Public Utilities Order Nov. 26, 2008), available at http:// njcleanenergy.com/files/file/Board%20Orders/11-21-08-8A.pdf (last visited April 29, 2014).

39 Press Release, New Jersey Board of Public Utilities, Board of Public Utilities Approves Grant of $4 Million for Offshore Wind Project Proposal (Oct. 3, 2008), http://www.njcleanenergy.com/files/file/Press% 20Releases/20081003.pdf (last visited April 29, 2014).

dard of sixteen percent by 2020.[40] To help meet this goal, Governor Donald Carcieri announced in September 2008 that the company Deepwater Wind was selected to construct a wind energy project off Rhode Island's coast.[41] The project will provide an estimated 1.3 million megawatt hours per year, which is approximately fifteen percent of the electricity used in the state.[42]

States are attracted to wind energy not only as a potential alternative energy source, but also as a potential generator of royalty revenues earned from the leasing of state-owned submerged lands. For example, Texas issued leases to state-owned submerged lands to two different companies.[43] Superior Renewable Energy, which subsequently was acquired by Babcock & Brown,[44] obtained the largest lease covering 39,900 acres of submerged lands located off Padre Island.[45] Texas officials stated that the State expected "to earn anywhere from $34 million to more than $100 million from the lease."[46]

Despite projections for having some of these proposed projects online by 2009,[47] no wind turbines have been placed in Texas waters. In fact, the Superior Renewable Energy lease was abandoned in 2007, with the company

---

40 See R.I. Gen. Laws §39-26-4 (2006).

41 Press Release, Office of the Governor, State of R.I., Carcieri Names Deepwater Wind as Developer for Rhode Island's Off-Shore Wind Farm (Sept. 25, 2008), http://www.ri.gov/press/view.php?id=7202 (last visited April 29, 2014).

42 Press Release, Office of the Governor, State of R.I., Carcieri Names Deepwater Wind as Developer for Rhode Island's Off-Shore Wind Farm (Sept. 25, 2008), http://www.ri.gov/press/view.php?id=7202 (last visited April 29, 2014).

43 Texas Bid Could be First U.S. Offshore Wind Farm, RenewableEnergyWorld.com, Oct. 31, 2005, http:// www.renewableenergyworld.com/rea/news/article/2005/10/texas-bid-could-be-first-u-s-offshore-wind-farm-38618 (last visited April 29, 2014).

44 Babcock & Brown Cancels Wind Farm off Texas, Reuters, June 13, 2007, http://www.reuters.com/article/ bondsNews/idUSN1335705620070613 (last visited April 29, 2014).

45 Texas Grants Lease for Gulf of Mexico Project, RenewableEnergyWorld.com, May 12, 2006, http:// www.renewableenergyworld.com/rea/news/article/2006/05/texas-grants-lease-for-gulf-of-mexico-wind-project-44884 (last visited April 29, 2014).

46 Erin Wayman, The Wind Over the Waves: Is Offshore Wind Power the Renewable Energy of the Future? Geotimes, Apr. 2008, http:// www.geotimes.org/apr08/article.html?id=feature_wind.html (last visited April 29, 2014).

47 Associated Press, Texas Plans Offshore Wind Farms, Fox News, Nov. 7, 2005, http://www.foxnews.com/story/0,2933,174806,00.html (last visited April 29, 2014).

citing the multibillion dollar cost for offshore construction as too high.[48] Texas would like to enter into more leases but is having trouble finding takers.[49] Recent hurricane activity in the Gulf of Mexico may have made other companies shy of putting billions of dollars in the path of future coastal storms that may have the strength of Hurricanes Katrina or Ike.

Each of the projects described above is proposed for location in waters relatively near the shore because of technology and cost limitations. Current technology allows wind facilities to be located in waters deeper than twenty to thirty meters.[50] In fact, existing technology would allow wind turbines to be sited in waters up to fifty meters in depth,[51] but at the present time, it is prohibitively expensive to construct the foundations for and to locate facilities in water much deeper than twenty to thirty meters.[52] For that reason, most of the 1470 MW of near shore and offshore wind energy capacity in Europe has been constructed in shallow waters that are less than twenty meters in depth.[53] Until the cost of deeper water technology drops significantly, twenty to thirty meters is close to the economically feasible limit for offshore wind energy facilities.[54] Water depth is significant to South Carolina because along the coast in the area of Horry and Georgetown Counties, the twenty-meter

48 Babcock & Brown Cancels Wind Farm off Texas, Reuters, June 13, 2007, http://www.reuters.com/article/bondsNews/idUSN1335705620070613 (last visited April 29, 2014).
49 http:// greeninc.blogs.nytimes.com/2008/10/10/a-few-snags-but-hopes-are-still-high-for-offshore-wind-in-texas/ (last visited April 29, 2014).
50 Peter Fairley, Wind Power That Floats, Technology Review, Apr. 2, 2008, http://www.technologyreview.com/energy/20500/ (last visited April 29, 2014).
51 Erin Wayman, The Wind Over the Waves: Is Offshore Wind Power the Renewable Energy of the Future? Geotimes, Apr. 2008, http:// www.geotimes.org/apr08/article.html?id=feature_wind.html (last visited April 29, 2014).
52 Emily Waltz, Offshore Wind May Power the Future, Scientific American, Oct. 20, 2008, available at http:// www.sciam.com/article.cfm?id=offshore-wind-may-power-the-future&page=2 (last visited April 29, 2014).
53 Emily Waltz, Offshore Wind May Power the Future, Scientific American, Oct. 20, 2008, available at http:// www.sciam.com/article.cfm?id=offshore-wind-may-power-the-future&page=2.
54 Peter Fairley, Wind Power That Floats, Technology Review, Apr. 2, 2008, http://www.technologyreview.com/energy/20500/ (last visited April 29, 2014).

line at times is within three miles of the shore.[55] At other places offshore, it is ten to fifteen miles out.[56] That means that water-based wind generating facilities may be visible from the shore.

Table 2: A picture of a windmill from different distances[57]

III. Who Regulates?

"Federal offshore waters" generally extend from 3 to 200 miles from the shore. Under the Submerged Lands Act (SLA), 43 U.S.C. § 1301 (2000), states have title to the submerged lands extending three nautical miles from the low water mark and control over natural resources within that three-mile belt (Florida's, on its Gulf coast, and Texas' ownership and control extends 3 marine leagues, which is approximately 10 nautical miles). The United States owns and controls the natural resources between three and two hundred miles from shore, and its control over the continental shelf (the seabed) may extend even further. However, as Table 1 illustrates, nearly one

---

55 Kevin C. Higgins et al., Utility-Related Statutory & Regulatory Barriers, in Coastal Wind: Energy for North Carolina's Future 207, 207-19 (2009) available at http://www.climate.unc.edu/coastal-wind/Coastal% 20Wind-%20Energy%20 for%C20NC2019s%20Future.pdf/at_download/file (last visited April 29, 2014).

56 Kevin C. Higgins et al., Utility-Related Statutory & Regulatory Barriers, in Coastal Wind: Energy for North Carolina's Future 207, 207-19 (2009) available at http://www.climate.unc.edu/coastal-wind/Coastal% 20Wind-%20Energy%20 for%C20NC2019s%20Future.pdf/at_download/file (last visited April 29, 2014).

57 http://blogs.app.com/inthemoney/2008/10/03/blowing-in-the-wind/ (last visited April 30, 2014).

hundred gigawatts of South Carolina's available wind energy is within 30m of water and therefore potentially under simultaneous control of the state.

A. History

Control and jurisdiction over such valuable offshore resources have been controversial. On September 28, 1945, the Truman Proclamation claimed U.S. jurisdiction and control over the natural resources of the subsoil and seabed of the continental shelf, essentially beginning the modern movement of coastal jurisdictional claims and Law of the Sea. Two years later, the U.S. Supreme Court issued its seminal opinion in United States v. California,[58] confirming the federal government's ownership of the submerged lands and associated natural resources from the tidelands to three miles from shore.[59] In 1953, though, under the Eisenhower Administration, Congress effectively reversed United States v. California. In passing the Submerged Lands Act[60], Congress gave the states exclusive rights to resources of the "marginal sea"— the band of water up to three nautical miles from shore.[61]

Thus, federal jurisdiction begins more than three nautical miles from the shore, along the Outer Continental Shelf, and ends two hundred nautical miles out to sea.[62] Analyses of offshore wind capacity typically assume that wind farms will be built in federal waters, more than five miles from the coast.[63] Therefore federal jurisdiction covers the generation component of

58 United States v. California, 332 U.S. 19 (1947).

59 United States v. California, 332 U.S. 19 (1947).

60 43 U.S.C. §§ 1301-1315 (1953).

61 The U.S. nevertheless retained the right to regulate, among other things, commerce, and navigation in these waters. See also 43 U.S.C. § 1314 (1953). For historical reasons, Texas, and Florida on the Gulf coast each maintain jurisdiction out to nine nautical miles. See id. § 1301.

62 Thomas C. Jensen, Offshore Renewable Energy Development after the Energy Policy Act of 2005, 1 (unpublished paper presented at the American Bar Association Section of Environment, Energy, and Resources 36th Annual Conference on Environmental Law, March 2007), available at http:// www.oceanrenewable.com/wp-content/uploads/2007/03/aba-ocs-paper-final.pdf (last visited April 29, 2014).

63 European Wind Energy Ass'n, The European Wind Industry: Key Trends and Statistics 2009 3, 5 (2010)http:// www.ewea.org/fileadmin/emag/statistics/2009offshore/pdf/offshore%20stats% 2020092.pdf (last visited April 29, 2014).

an offshore wind project, mainly the turbines.[64] This includes site approval and permitting for project construction.[65]

B. Modern Developments

Section 388 of the Energy Policy Act of 2005 grants the Department of the Interior (DOI) primary authority over offshore wind farm approval and permitting.[66] Section 388 specifies that the Minerals Management Service (MMS), a branch of DOI, controls the offshore wind facility permitting process; the Secretary of the Interior makes the final permitting decision.[67] This grant of authority extends MMS's existing authority under the Outer Continental Shelf Lands Act (OCSLA), which gives it management rights over the Outer Continental Shelf primarily for offshore fossil fuel extraction.[68] Because of MMS's experience with managing offshore oil and gas extraction, Congress deemed it the proper body for offshore wind permitting as well.[69] Opponents of the decision have been concerned with MMS's lack of experience with marine habitat regulation and protection.[70] As a result, MMS appears receptive to coordinating with other agencies with relevant experience, like the Army Corps of Engineers, National Marine Fisheries Service,

---

64 Thomas C. Jensen, Offshore Renewable Energy Development after the Energy Policy Act of 2005, 1 (unpublished paper presented at the American Bar Association Section of Environment, Energy, and Resources 36th Annual Conference on Environmental Law, March 2007), available at http:// www.oceanrenewable.com/wp-content/uploads/2007/03/aba-ocs-paper-final.pdf (last visited April 29, 2014).

65 Thomas C. Jensen, Offshore Renewable Energy Development after the Energy Policy Act of 2005,1 (unpublished paper presented at the American Bar Association Section of Environment, Energy, and Resources 36th Annual Conference on Environmental Law, March 2007), available at http:// www.oceanrenewable.com/wp-content/uploads/2007/03/aba-ocs-paper-final.pdf (last visited April 29, 2014).

66 43 U.S.C. § 1337 (2006).

67 43 U.S.C. § 1337 (2006).

68 43 U.S.C. § 1337 (2006).

69 Carolyn S. Kaplan, Congress, the Courts, and the Army Corps: Siting the First Offshore Wind Farm in the United States, 31 B.C. Envtl. Aff. L. Rev. 177, 213 (2004).

70 Carolyn S. Kaplan, Congress, the Courts, and the Army Corps: Siting the First Offshore Wind Farm in the United States, 31 B.C. Envtl. Aff. L. Rev. 177, 191 (2004).

Coast Guard, Department of Energy, and Environmental Protection Agency, as well as appropriate state actors.[71]

Section 388 came in response to controversy over which federal agency had permitting authority during the early stages of the Cape Wind project. While Section 388 does not resolve all of the issues relating to federal jurisdiction over offshore wind,[72] its designation of MMS as the primary permitting agency marks Congress's first step toward a unified review process for offshore alternative energy.[73] Nonetheless, the current federal regulatory environment for offshore wind remains confusing. In April 2009, President Barack Obama took a first step toward remedying some of that confusion by announcing a coordinated program, headed by DOI, for federal offshore renewable energy permitting. The program will cover not only offshore wind power generation, but also other offshore renewable energy, such as electricity generated from ocean currents.[74] Despite this progress toward an improved federal regulatory program, barriers to offshore wind power still exist, largely due to the absence of a strong and effective federal mandate promoting offshore wind power development and the powers that states retain over project siting.[75]

---

71 Minerals Mgmt. Serv., U.S. Dep't of the Interior, Cape Wind Cooperating Agency Contacts & Responsibilities, available at http:// www.mms.gov/offshore/RenewableEnergy/PDF/CapeWindCooperatingAgencyContacts.pdf (MMS's list of federal, state, and local agencies with which it is cooperating regarding the Cape Wind project) (last visited April 29, 2014).

72 Thomas C. Jensen, Offshore Renewable Energy Development after the Energy Policy Act of 2005, 1 (unpublished paper presented at the American Bar Association Section of Environment, Energy, and Resources 36th Annual Conference on Environmental Law, March 2007), available at http:// www.oceanrenewable.com/wp-content/uploads/2007/03/aba-ocs-paper-final.pdf (last visited April 29, 2014).

73 Adam M. Dinnell & Adam J. Russ, The Legal Hurdles to Developing Wind Power as an Alternative Energy Source in the United States: Creative and Comparative Solutions, 27 Nw. J. Int'l L. & Bus. 535, 578 (2007).

74 Remarks at Trinity Structural Towers Manufacturing Plant in Newton, Iowa, 2009 Daily Comp. Pres. Doc. 282 (Apr. 22, 2009).

75 Thomas C. Jensen, Offshore Renewable Energy Development after the Energy Policy Act of 2005 1 (unpublished paper presented at the American Bar Association Section of Environment, Energy, and Resources 36th Annual Conference on Environmental Law, March 2007), available at http:// www.oceanrenewable.com/wp-content/uploads/2007/03/aba-ocs-paper-final.pdf (last visited April 29, 2014).

C. State Jurisdiction

Any electricity generated in an offshore facility must be transmitted to land through the state controlled Coastal Zone. Therefore, state—and sometimes local—authorities ultimately have a role to play in any offshore wind project through the siting and permitting of transmission cables that are necessary to bring electricity from the turbines to land, vessel passage, and other necessities. Although state and localities may only exert direct control over the permitting of transmission cables, they will almost certainly consider the impact of the generation turbines on their aesthetic impact on the environment. They know that denying transmission permits effectively stalls or destroys the construction of generation facilities. States will also likely consider such aesthetic and environmental considerations in the federal consistency review process, with which they may also block federal activities and permits.[76] Federal consistency review is a component of the CZMA and will be described in more detail below.

Because most of the costs of offshore wind power development are local, there is a strong argument for state and local control over offshore wind project siting: because localities must deal with the downsides of offshore wind projects, they should control where those projects are placed.[77] On the other hand, there are broader, positive effects of offshore wind power development—such as energy security improvement and environmental benefits like climate change mitigation—that imply a need for stronger federal intervention to balance appropriately the costs and benefits of offshore wind. The CZMA attempts to provide a formal structure for such balancing, but it ultimately leaves the states with too much power, and the federal government and offshore wind farm proponents with no formal federal encouragement or support.[78]

---

76 16 U.S.C. § 1456(c)(1)(A), (1)(C), (3)(A) (2006).
77 Robert W. Eberhardt, Note, Federalism and the Siting of Offshore Wind Energy Facilities, 14 N.Y.U. Envtl. L.J. 374, 411-417 (2006).
78 Robert W. Eberhardt, Note, Federalism and the Siting of Offshore Wind Energy Facilities, 14 N.Y.U. Envtl. L.J. 374, 411-417 (2006).

IV. The Coastal Zone Management Act: Reconciling Local Interests with National Priorities

The overarching goal of the Coastal Zone Management Act (CZMA) is "to preserve, protect, develop, and where possible, to restore or enhance, the resources of the Nation's coastal zone for this and succeeding generations."[79] The CZMA mentions the development of energy facilities in the Coastal Zone, but its language is vague, and generally requires only that states undertake "adequate consideration of the national interest" in siting energy facilities, and "give consideration" to any applicable national or interstate energy plan or program.[80] The CZMA also mentions energy with regard to funding for development: "The national objective of attaining a greater degree of energy self-sufficiency would be advanced by providing Federal financial assistance to meet state and local needs resulting from new or expanded energy activity in or affecting the coastal zone."[81] However, the CZMA does not mention offshore wind energy or renewable energy at all.

Although the CZMA acknowledges the "national interest in the effective management, beneficial use, protection, and development of the coastal zone,"[82] it allows states substantial discretion over their coastal zone management through CZMPs, which the Secretary of Commerce oversees.[83] As noted previously, the Submerged Lands Act defines state coastal zones as three miles from the shoreline.[84] The CZMA mechanism of federal consistency review extends state power further, past their coastal zones, by allowing states to review and sometimes overrule federal actions and permits in federal waters.[85]

Before the CZMA was promulgated, the coastal zone had long been

---

79 16 U.S.C. § 1452(1) (2006).
80 16 U.S.C. § 1455(d)(8) (2006).
81 16 U.S.C. § 1451(j) (2006).
82 16 U.S.C. § 1451(a) (2006).
83 16 U.S.C. §§ 1452(2), 1455(d) (2006).
84 43 U.S.C. §§ 1311-1312 (2006).
85 16 U.S.C. § 1456(c)(1)(A), (1)(C), (3)(A) (2006).

subject to decentralized management.[86] The CZMA continues this tradition with its own approach to federalism, explicitly encouraging cooperation between local, state, and federal levels of government in their management of coastal resources.[87] Specifically, under the CZMA, each state makes its own CZMP.[88] The CZMA provides a variety of policy considerations for states to incorporate into their management programs. Prioritizing construction of certain facilities, specifically energy facilities, in states' coastal zones is one of several listed considerations.[89] Others include protecting natural resources; minimizing the loss of life and property to flooding and sea level rise; improving coastal water quality; allowing public recreational access to the coast; restoring urban waterfronts and preserving coastal features; coordinating and simplifying governmental management procedures for coastal resources; consulting and coordinating with federal agencies; giving timely and effective notice for public and local participation in governmental decision making; comprehensive planning for marine resource preservation; and studying sea level rise and land subsidence.[90] The Secretary of Commerce examines states' CZMPs, making sure they are in accordance with the CZMA's policy considerations and other mandates, and any other federal regulations.[91] In particular, the CZMA requires that states adequately consider the national interest in "siting of facilities such as energy facilities which are of greater than local significance. In the case of energy facilities, the Secretary shall find that the State has given consideration to any applicable national or interstate energy plan or program."[92] Once approved by the Secretary of Commerce, however, state CZMPs are subject to very little federal constraint under the CZMA, leaving states with nearly complete discretion within their coastal zones.

---

86 Rusty Russell, Neither Out Far nor In Deep: The Prospects for Utility-Scale Wind Power in the Coastal Zone, 31 B.C. Envtl. Aff. L. Rev. 221, 232-233 (2004).
87 16 U.S.C. § 1452(4)-(5) (2006).
88 16 U.S.C. §§ 1452(2), 1455(d) (2006).
89 16 U.S.C. § 1452(2)(A)-(K) (2006).
90 16 U.S.C. § 1452(2)(A)-(K) (2006).
91 16 U.S.C. §§ 1454, 1455(d) (2006).
92 16 U.S.C. § 1455(d)(8) (2006).

State control is expanded by federal consistency review,[93] a mechanism unique to the CZMA. Consistency review allows a state to review a federal agency activity or permit within or outside of the coastal zone for compatibility with the state's CZMP when the activity or permit affects the state's coastal zone.[94] Under this mechanism, the federal agency must submit a "consistency determination" (for an activity) or "consistency certification" (for a permit) to the state before moving forward with the project.[95] For federal permits, which would be more relevant to offshore renewable development than federal actions, the state then has the opportunity to concur with or object to the agency's certification.[96] "No license or permit shall be granted by the Federal agency until the state . . . has concurred with the applicant's certification."[97] Thus, a coastal state's control extends beyond its own coastal zone into federal waters, as it has the ability to review—and potentially block—any project that affects their coastal zone. In the end, however, the Secretary of Commerce—by her own initiative or in response to an appeal—can overrule the state's protest by finding that a permit is consistent with the objectives of the CZMA or otherwise in the interest of national security.[98]

Since the passage of the CZMA in 1972 until March 2010, states had filed 141 appeals with the Secretary protesting federal permits affecting their coastal zones.[99] States settled their issues with the federal government in 64 instances, or 45 percent of these cases.[100] The Secretary dismissed or

---

93 16 U.S.C. § 1456(c)(1)(A), (1)(C), (3)(A) (2006).
94 16 U.S.C. § 1456(c)(1)(A), (1)(C), (3)(A) (2006).
95 16 U.S.C. § 1456(c)(1)(C), (3)(A) (2006).
96 16 U.S.C. § 1456(c)(3)(A) (2006).
97 16 U.S.C. § 1456(c)(3)(A) (2006).
98 16 U.S.C. § 1456(c)(3)(A).
99 Office of Ocean & Coastal Resource Mgmt., Nat'l Oceanic & Atmospheric Admin., Appeals to the Secretary of Commerce Under the Coastal Zone Management Act (CZMA) 1 (2010), available at http:// coastalmanagement.noaa.gov/consistency/ media/appealslist.pdf (last visited April 29, 2014).
100 Office of Ocean & Coastal Resource Mgmt., Nat'l Oceanic & Atmospheric Admin., Appeals to the Secretary of Commerce Under the Coastal Zone Management Act (CZMA) 1 (2010), available at http:// coastalmanagement.noaa.gov/consistency/ media/appealslist.pdf (last visited April 29, 2014).

overrode state appeals in 32 instances, or 23 percent of these cases.[101] Of the remaining 45 appeals that the Secretary considered for their substance, the Secretary overrode the state's objection in 14 cases, or 31 percent of the time, and accepted the state's objection in 30 cases, or 67 percent of the time.[102] Only 19 of the 45 appeals related to energy facilities, but all of these related to oil or natural gas projects; the Secretary overrode these appeals about half of the time.[103] Although states do not choose to use their federal consistency review power over federal permits frequently, as these numbers show, it is nonetheless a powerful tool that extends their power beyond their coastal zones.

V. Starting the Offshore Energy Process

In 2009, President Barack Obama announced the final regulations for the Outer Continental Shelf (OCS) Renewable Energy Program, which was authorized by the Energy Policy Act of 2005 (EPAct).[104] These regulations provide a framework for issuing leases, easements and rights-of-way for OCS activities that support production and transmission of energy from sources other than oil and natural gas. Department of the Interior's Bureau of Ocean Energy Management (BOEM) is responsible for offshore renewable energy development in Federal waters and anticipates future development on the OCS from three general sources: offshore wind energy, ocean wave energy, and current wave energy.[105]

---

101 Office of Ocean & Coastal Resource Mgmt., Nat'l Oceanic & Atmospheric Admin., Appeals to the Secretary of Commerce Under the Coastal Zone Management Act (CZMA) 1 (2010), available at http:// coastalmanagement.noaa.gov/consistency/ media/appealslist.pdf (last visited April 29, 2014).

102 Office of Ocean & Coastal Resource Mgmt., Nat'l Oceanic & Atmospheric Admin., Appeals to the Secretary of Commerce Under the Coastal Zone Management Act (CZMA) 1 (2010), available at http:// coastalmanagement.noaa.gov/consistency/ media/appealslist.pdf (last visited April 29, 2014).

103 Office of Ocean & Coastal Resource Mgmt., Nat'l Oceanic & Atmospheric Admin., Appeals to the Secretary of Commerce Under the Coastal Zone Management Act (CZMA) 1 (2010), available at http:// coastalmanagement.noaa.gov/consistency/ media/appealslist.pdf (last visited April 29, 2014).

104 http://www.boem.gov/Renewable-Energy/ (last visited April 29, 2014).

105 http://www.boem.gov/uploadedFiles/30_CFR_585.pdf (last visited April 29, 2014).

- **Offshore Wind Energy.** Wind turbines have been installed off-shore in a number of countries to harness the energy of the moving air over the oceans and convert it to electricity. Offshore winds tend to flow at higher sustained speeds than onshore winds, making turbines more efficient.[106]

- **Ocean Wave Energy (Hydrokinetic).** There is tremendous energy in ocean waves. Wave power devices extract energy directly from the surface motion of ocean waves. A variety of technologies have been proposed to capture that energy, and some of the more promising designs are undergoing demonstration testing. The Northwestern Coast of the United States has especially high potential for wave energy development and is one of only a few areas in the world with abundant available wave power resources.[107]

- **Ocean Current Energy (Hydrokinetic).** Ocean currents contain an enormous amount of energy that can be captured and converted to a usable form. Some of the ocean currents on the OCS are the Gulf Stream, Florida Straits Current, and California Current. Submerged water turbines, similar to wind turbines, may be deployed on the OCS in the coming years to extract energy from ocean currents.[108]

The BOEM process is not a simplistic plan, but a rigorous study in everything from land surveying to loggerhead sonic sensitivity.[109]

---

106 http://www.boem.gov/Renewable-Energy/ (last visited April 29, 2014).
107 http://www.boem.gov/Renewable-Energy/ (last visited April 29, 2014).
108 http://www.boem.gov/Renewable-Energy/ (last visited April 29, 2014).
109 http://www.data.boem.gov/PI/PDFImages/ESPIS/5/5296.pdf (last visited April 29, 2014).

Table 3: Offshore Alternative Energy Process[110]

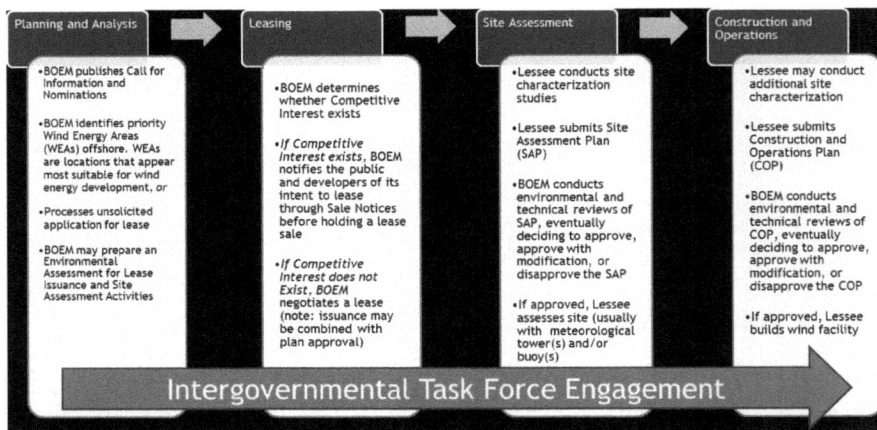

Planning and Analysis	Leasing	Site Assessment	Construction and Operations
•BOEM publishes Call for Information and Nominations	•BOEM determines whether Competitive Interest exists	•Lessee conducts site characterization studies	•Lessee may conduct additional site characterization
•BOEM identifies priority Wind Energy Areas (WEAs) offshore. WEAs are locations that appear most suitable for wind energy development, *or*	•*If Competitive Interest exists*, BOEM notifies the public and developers of its intent to lease through Sale Notices before holding a lease sale	•Lessee submits Site Assessment Plan (SAP)	•Lessee submits Construction and Operations Plan (COP)
•Processes unsolicited application for lease		•BOEM conducts environmental and technical reviews of SAP, eventually deciding to approve, approve with modification, or disapprove the SAP	•BOEM conducts environmental and technical reviews of COP, eventually deciding to approve, approve with modification, or disapprove the COP
•BOEM may prepare an Environmental Assessment for Lease Issuance and Site Assessment Activities	•*If Competitive Interest does not Exist, BOEM* negotiates a lease (note: issuance may be combined with plan approval)	•If approved, Lessee assesses site (usually with meteorological tower(s) and/or buoy(s)	•If approved, Lessee builds wind facility

Intergovernmental Task Force Engagement

A. State Participation

This federal process in South Carolina will be completed in cooperation with the South Carolina Department of Health and Environmental Concerns (DHEC). DHEC is responsible for managing ocean resources within South Carolina's state waters which extend out to three (3) nautical miles offshore. State marine waters include critical habitats for commercially and recreationally important fisheries, as well as significant mineral and sand resources. Due to their proximity to land, state waters are also subject to a growing range of potential human activities including sand mining, submerged transmission cables and energy facilities. In 2008, DHEC established an Ocean Planning Work Group to consider emerging ocean resource issues and develop a plan to guide future ocean research, data collection and mapping, and decision making.[111] As previously mentioned, two bills have been introduced to begin the state (3 mile) process for implementing the application/permitting process within state waters.

A collaboration between state, federal, and even local governments will

---

110 http://www.data.boem.gov/PI/PDFImages/ESPIS/5/5296.pdf (last visited April 29, 2014).
111 http://www.scdhec.gov/environment/ocrm/ocean_management.htm (last visited April 29, 2014).

need to be created in order to simplify this process. If a wind farm is installed on the Outer Continental Shelf, with transmission tubes carrying the energy over South Carolina submerged lands and filtered into local utility/municipal electrical grids then each party is central to the success of this energy source. If a company is to invest in this process, a simplified application and study must be used, or the costs/risks will overwhelm the benefit/potential.

B. Offshore Regulatory Task Force

The Bureau of Energy Management (BOEM) established a South Carolina Renewable Energy Task Force to assist government decision-making within the umbrella of the established BOEM regulatory framework regarding renewable energy leasing and development on the OCS off the coast of South Carolina. Membership of the BOEM South Carolina Task Force is mostly governmental and includes representatives from federal, state, local and tribal governments. The goal is to facilitate intergovernmental communications regarding OCS renewable energy activities.[112] This task force met March 29, 2012, for its first and only meeting (another meeting was set for May 16, 2014) to discuss initiatives and the offshore leasing process.[113]

A list of the members for this task force is comprised of:

- U.S. Army Corps of Engineers
- U.S. Coast Guard
- U.S. Environmental Protection Agency
- U.S. Fish & Wildlife Service
- Minerals Management Service
- National Marine Fisheries Service, NOAA
- Federal Aviation Administration
- S.C. DHEC, Bureau of Water
- S.C. DHEC, Office of Coastal Resource Management
- S.C. Department of Archives & History
- S.C. Department of Natural Resources
- Clemson University Restoration Institute

---

112 http://www.boem.gov/State-Activities-South-Carolina/ (last visited April 29, 2014).
113 http://www.boem.gov/State-Activities-South-Carolina/ (last visited April 29, 2014).

- Coastal Carolina University
- EcoEnergy, LLC
- North Carolina State University
- Research Planning, Inc.
- SCANA
- Santee Cooper
- Savannah River Ecology Lab
- Southern Environmental Law Center
- S.C. Coastal Conservation League
- S.C. Sea Grant Consortium
- University of South Carolina, Marine Science Program
- University of South Carolina, School of the Environment[114]

The objectives of this group are to identify the proper permitting authorities, identify timeframes for permitting, and identifying the regulatory gaps. As a result, the below table was generated for offshore permitting in South Carolina.

---

114 http://www.boem.gov/uploadedFiles/BOEM/Renewable_Energy_Program/State_ Activities/ SC%20Offshore%20Wind%20Initiatives_Energy%20Office_Vanden- Houten.pdf (last visited April 29, 2014).

Table 4: South Carolina Territorial Waters Permitting Process[115]

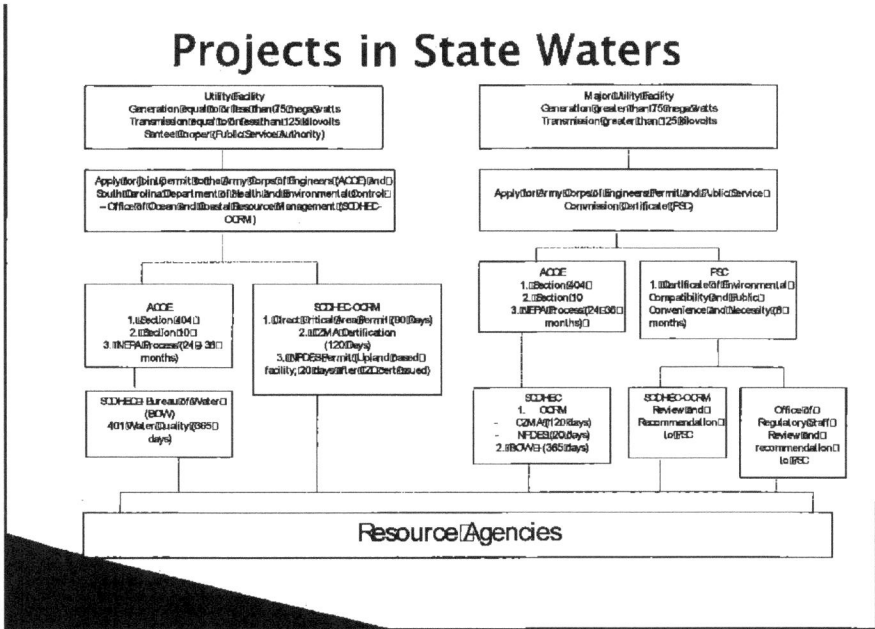

Projects in State Waters

Utility Facility	Major Utility Facility
Generation equal to or less than 75 megawatts Transmission equal to or less than 125 kilovolts Santee Cooper (Public Service Authority)	Generation greater than 75 megawatts Transmission greater than 125 kilovolts

| Apply for joint permit to the Army Corps of Engineers (ACOE) and South Carolina Department of Health and Environmental Control – Office of Ocean and Coastal Resource Management (SCDHEC-OCRM) | Apply for Army Corps of Engineers Permit and Public Service Commission Certificate (PSC) |

ACOE
1. Section 404
2. Section 10
3. NEPA Process (24-36 months)

SCDHEC-OCRM
1. Critical Area Permit (90 Days)
2. CZMA Certification (120 Days)
3. NPDES Permit (Upland based facility; 20 days after 401 Cert issued)

ACOE
1. Section 404
2. Section 10
3. NEPA Process (24-36 months)

PSC
1. Certificate of Environmental Compatibility and Public Convenience and Necessity (6 months)

SCDHEC Bureau of Water (BOW) 401 Water Quality (365 days)

SCDHEC
1. OCRM
   - CZMA (120 days)
   - NPDES (20 days)
2. BOW (365 days)

SCDHEC-OCRM Review and Recommendation to PSC

Office of Regulatory Staff Review and recommendation to PSC

Resource Agencies

As the table illustrates the proposed permitting is an intergovernmental process requiring compliance with both federal and state law. This conundrum of requirements makes the already costly wind energy prospects seem improbable. At least the local environmental groups support the implementation of wind, with a caveat that the marine wildlife be protected during the studies and the implementation of the wind farms.[116]

---

115 http://www.boem.gov/uploadedFiles/BOEM/Renewable_Energy_Program/ State_Activities/ SC%20Offshore%20Wind%20Initiatives_Energy%20Office_VandenHouten.pdf (last visited April 29, 2014).

116 Hamilton Davis, Coastal Conservation League (South Carolina), April 3, 2014, Interview (Natural Gas is also being studied and considered. The same concerns for marine wildlife wellbeing are being explored as with wind energy. Environmental Groups in SC are not as concerned with leakage/spills based on the consistence of the natural gas, but with disruption of the ocean floor and with the marine life.)

V. Applicable Maritime Regulations and Laws

When reviewing the permitting structures for offshore wind in the United States of America, three things should be kept in mind: 1) who is holding the land/seabed in title upon which the project will be built, 2) what are the administrative structures/agencies that oversee the application process, and (3) who do these administrative agencies answer to?[117]

The United States has the most cumbersome and entangled system of permitting regulations for an offshore wind project currently in the World.[118] First, in comparison to the British and German regimes, the United States holds land submerged in a public trust.[119] The Public Trust Doctrine[120] makes such lands open to all, and therefore activities conducted in these areas have to conform to the desire/needs of society as a whole.[121] On top of this abstract protection, a wind farm project must navigate regulations and issues of multi-level governance as well as multiple agencies involved in the process. For example, the federal permitting regime requires compliance with the National Environmental Policy Act ("NEPA"),[122] Coastal Zone Management Act ("CZMA"),[123] Clean Water Act ("CWA"),[124] Rivers and Harbors Act ("RHA"),[125] and species-protecting statutes such as the

---

117 Marc R. Fialkoff, Shipping Lanes and Power Lines: The Port of Davisville and the Dynamic Role of Infrastructure, 18 Roger Williams U. L. Rev. 220, 241-54 (2013).
118 Kurt E. Thomsen, Offshore Wind: A Comprehensive Guide to Successful Offshore Wind Farm Installation 9, 17, 21, 23 (2012).
119 Christine Santora, Nicole Hade, & Jackie Odell, managing offshore wind developments in the United States: Legal, environmental, and social considerations using a case study in Nantucket Sound, 47 Ocean & Coastal Mgmt. 141, 153 (2004).
120 Christine Santora, Nicole Hade, & Jackie Odell, managing offshore wind developments in the United States: Legal, environmental, and social considerations using a case study in Nantucket Sound, 47 Ocean & Coastal Mgmt. 141, 143 (2004).
121 Christine Santora, Nicole Hade, & Jackie Odell, managing offshore wind developments in the United States: Legal, environmental, and social considerations using a case study in Nantucket Sound, 47 Ocean & Coastal Mgmt. 141, 153 (2004).
122 42 U.S.C. §§ 4321-4370f (2006).
123 42 U.S.C. §§ 4321-4370f (2006).
124 33 U.S.C. §§ 1251-1387 (2006).
125 33 U.S.C. §§ 401-467 (2006).

Endangered Species Act ("ESA")[126] and the Marine Mammal Protection Act ("MMPA").[127]

Within each of these statutes are various applications, permitting requirements and impact analyses to ensure the project is in compliance with each of the regimes. The U.S. has a pseudo-centralized agency, the Bureau of Ocean Energy Management Regulation and Enforcement ("BOEMRE") that focuses on the development of wind farms on the outer continental shelf. However, final approval requires multi-level governmental cooperation and communication as well as support from the communities potentially impacted by the project.[128]

A. The US Energy Policy Act and 30 CFR § 585—"RENEWABLE ENERGY AND ALTERNATE USES OF EXISTING FACILITIES ON THE OUTER CONTINENTAL SHELF"

In 2005, after the Alliance case[129] but before the Army Corps could issue a Final EIS in the Cape Wind Project, Congress shifted authority over offshore wind from the Army Corps to Mineral Management Services (MMS) by passing Section 388 of the Energy Policy Act.[130] MMS has since taken over the NEPA environmental review process from the Army Corps.[131] Now that Congress has designated MMS as the primary agency overseeing Cape Wind and other offshore development, it appears to have resolved the question of who has primary jurisdiction over offshore wind regulation at the federal level. Further, 30 CFR § 585—"RENEWABLE ENERGY AND ALTERNATE USES OF EXISTING FACILITIES ON THE OUTER CONTINEN-

---

126 7 U.S.C. §§ 136-136y (2006).

127 16 U.S.C. §§ 1361-1423h (2006).

128 Marc R. Fialkoff, Shipping Lanes and Power Lines: The Port of Davisville and the Dynamic Role of Infrastructure, 18 Roger Williams U. L. Rev. 220, 241-54 (2013).

129 Alliance to Protect Nantucket Sound, Inc. v. U.S. Dep't of the Army (Alliance II), 398 F.3d 105, 116 (1st Cir. 2005).

130 Energy Policy Act of 2005, Pub. L. No. 109-58, § 388, 119 Stat. 594, 745 (codified at 43 U.S.C. § 1337 (2006)).

131 See Notice of Availability of Draft Environmental Impact Statement and Public Hearings for the Cape Wind Project Energy Project, 73 Fed. Reg. 3482 (Jan. 18, 2008); Notice of Intent to Prepare an Environmental Impact Statement, 71 Fed. Reg. 30693 (May 30, 2006).

TAL SHELF" provides the outline of authority to regulate offshore energy derives from amendments to subsection 8 of the Outer Continental Shelf Lands Act (OCSLA) (43 U.S.C. 1337), as set forth in section 388(a) of the Energy Policy Act of 2005 (EPAct) (Pub. L. 109–58). The Secretary of the Interior delegated to the Bureau of Ocean Energy Management (BOEM) the authority to regulate activities under section 388(a) of the EPA act.[132]

These regulations specifically apply to activities that:

(a) Produce or support production, transportation, or transmission of energy from sources other than oil and gas; or

(b) Use, for energy-related purposes or for other authorized marine-related purposes, facilities currently or previously used for activities authorized under the OCS Lands Act.[133]

The offshore energy regulations for BOEM's renewable energy program under 30 CFR § 585 occur in four distinct phases: (1) planning and analysis,(2) lease issuance, (3) site assessment, and (4) construction and operations. These phases must be worked in cooperation with SC DHEC.

The Planning and Analysis phase seeks to identify suitable areas for wind energy leasing consideration through collaborative, consultative, and analytical processes that engage stakeholders, tribes, and State and Federal government agencies. This is the phase when BOEM conducts environmental compliance reviews and consultations with Tribes, States, and natural resource agencies. In this phase the environmental consequences associated with issuing commercial wind leases and approving site assessment activities on those leases. Environmental and Socioeconomic resources and issues to be considered include, but are not limited to: [134]

- Air Quality
- Water Quality
- Marine Mammals

---

132 30 CFR § 585—"RENEWABLE ENERGY AND ALTERNATE USES OF EX-
    ISTING FACILITIES ON THE OUTER CONTINENTAL SHELF".
133 http://www.boem.gov/uploadedFiles/30_CFR_585.pdf (last visited April 29, 2014).
134 http://www.boem.gov/RE-Commercial-Leasing-Process-Fact-Sheet/ (last visited
    April 29, 2014).

- Sea Turtles
- Birds
- Bats
- Seafloor Habitats
- Physical Oceanography
- Coastal Habitats
- Socioeconomics
- Cultural Resources
- Fisheries
- Multiple Use Conflicts

The Environmental impact study is likely to take between 12-14 months.[135] In which time they will consult the:

- Endangered Species Act (Section 7)
- National Historic Preservation Act (Section 106)
- Government to Government (Federally Recognized Tribes)
- Magnuson-Stevens Fishery Conservation and Management Act (Essential Fish Habitat)
- Coastal Zone Management Act (Consistency Determination)
- Clean Air Act General Conformity Determination
- Migratory Birds Treaty Act/Executive Order Analysis[136]

If the proposed action has no significant environmental impact, BOEM will issue a Finding of No Significant Impact (FONSI).[137] Of course, this only comes after they decide to allow offshore leasing and have received application for such structures.

The Leasing phase results in the issuance of a commercial wind energy lease. Leases may be issued either through a competitive or noncompetitive process. A commercial lease gives the lessee the exclusive right to subsequently seek BOEM approval for the development of the leasehold. The lease does

---

135 http://www.boem.gov/RE-Commercial-Leasing-Process-Fact-Sheet/ (last visited April 29, 2014).

136 http://www.boem.gov/RE-Commercial-Leasing-Process-Fact-Sheet/ (last visited April 29, 2014).

137 http://www.boem.gov/RE-Commercial-Leasing-Process-Fact-Sheet/ (last visited April 29, 2014).

not grant the lessee the right to construct any facilities; rather, the lease grants the right to use the lease area to develop its plans, which must be approved by BOEM before the lessee can move on to the next stage of the process.[138] The process for lease approval includes the following meetings and documents mandatory for approval:

- Task Force meetings;
- Stakeholder meetings;
- National Environmental Policy Act scoping meetings and hearings;
- Federal Register notices;
- Request for Information (RFI);
- Notice of Proposed Lease Area and Request for Competitive Interest(RFCI);
- Call for Information and Nominations(Call); Proposed Sale Notice (PSN);
- Notice of Intent (NOI) to prepare a NEPA document; and
- NEPA document.[139]

The Site Assessment phase includes the submission of a site assessment plan (SAP), which contains the lessee's detailed proposal for the construction of a meteorological tower and/or the installation of meteorological buoys on the leasehold. The lessee's SAP must be approved by BOEM before it conducts these "site assessment" activities on the leasehold. BOEM may approve, approve with modification, or disapprove a lessee's SAP. It is also during this phase that the lessee would conduct site characterization surveys and studies (e.g., avian, marine mammal, archeological).[140]

The Construction and Operations phase consists of the submission of a Construction and Operations Plan (COP), which is a detailed plan for the construction and operation of a wind energy project on the lease. BOEM conducts environmental and technical reviews of the COP and decides whether to approve, approve with modification, or disapprove the COP. Prior to the

---

138 http://www.boem.gov/RE-Commercial-Leasing-Process-Fact-Sheet/ (last visited April 29, 2014).

139 http://www.energy.sc.gov/search/node/wind?page=1(last visited April 29, 2014).

140 http://www.boem.gov/RE-Commercial-Leasing-Process-Fact-Sheet/(last visited April 29, 2014).

end of the lease term, the developer must submit a plan to decommission facilities.[141] Unlike, many Oil and Gas Structures all Wind related construction must be removed from open waters.

VI. More on the Mineral Management Services Alternative Energy Regulations

Although implementing regulations were called for within 270 days of the August 8, 2005, enactment of the Energy Policy Act, and although MMS issued an Advance Notice of Proposed Rulemaking on December 30, 2005,[142] final regulations were not published until April 29, 2009.[143] Among other issues, the MMS and the Federal Energy Regulatory Commission (FERC) disputed which agency had authority over wave and current energy development.[144] Several issues lay at the heart of the dispute, including the savings provision in OCSLA section 8(p)(9), the congressional reservation of "water power" in SLA section 2, and FERC's existing water power authority in the Federal Power Act (FPA).[145]

Nevertheless, there was some intervening regulatory progress. In March 2006, the Department of the Interior (DOI) designated the MMS to implement the new Outer Continental Shelf Lands Act (OCSLA) section 8(p) provisions. On November 6, 2007, MMS announced an interim policy for authorization of installation of offshore data collection and technology testing facilities and a proposed lease form for limited-term leases.[146] In July 2008, MMS also issued a Notice of Proposed Rulemaking on the OCSLA section 8(p) leasing rules.[147] MMS reported that it received 280 written comments in response to the draft regulations.[148]

---

141 http://www.boem.gov/RE-Commercial-Leasing-Process-Fact-Sheet/(last visited April 29, 2014).
142 70 Fed. Reg. 77,345 (Dec. 30, 2005).
143 74 Fed. Reg. 19,638 (Apr. 29, 2009).
144 74 Fed. Reg. 19,638 (Apr. 29, 2009).
145 43 U.S.C. §1337(p)(9) (2006).
146 72 Fed. Reg. 71,152 (Dec. 14, 2007).
147 73 Fed. Reg. 39,376 (July 9, 2008).
148 74 Fed. Reg. 19,638 (Apr. 29, 2009).

The MMS-FERC dispute was eventually resolved and memorialized in an April 2009 Memorandum of Understanding between DOI and FERC.[149] The final regulations, referred to by the MMS as the "Final Renewable Energy Framework" followed on April 29, 2009.[150] MMS also proceeded with the interim lease process, issuing an environmental assessment and issuing an affirmative lease decision on certain interim leases in June 2009. In August 2009, MMS issued further implementing guidance on the renewable energy leasing framework.[151] The regulatory materials outlined above do not directly address the applicability of Maritime Cabotage Laws to U.S. OCS alternative energy activities. However, the regulations require compliance with "all applicable laws" at virtually every material stage of the regulatory process and project life cycle, but no definition expressly defines the "applicable laws."[152]

MMS describes its overarching regulatory authority as "requiring compliance with all applicable laws, regulations, and other requirements."[153] In each of the required plan submissions, SAP, COP, and GAP, MMS similarly requires that the plans "must demonstrate that you have planned and are prepared to conduct the proposed . . . activities in a manner that conforms to your responsibilities listed in § 285.105(a) [for SAP and COP] and: (1)Conforms to all applicable laws, regulations, and lease provisions of your commercial lease."[154] MMS also describes its inspection authority in a manner covering all applicable laws and regulations:

The MMS conducts inspections of OCS facilities and any vessels engaged in activities authorized under this part to verify that the applicant is operating in accordance with the OCS Lands Act, the regulations, lease stipulations, conditions of the grant, approved plans, and other applicable

---

149 Memorandum of Understanding Between the U.S. DOI and FERC (Apr. 9, 2009), http://www.mms.gov/offshore/AlternativeEnergy/PDFs/DOI_FERC_MOU.pdf. (Last visited April 29, 2014).

150 74 Fed. Reg. 19,638 (Apr. 29, 2009).

151 Minerals Mgmt. Serv. Office of Offshore Alternative Energy Programs, U.S. Dep't of the Interior, Guidelines for the Minerals Management Service Renewable Energy Framework (2009).

152 74 Fed. Reg. 19,638 (Apr. 29, 2009).

153 30 C.F.R. §285.102(b) (2009).

154 30 C.F.R. §§285.606, .621, .641 (Apr. 29, 2009).

laws and regulations, and to determine whether the proper safety equipment is installed and operating properly.[155]

MMS similarly describes its cessation and cancellation authority to include, among other things, "failure to comply with the OCS Lands Act and other applicable laws."[156] Whether "failure to comply with OCS Lands Act" is meant to subject alternative energy activities to OCSLA section 4(a) and thus all federal laws is not clear. The regulations contain at least a suggestion of support for that view. The definition of "natural resources" for the purpose of section 8(p) leasing authority "include[s], without limiting the generality thereof, renewable energy, oil, gas, and all other minerals (as defined in section 2(q) of the OCS Lands Act), and marine animal and marine plant life."[157] Thus, if MMS applies its regulatory definition of resources in section 8(p) to the administration of OCSLA section 4(a), it may conclude that a wind installation is therefore "for the purpose of exploring for, developing, or producing" a resource covered by OCSLA section 4(a).[158]

The MMS comments on the final rule also provide some guidance on the meaning of "applicable laws." The comments include a list of federal laws and executive orders to which MMS will require compliance.[159] The (long) list is expressly not exclusive, and therefore not determinative of all applicable laws, but it is nevertheless instructive for three reasons. First, it does not list any Maritime Cabotage Laws. Second, MMS does not expressly assert the applicability of a law pursuant to OCSLA section 4(a). And third, the laws on the list would not necessarily rely on OCSLA section 4(a) to apply to at least some US OCS alternative energy activities. The identified laws are:

- National Environmental Policy Act of 1969 (MMS cites 42 U.S.C. § 4321 et seq., which applies to any major federal action that may affect the marine environment);
- Endangered Species Act of 1973 (MMS cites 16 U.S.C. § 1531 et seq.,

---

155 74 Fed. Reg. 19,706 (Apr. 29, 2009).
156 74 Fed. Reg. 19,706 (Apr. 29, 2009).
157 30 C.F.R. §285.112 (2009).
158 OCSLA §4(a), 67 Stat. 462, 462 (1953) (codified as amended at 43 U.S.C. §1333(a) (2006)).
159 74 Fed. Reg. 19,647 (Apr. 29, 2009).

which applies to all federal agency activities and which prohibits without a permit the taking by any person of an endangered species in the territorial sea, and for any person subject to the jurisdiction of the U.S., the taking of an endangered species on the high seas);

- Marine Mammal Protection Act of 1972, (MMS cites 16 U.S.C. §§ 1361-1407, which prohibits, with certain exceptions, the taking of a marine mammal in the territorial sea, and for any person subject to the jurisdiction of the United States, the taking of a marine mammal on the high seas);

- Magnuson-Stevens Fishery Conservation and Management Act (MMS cites 16 U.S.C. § 1801 et seq., which applies within the Exclusive Economic Zone (EEZ);

- Marine Protection, Research, and Sanctuaries Act of 1972 (the Ocean Dumping Act) (MMS cites 33 U.S.C. § 1401 et seq., which generally prohibits the dumping of U.S.-sourced material anywhere in the ocean and foreign-sourced dumping out to twelve miles);

- National Marine Sanctuaries Act (MMS cites 16 U.S.C. § 1431 et seq., which applies in the 12-mile territorial sea and the EEZ);

- Executive Order No. 13,186, "Responsibilities of Federal Agencies to Protect Migratory Birds" (January 10, 2001), and Migratory Bird Treaty Act (16 U.S.C. §§ 703-711, which applies to federal actions that have, or are likely to have, a measurable negative effect on migratory bird populations);

- Coastal Zone Management Act of 1972 (MMS cites 16 U.S.C. § 1451 et seq., which applies to federal actions within or outside the coastal zone that affects any land or water use or natural resources of the coastal zone);

- Clean Air Act (CAA), title I (MMS cites 42 U.S.C. § 7401 et seq. and discusses the CAA title I requirements, which applies to any equipment, activity, or facility that has the potential to emit any air pollutant and is regulated or authorized under OCSLA);

- Clean Water Act (CWA), section 311 (MMS cites 33 U.S.C. § 1321 and Executive Order No. 12,777, "Implementation of Section 311 of the Federal Water Pollution Control Act of October 18, 1972," which regulates any offshore facility subject to U.S. jurisdiction and prohibits discharges of oil in the territorial sea, contiguous zone, in connection with OCSLA activities, or that may affect natural resources of the United States in the EEZ);

- CWA, sections 402 and 403 (MMS cites 33 U.S.C. §§ 1342 and 1343, pertaining to national pollutant discharge elimination system permits, which regulate pollution discharge permits in the 3-mile territorial sea, the 24-mile contiguous zone, and the high seas);
- CWA, section 404 (MMS cites 33 U.S.C. § 1344, which regulates dredge and fill permits for disposal of dredged material in navigable waters that may implicate shore side connection activities);
- Marking of Obstructions (MMS cites 14 U.S.C. § 86, which applies to marking obstructions on the navigable waters and waters above the continental shelf of the United States);
- Ports and Waterways Safety Act (MMS cites 33 U.S.C. 1221 et seq., which applies within the 12-mile territorial sea);
- Rivers and Harbors Appropriation Act of 1899 (MMS cites 33 U.S.C. § 401 et seq. and discusses the applicability of section 10, which applies to construction in navigable waters and any structure on the OCS);
- Resource Conservation and Recovery Act, as amended by the Hazardous and Solid Waste Amendments of 1984 (MMS cites 42 U.S.C. § 6901 et seq., which applies to generation and transportation of hazardous waste);
- National Historic Preservation Act of 1966 (MMS cites 16 U.S.C. §§ 470-470t, which applies to federal undertakings that may affect historic properties);
- Archaeological and Historical Preservation Act of 1974 (MMS cites 16 U.S.C. §§ 469-469c-2, which applies to any federally licensed activity or program);
- American Indian Religious Freedom Act of 1978 (MMS cites 42 U.S.C. § 1996 and Executive Order 13,007, "Indian Sacred Sites" (May 24, 1996) which apply to federal actions and federal lands);
- Federal Aviation Act of 1958 (MMS cites 49 U.S.C. § 44718 and 14

C.F.R. part 77, which regulate objects affecting "navigable airspace" on land and in the 12-mile territorial sea).[160]

The MMS comments on the intended application of the regulations also provide some insight into the meaning of "applicable laws." The various regulatory plan requirements "serve as a blueprint for site development, construction, operations, and decommissioning."[161] The General Activities Plan (GAP) requirements characterize "all applicable laws" as the environmental laws relevant for the NEPA review and environmentally safe operation: "The GAP must demonstrate that the applicant plans and is prepared to conduct the proposed activities in a manner that conforms to all applicable laws (e.g., NEPA, MSA, ESA, and CZMA), implementing regulations, lease provisions, and stipulations."[162] Similar comments focusing on environmental laws are provided with respect to a Site Assessment Plan (SAP) and Construction and Operations Plan (COP).[163]

The regulations regarding operations also appear focused on environmental law compliance:

> The regulations that address operations cover environmental management, safety management, inspections, facility assessments, and decommissioning. The regulations on operations are designed to ensure safety and prevent or minimize the likelihood of harm or damage to the marine and coastal environments. . . . In addition, the company will be required to comply with regulations regarding air quality, safety, maintenance and shutdowns, equipment failure, adverse environmental effects, inspections, facility assessments, and incident reporting.[164]

In addition, the specific plan submission requirements do not appear to request information that would be necessary to evaluate compliance with maritime cabotage laws (for example, vessel ownership, construction, or

---

160 74 Fed. Reg. 19,648-652 (Apr. 29, 2009).
161 74 Fed. Reg. 19,652 (Apr. 29, 2009).
162 74 Fed. Reg. 19,698 (Apr. 29, 2009).
163 74 Fed. Reg. 19,688 (Apr. 29, 2009).
164 74 Fed. Reg. 19,652-653 (Apr. 29, 2009).

documentation). For example, a COP must contain "[a] description of any vessels, vehicles, and aircraft that will be used to support the activities."[165] But the only vessel information specifically requested is "[a]n estimate of the frequency and duration of vessel/vehicle/aircraft traffic."[166] Unlike the requirement to identify and evidence the U.S. citizenship (or permanent resident alien status) of prospective lessees,[167] the regulations do not require or request information on vessel ownership, construction, or documentation.

In August 2009, MMS released guidance for implementing the alternative energy regulations.[168] MMS created the interpretive guidelines to "provide program details and describe the type of information that we are looking for in various submittals that are required."[169] The approximately 100 pages of guidelines and appendices do not address vessel operations or the question of applicable laws.[170]

VII.   More than just Regulations – American Cabotage

U.S. maritime cabotage laws are often popularly referred to as a group as the "Jones Act." There are in fact several laws to consider whenever an offshore project is undertaken, whether in waters adjacent to the United States or on the U.S. outer continental shelf (US OCS). Those principal laws are the Jones Act proper, which was enacted as section 27 of the Merchant Marine Act of 1920,[171] and separate acts governing the transportation of passengers, towing,

---

165 74 Fed. Reg. 19,696 (Apr. 29, 2009).

166 74 Fed. Reg. 19,848 (Apr. 29, 2009).

167 30 C.F.R. §285.106 (2009).

168 Minerals Mgmt. Serv. Office of Offshore Alternative Energy Programs, U.S. Dep't of the Interior, Guidelines for the Minerals Management Service Renewable Energy Framework (2009).

169 Minerals Mgmt. Serv. Office of Offshore Alternative Energy Programs, U.S. Dep't of the Interior, Guidelines for the Minerals Management Service Renewable Energy Framework (2009).

170 Constantine G. Papavizas & Gerald A. Morrissey III, Does the Jones Act Apply to Offshore Alternative Energy Projects? 34 Tul. Mar. L.J. 377, 407-13 (2010).

171 Constantine G. Papavizas & Bryant E. Gardner, Is the Jones Act Redundant? 21 U.S.F. Mar. L.J. 95 (2008).

and dredging.[172] Specifically, those acts, as amended, are the Act of June 19, 1886 (Passenger Vessel Services Act or Passenger Act),[173] the Act of June 11, 1940 (Towing Statute),[174] and the Dredging Act of 1906 (Dredging Act).[175]

All of these laws have potential applicability to offshore construction and maintenance of facilities or devices. The Jones Act potentially applies to the transportation of all items to a work site, the Passenger Act potentially applies to any person who might be considered a "passenger" traveling to the work site, the Towing Statute potentially applies to the towing of a barge to a work site, and the Dredging Act potentially applies to the installation of cable on the seabed or other actions taken at the work site.

All of the maritime cabotage laws also require, with some differences, the use of a U.S.-built vessel documented in the United States and owned and operated by a U.S. citizen.[176] These requirements, particularly the U.S.-built requirement, have been mentioned by commentators as potential impediments to offshore alternative energy projects and a potential source of business for shipyards.[177]

The Jones Act gets its name from the principal sponsor of the Merchant Marine Act of 1920, Senator Wesley L. Jones from the State of Washington.[178] Adding confusion, another section of the 1920 Act—section 33, which governs claims made by seamen for personal injuries suffered in the course of their employment—is also commonly referred to as the "Jones Act."[179] We will use the term "Jones Act" to mean section 27, which treats cabotage,

---

172 Act of June 5, 1920, ch. 250, 41 Stat. 988.

173 Ch. 421, §8, 24 Stat. 79, 81 (codified as amended at 46 U.S.C. §55103).

174 Ch. 324, 54 Stat. 304 (codified as amended at 46 U.S.C. §§55111 and 55118) (formerly 46 U.S.C. §316).

175 Ch. 2566, 34 Stat. 204 (codified as amended at 46 U.S.C. §55109) (formerly 46 U.S.C. app. §292).

176 46 U.S.C. §12112 (setting forth requirements for a "coastwise endorsement" on a vessel's Certificate of Documentation).

177 DSME Wins Order for Offshore Wind Farm Planter, Marine Log, Dec. 4, 2009, http://www.marinelog.com/DOCS/NEWSMMIX/2009dec00041.html (last visited April 29, 2014).

178 Andrew Gibson & Arthur Donovan, The Abandoned Ocean: A History of United States Maritime Policy, 119 (2000).

179 Constantine G. Papavizas & Gerald A. Morrissey III, Does the Jones Act Apply to Offshore Alternative Energy Projects? 34 Tul. Mar. L.J. 377, 379-80 (2010).

as it is presently codified with a number of important amplifications and exceptions enacted since 1920.[180] When we consider the Jones Act together with the other principal U.S. maritime cabotage laws as a group, we will refer to them as the "Maritime Cabotage Laws."

A. The Jones Act

The Jones Act covers "transportation of merchandise by water . . . between points in the United States to which the coastwise laws apply."[181] A related statute provides that "the coastwise laws apply to the United States, including the island territories and possessions of the United States [with several significant exceptions such as the U.S. Virgin Islands]."[182] The general definition of the "United States" restricts it to "the States of the United States, the District of Columbia, Guam, Puerto Rico," and several U.S. possessions (the Virgin Islands, American Samoa, and the Northern Mariana Islands) that are elsewhere statutorily exempted from the coastwise laws.[183]

Customs and Border Protection (CBP), which is charged with determining which voyages or vessel movements are covered by the Jones Act (and the other Maritime Cabotage Laws),[184] has promulgated a regulation that similarly provides, "No vessel shall transport, either directly or by way of a foreign port, any passenger or merchandise between points in the United States embraced within the coastwise laws, including points within a harbor . . . ."[185]

Although there is some circularity in these formulations, CBP rulings have consistently applied the Jones Act to any point within U.S. navigable waters or "territorial waters."[186] CBP itself has opined, "CBP has consistently ruled that a point in the United States territorial waters is a point in the

---

180 United States v. California, 332 U.S. 19, 34 n.16, 1947 AMC 1579, 1590 n.16 (1947).
181 46 U.S.C. §55102(b) (2006).
182 46 U.S.C. §55101 (a)-(b) (2006).
183 46 U.S.C. §114 (2006).
184 . 31 U.S.C. §308 (2006); 19 C.F.R. Pt. 0, App. (2009)
185 19 C.F.R. §4.80(a) (2013).
186 CBP, HQ 112023 (Dece. 23, 1991)

United States embraced within the coastwise laws."[187] For example, CBP recently indicated that the Jones Act applies in U.S. waters "defined as the belt, three nautical miles wide, seaward of the territorial sea baseline, and to points located in internal waters, landward of the territorial sea baseline."[188]

Just as consistently, CBP has only applied the Jones Act outside of U.S. navigable waters based upon the extension of federal jurisdiction granted by Outer Continental Shelf Lands Act (OCSLA). According to CBP: "In order for an activity to constitute coastwise trade, there must be a transportation between 'coastwise points.' In addition to the U.S. territorial waters . . . coastwise points also include certain points on the Outer Continental Shelf (OCS)."[189]

CBP has rejected the notion that the 12-mile Proclamation extends the navigable waters for Jones Act purposes to twelve miles.[190] According to CBP, "[I]t is our position that the 3-mile territorial sea Customs recognizes for the purposes of the administration of the navigation laws was not affected [by the 12-mile Proclamation.]"[191]

CBP has been careful to limit the Jones Act to the OCSLA governing law provision, giving effect to the "installations and other devices," "attachment," and "exploration, development, or production" purpose provisions in section 4(a).[192] CBP has determined, for example, that marker buoys are not installations and other devices and therefore they are not points embraced by the Maritime Cabotage Laws.[193] Similarly, dynamically positioned vessels are not coastwise points pursuant to OCSLA because they are not "permanently or temporarily attached to the seabed."[194]

---

187 http://www.cbp.gov/linkhandler/cgov/trade/legal/informed_ compliance_pubs/ merchandise.ctt/merchandise.pdf. (Last visited April 29, 2014).

188 CBP, HQ H032257 (Aug. 1, 2008).

189 http://www.cbp.gov/linkhandler/cgov/trade/legal/informed_ compliance_pubs/ merchandise.ctt/merchandise.pdf. (Last visited April 29, 2014).

190 http://www.cbp.gov/linkhandler/cgov/trade/legal/informed_ compliance_pubs/ merchandise.ctt/merchandise.pdf. (Last visited April 29, 2014).

191 http://www.cbp.gov/linkhandler/cgov/trade/legal/informed_ compliance_pubs/ merchandise.ctt/merchandise.pdf. (Last visited April 29, 2014).

192 42 U.S.C. §1333(a) (2006).

193 E.g., CBP, HQ 015078 (Nov. 7, 2007); CBP, HQ 110959 (Aug. 8, 1990).

194 CBP, HQ H010211 (Dec. 30, 2007); CBP, HQ 113838 (Feb. 25, 1997).

CBP has also reasoned that certain activities are not for the purpose of "exploration, development, or production."[199] For example, CBP has determined that wreckage or debris, even if attached to the seafloor, "can in no way be legally perceived as being affixed to the seafloor for exploration, development, or production, purposes as required by the OSCLA."[200] CBP has also determined that a "vessel used solely for pipe laying purposes and not for the purpose of 'exploring for, developing, or producing resources' from the OCS is not considered 'attached' to the seabed as that term is used in OCSLA and therefore is not a coastwise point."[201] Thus, CBP concludes, "The installation or device must be permanently or temporarily attached, and it must be used for the purpose of exploring for, developing or producing resources therefrom, in order to be considered a coastwise point."[202]

In making these judgments, CBP focuses on the 1978 OCSLA amendments.[203] CBP frequently cites to the amended section 4(a) and related legislative history indicating that "federal law" applies to installations and devices "when they are connected to the seabed by drillstring, pipes, or other appurtenances, on the OCS for exploration, development, or production purposes."[204]

This jurisdictional review is aside from the fact that the Jones Act in its own terms does not apply to all US OCS maritime activity. As noted earlier, however, the exact application of Maritime Cabotage Laws to the marine activities likely to arise in alternative energy offshore projects is outside the scope of this Article.

B. Other Maritime Cabotage Laws
1. Passenger Vessel Services Act

The jurisdiction of the Passenger Act overlaps with that of the Jones Act. The Passenger Act provides that "a vessel may not transport passengers between ports or places in the United States to which the coastwise laws apply, either directly or via a foreign port, unless the vessel" is a qualified U.S.-flagged vessel.[205] As with the Jones Act, CBP implementing regulations closely follow the statute by defining a "coastwise port" as "a port in the U.S., its territories, or possessions embraced within the coastwise laws."[206]

Regarding the US OCS, CBP has also carefully limited the application of the Passenger Act consistent with OCSLA section 4(a).[207]

2. Towing Statute

The Towing Statute requires the use of a qualified U.S.-flagged vessel for the towing of another vessel "between ports or places in the United States to which the coastwise laws apply, either directly or via a foreign port or place" and "from point to point within the harbors of ports or places to which the coastwise laws apply" unless a vessel is in distress.[208] In its rulings relating to the Towing Statute, CBP "has taken the position that the statute is to be construed consistently with the Jones Act."[195] Thus, the concept of "places in the United States to which the coastwise laws apply" encompasses points on the US OCS as defined in OCSLA.

The Towing Statute also applies to some vessel movements regardless of the applicability of the Jones Act to the US OCS. As a result of the twelfth proviso to the Jones Act enacted in 1988,[196] a qualified U.S. towing vessel is required if the towed vessel is transporting "valueless material or dredged material, regardless of whether it has commercial value" between any point in the United States and any point within the U.S. EEZ and vice versa.[197]

3. Dredging Act

The Dredging Act restricts "dredging," which includes certain pipe or cable laying activities as well as foundation excavations, "in the navigable waters of the United States" to qualified U.S.-flagged vessels.[198] According to CBP, it "has long-held that 'dredging' . . . is the use of a vessel equipped with excavating machinery in digging up or otherwise removing submarine material."[199] As with the Jones Act, CBP has limited the applicability

---

195 CBP, HQ H026282 (May 13, 2008).
196 Act of June 7, 1988, Pub. L. No. 100-329, §5, 102 Stat. 588, 589 (1988).
197 46 U.S.C. §55111(b)(3) (2006).
198 46 U.S.C. §55109 (2006).
199 CBP, HQ H012082 (Aug. 27, 2007).

of the Dredging Act beyond navigable waters to locations on the US OCS consistent with OCSLA section 4(a):

> With respect to the applicability of [the Dredging Act] to the OCS, we have held that statute to apply only to dredging on the OCS for the purposes described in section 4 of the OCSLA, and not to dredging done to prepare the seabed of the OCS for the laying of trans-oceanic cable.[200]

Thus, because dredging for a trans-oceanic cable on the US OCS was not within the purposes outlined in OCSLA section 4(a), the Dredging Act was not implicated, although any subsequent transportation of valueless dredged material would be implicated, pursuant to the extension of the Jones Act to the EEZ for valueless material and dredged material.[201]

C. Waiver Authority

All of the Maritime Cabotage Laws, and certain other "navigation and vessel-inspection" related laws, can be waived by the U.S. government in certain limited circumstances, which could come into play if those laws were found to apply to offshore alternative energy projects. Specifically the waiver law provides: "On request of the Secretary of Defense, the head of an agency responsible for the administration of the navigation or vessel-inspection laws shall waive compliance with those laws to the extent the Secretary considers necessary in the interest of national defense."[202] The phrase "navigation and vessel inspection-laws" has been found to include the Maritime Cabotage Laws, as it is "a broad, general description of laws administered by the Coast Guard that must be read expansively."[203] The general waiver authority was utilized by President George W. Bush to waive the Jones Act in limited circumstances following Hurricanes Katrina and Rita in 2005.[204]

---

200 U.S. Customs & Border Protection (CBP), HQ 114715 (June 16, 1999)
201 46 U.S.C. §55109 (2006).
202 Act of Dec. 27, 1950, ch. 1155, §§1, 2, 46 U.S.C. §501
203 Nat'l Marine Eng'rs Beneficial Ass'n v. Burnley, 684 F. Supp. 6, 8 (D.D.C. 1988).
204 Waiver of Compliance with Navigation and Inspection Laws, 70 Fed. Reg. 53,236 (Sept. 7, 2005) (Office of the Sec'y, Dep't of Homeland Sec.); Waiver of Compliance with Navigation and Inspection Laws; Gulf Coast States, 70 Fed. Reg. 57,611 (Oct. 3, 2005) (Office of the Sec'y, Dep't of Homeland Sec.).

Certain commentators have highlighted the waiver authority to apply potentially to offshore energy projects.[205] They cite to a relatively recent waiver granted to Escopeta Energy in connection with the use of foreign vessels to relocate a jack-up rig from the U.S. Gulf of Mexico to the Bering Sea off of Alaska as support for the possible use of waivers for offshore energy projects.[206]

However, the phrase "in the interest of national defense" has historically been interpreted by CBP as placing a heavy burden on any waiver requestor.[207] According to CBP, "Owing to the necessity for some national defense justification, requests for waiver of the coastwise laws are infrequently granted."[208] Further, "[A] waiver of the provisions of the coastwise laws cannot be issued solely for economic reasons."[209] Secretary of Homeland Security Chertoff, made findings in support of each of the hurricane waivers that the waivers were in the interest of national defense.[210]

Moreover, the existing policy relating to energy-related waivers does not fit the alternative energy project circumstances well. Executed in 1990, the agreement among CBP (then the Customs Service), the United States Maritime Administration, and the United States Department of Energy provides for voyage-by-voyage waivers of the Jones Act to carry petroleum

205 Memorandum from Brian Eisenhower to Erich Stephens, Rhode Island Project Director, Regarding U.S. Cabotage Laws and Offshore Energy Projects 2 (June 15, 2007), available at http:// law.rwu.edu/sites/marineaffairs/content/pdf/Eisenhower.pdf. (Last visited April 30, 2014).

206 Kay Cashman, They Got It! Stevens: Escopeta Has Its Jones Act Waiver to Bring Jack-Up Rig to Alaska, Petroleum News, July 16, 2006, at 1, 9-10.

207 CBP, HQ H059376 (May 22, 2009); CBP, HQ H046797 (Dec. 12, 2008); CBP, HQ H045777 (Dec. 4, 2008); CBP, HQ 115613 (Mar. 6, 2002). In 1995, CBP denied a waiver request relating to the movement of refrigerated containers from the U.S. Virgin Islands (which originated from the lower forty-eight states) to Puerto Rico, stranded in the Virgin Islands as a result of Hurricane Marilyn. CBP was not persuaded to grant a waiver by the facts that the Virgin Islands would be without electricity for months and therefore the cargo would spoil. CBP, HQ 113569 (May 21, 1995).

208 CBP, HQ 112085 (Mar. 10, 1992).

209 CBP, HQ 111867 (Sept. 24, 1991).

210 Waiver of Compliance with Navigation and Inspection Laws, 70 Fed. Reg. 53,236 (Sept. 7, 2005) (Office of the Sec'y, Dep't of Homeland Sec.); Waiver of Compliance with Navigation and Inspection Laws; Gulf Coast States, 70 Fed. Reg. 57,611 (Oct. 3, 2005) (Office of the Sec'y, Dep't of Homeland Sec.).

products when the Maritime Administration confirms that no qualified U.S.-flagged vessel is available.[211] The agreement provides by its own terms that it is intended "to facilitate consideration . . . of case-by-case waivers of the Jones Act during a period of actual or imminent shortage of energy supplies."[212] Therefore, if the Maritime Cabotage Laws apply to offshore alternative energy projects, any waiver consideration would have to demonstrate that the project could fit within the circumstance of solving an "actual or imminent shortage of energy supplies," which may be difficult for long-term alternative energy projects absent unusual circumstances.

VIII. Placement matters: The United States Continental Shelf

In OCSLA,[213] the federal government asserted jurisdiction over the seabed and subsoil of the continental shelf beyond the area ceded to the states in the SLA, established a leasing policy for US OCS minerals, and defined the law applicable to the US OCS.[214] Congress indicated that with OCSLA, it wanted to "assert the exclusive jurisdiction and control of the Federal Government of the United States over the seabed and subsoil of the outer continental shelf, and to provide for the development of its vast mineral resources."[215] The United States House of Representatives Judiciary Committee report indicates, "The purpose of [the legislation] is to amend the Submerged Lands Act in order that the area in the outer Continental Shelf beyond boundaries of the States may be leased and developed by the Federal

---

211 Agreement Among the U.S. Customs Service of the Department of the Treasury, the Maritime Administration of the Department of Transportation, and the Department of Energy to Expedite Requests for Waivers of the Jones Act During Periods of Actual or Imminent Shortages of Energy (July 26, 1990).

212 Agreement Among the U.S. Customs Service of the Department of the Treasury, the Maritime Administration of the Department of Transportation, and the Department of Energy to Expedite Requests for Waivers of the Jones Act During Periods of Actual or Imminent Shortages of Energy (July 26, 1990)

213 Outer Continental Shelf Lands Act (OCSLA), Pub. L. No. 83-212, 67 Stat. 462 (1953) (codified as amended at 43 U.S.C. §§1331-1356a).

214 Outer Continental Shelf Lands Act (OCSLA), Pub. L. No. 83-212, 67 Stat. 462 (1953) (codified as amended at 43 U.S.C. §§1331-1356a).

215 S. Rep. No. 411, at 2 (1953).

Government."[216] Further, the Judiciary Committee reported that the lack of legislation governing leasing in the US OCS had to be remedied and it was "the duty of the Congress to enact promptly a leasing policy for the purpose of encouraging the discovery and development of the oil potential of the Continental Shelf."[217] And as stated by the Supreme Court, "The purpose of the Lands Act was to define a body of law applicable to the seabed, the subsoil, and the fixed structures . . . on the outer Continental Shelf."[218]

OCSLA defined "Outer Continental Shelf" to mean "all submerged lands lying seaward and outside of the area of lands beneath navigable waters as defined in section 2 of the Submerged Lands Act [43 U.S.C. 1301], and of which the subsoil and seabed appertain to the United States and are subject to its jurisdiction and control."[219]

Section 3 of OCSLA reaffirmed and expanded upon the Truman Proclamation: "It is hereby declared to be the policy of the United States that the subsoil and seabed of the outer Continental Shelf appertain to the United States and are subject to its jurisdiction, control, and power of disposition as provided in this Act."[220] What had been an assertion of jurisdiction and control over the natural resources of the subsoil and seabed was expanded, at least linguistically, to include the subsoil and seabed itself.[221] The expanded jurisdictional claim was, however, limited by OCSLA section 3(b), which provided that the "character as high seas of the waters above the [US OCS] . . . shall not be affected."[222] The intent of section 3(b) was to limit the jurisdictional claim of the United States over the US OCS solely to what was

---

216 H.R. Rep. No. 83-413 (1953), as reprinted in 1953 U.S.C.C.A.N. 2177, 2177.
217 H.R. Rep. No. 83-413 (1953), as reprinted in 1953 U.S.C.C.A.N. 2177, 2177.
218 Rodrigue v. Aetna Cas. & Surety Co., 395 U.S. 352, 355, 1969 AMC 1082, 1085 (1969).
219 OCSLA §2(a), 67 Stat. at 462 (codified as amended at 43 U.S.C. §1331(a)).
220 OCSLA §3, 67 Stat. at 462 (codified as amended at 43 U.S.C. §1331(a)).
221 Hearings on S. 1901 Before the S. Comm. on Senate Interior and Insular Affairs, 83d Cong. 586, 587 (1953) (testimony of J. Tate, Deputy Legal Advisor, Dep't of State)).
222 OCSLA §3(b), 67 Stat. at 462 (codified as amended at 43 U.S.C. §1332(2)).

described as "horizontal jurisdiction," that is, jurisdiction over the seabed, not the waters or airspace above.[223]

Having asserted jurisdiction and control over the US OCS, Congress had to grapple with the question of what law to apply to the vast area. The governing law issue was a subject of considerable debate that "presented the most challenging question of legal theory involved in the drafting of the Act."[224] The Supreme Court in Rodrigue v. Aetna Casualty & Surety Co. provides an informative capsule summary of key proposals and the resulting federal-state law compromise:

> In introducing the bill to the Senate, Senator Cordon explained its inception as follows:
>
> "The committee first attempted to provide housekeeping law for the outer shelf by applying to the structures necessary for the removal of the minerals in the area under the maritime law of the United States. This was first attempted by incorporating by reference the admiralty statutes. This solution at first seemed to be a reasonably complete answer . . . inasmuch as the drilling platforms would have been treated as vessels. Maritime law, which applies to American vessels, would have applied under that theory to the structures themselves.
>
> "However, further consideration clearly showed that this approach was not an adequate and complete answer to the problem. The so-called social laws necessary for protection of the workers and their families would not apply. I refer to such things as unemployment laws, industrial-accident laws, fair-labor-standard laws, and so forth. . . .
>
> . . . .
>
> "[Ultimately, instead,] the whole body of Federal law [was made applicable] to the area [as well as state law where necessary].

---

223 Warren M. Christopher, The Outer Continental Shelf Lands Act: Key to a New Frontier, 6 Stan. L. Rev. 23, 28-29 (1953).
224 Rodrigue v. Aetna Cas. & Surety Co., 395 U.S. 352, 361-66, 1969 AMC 1082, 1089-92 (1969).

Thus, the legal situation is comparable to that in the areas owned by the Federal Government under the exclusive jurisdiction of the Federal Government and lying within the boundaries of a State in the uplands."

Similarly, Senator Ellender asserted that in the first draft it "was sought to treat the platforms or artificial islands created in the water as ships" but now the "islands are made subject to our domestic law" instead so as to be "treated just as though they were islands created by nature, insofar as the application of our domestic laws is concerned."

The House bill, H.R. 5134, had made federal law applicable, but also provided that the not "inconsistent . . . laws of each coastal State which so provides shall be applicable," at least if adopted by the Secretary of the Interior. The Senate bill, as it read before committee amendments, provided instead that acts "on any structure (other than a vessel)" located on the Continental Shelf for exploring or exploiting its resources "shall be deemed to have occurred or been committed aboard a vessel of the United States on the high seas and shall be adjudicated . . . according to the laws relating to such acts . . . on vessels of the United States on the high seas." When the Senate bill was reported from committee, this section had been replaced by the present language, omitting entirely any reference to treating the islands as though they were vessels.[225]

Section 4(a)(1) and (2) of OCSLA applied the governing law compromise:

(1) The Constitution and laws and civil and political jurisdiction of the United States are hereby extended to the subsoil and seabed of the outer Continental Shelf and to all artificial islands and fixed structures which may be erected thereon for the purpose of exploring for, developing, removing, and transporting resources therefrom, to the same extent as if the outer Continental Shelf were an area of exclusive Federal jurisdiction located within a State . . . .

---

225 Rodrigue v. Aetna Cas. & Surety Co., 395 U.S. 352, 361-63, 1969 AMC 1082, 1089-90 (1969).

(2) To the extent that they are applicable and not inconsistent with this Act or with other Federal laws and regulations of the Secretary now in effect or hereafter adopted, the civil and criminal laws of each adjacent State as of the effective date of this Act are hereby declared to be the law of the United States for that portion of the subsoil and seabed of the outer Continental Shelf, and artificial islands and fixed structures erected thereon, which would be within the area of the State if its boundaries were extended seaward to the outer margin of the outer Continental Shelf . . . . All of such applicable laws shall be administered and enforced by the appropriate officers and courts of the United States. State taxation laws shall not apply to the outer Continental Shelf.[226]

Thus, pursuant to section 4(a)(1), all federal laws were extended to "artificial islands and fixed structures which may be erected thereon for the purpose of exploring for, developing, removing, and transporting resources therefrom," and pursuant to section 4(a)(2), adjacent state laws were extended as surrogate federal law to "artificial islands and fixed structures erected [on the US OCS]" to the extent not inconsistent with other Federal laws and regulations of the Secretary. OCSLA did not define the term "resources" used in section 4(a).

A. *United Nations Convention on the Continental Shelf*

The Truman Proclamation brought international attention to continental shelf mineral resources, including precipitating follow-on claims by coastal nations well in excess of that asserted in the Truman Proclamation.[227] In 1950 the United Nations, through its International Law Commission (ILC), sought to address the unilateral and inconsistent claims.[228] The result was the United Nations Convention on the Continental Shelf, adopted in Geneva

---

226 OCSLA §4(a), 67 Stat. at 462 (codified as amended at 43 U.S.C. §1333).
227 Treasure Salvors, Inc. v. Unidentified Wrecked & Abandoned Sailing Vessel, 569 F.2d 330, 338, 1978 AMC 1404, 1414-15 (5th Cir. 1978).
228 Arron L. Shalowitz, Shore and Sea Boundaries, 187-91 (1962).

in 1958 at the First United Nations Conference on the Law of the Sea.[229] The United States signed the Convention in 1958 and ratified it in 1961.[230]

The Convention recognized the right of coastal states to exercise over the continental shelf "sovereign rights for the purpose of exploring it and exploiting its natural resources."[231] The term "natural resources" is defined in the Convention as the mineral and other non-living resources of the seabed and subsoil together with living organisms belonging to sedentary species, that is to say, organisms which, at the harvestable stage, either are immobile on or under the seabed or are unable to move except in constant physical contact with the seabed or the subsoil.[232]

Coastal state jurisdiction does not include sovereignty over the "super-jacent waters as high seas, or that of the airspace above those waters,"[233] nor the right to impede the laying of submarine cables or pipelines on the outer continental shelf.[234] In order to explore and extract natural resources, the Convention recognized the right of coastal states to "construct and maintain or operate on the continental shelf installations and other devices necessary for its exploration and the exploitation of its natural resources."[235]

The United States supported both the jurisdictional scope and the definition of natural resources embodied in the Continental Shelf Convention. The ILC convened in 1950, reported draft articles pertaining to the continental shelf in 1951, 1953, and 1956, and conducted negotiations on the final draft

---

229 United Nations Convention on the Continental Shelf, Apr. 29, 1958, 15 U.S.T. 471, U.N.T.S. 312.

230 United Nations Convention on the Continental Shelf, Apr. 29, 1958, 15 U.S.T. 471§2.1, U.N.T.S. 312.

231 United Nations Convention on the Continental Shelf, Apr. 29, 1958, 15 U.S.T. 471§2.4, U.N.T.S. 312.

232 United Nations Convention on the Continental Shelf, Apr. 29, 1958, 15 U.S.T. 471§3, U.N.T.S. 312.

233 United Nations Convention on the Continental Shelf, Apr. 29, 1958, 15 U.S.T. 471 §4, U.N.T.S. 312.

234 United Nations Convention on the Continental Shelf, Apr. 29, 1958, 15 U.S.T. 471§5.2, U.N.T.S. 312.

235 United Nations Convention on the Continental Shelf, Apr. 29, 1958, 15 U.S.T. 471§5.2, U.N.T.S. 312.

at the United Nations Conference on the Law of the Sea in Geneva between February 24 and April 27, 1958.[236]

The continental shelf provisions were assigned to Committee IV at the conference. An underlying dispute concerned competing views of the scope of jurisdiction: one group of states sought to extend what was in effect territorial jurisdiction over the continental shelf and the water and airspace above it, while another group sought jurisdiction to control seabed resources, but without extending coastal state territory.[237] The United States was in the latter camp. The U.S. delegation stated that it sought "an expansion of international law" with respect to the jurisdictional claims asserted in the Truman Proclamation and section 3 of OCSLA.[238] However, the United States was "opposed to anything which might even remotely cast doubt upon the status of the superjacent waters and airspace."[239] The U.S. delegation expressed its commitment to limiting jurisdiction to the seabed and subsoil by citing the protection of the high seas embodied in section 3(b) of OCSLA.[240]

The committee debates also addressed at length the meaning of "natural resources," which as quoted above, ultimately included "minerals," "other non-living resources," and "sedentary species" of the seabed and subsoil. As an initial matter, the earlier draft used the term "mineral resources." "Natural" was substituted in place of "mineral" so that the term would not suggest the exclusion of certain living resources that were permanently attached to the seabed, that is, "sedentary species":

[T]the Commission decided after long discussion to retain the term "natural resources," as distinct from the more limited term "mineral resources" . . . and some members proposed adhering to that course. The Commission, however, came to the conclusion that the products of "sedentary" fisheries,

236 Marjorie M. Whiteman, Conference on the Law of the Sea: Convention on the Continental Shelf, 52 Am. J. Int'l L. 629 (1958).

237 J.A.C. Gutteridge, The 1958 Geneva Convention on the Continental Shelf, 35 Brit. Y.B. Int'l L. 102, 111-112 (1959).

238 J.A.C. Gutteridge, The 1958 Geneva Convention on the Continental Shelf, 35 Brit. Y.B. Int'l L. 102, 631-632 (1959).

239 J.A.C. Gutteridge, The 1958 Geneva Convention on the Continental Shelf, 35 Brit. Y.B. Int'l L. 102, 636 (1959).

240 J.A.C. Gutteridge, The 1958 Geneva Convention on the Continental Shelf, 35 Brit. Y.B. Int'l L. 102, 636 (1959).

in particular, to the extent that they were natural resources permanently attached to the bed of the sea should not be left outside the scope of the regime adopted, and that this aim could be achieved by using the term "natural resources." It is clearly understood that the rights in question do not cover so-called bottom-fish and other fish which, although living in the sea, occasionally have their habitat at the bottom of the sea or are bred there.[241]

The phrase "other non-living resources of the seabed and subsoil" was included to capture certain non-living seabed resources that were non-mineral, for example, shells of dead organisms. The committee debate on the final version of the definition explained:

> Most of the non-living resources of the seabed and the subsoil were, of course, mineral resources, but the words "and other non-living resources" had been added so that the article would apply to resources such as the shells of dead organisms. As far as the living resources in question were concerned, . . . it was the permanent intimate association of certain living organisms with the seabed which justified giving the coastal States exclusive rights in regard to such organisms. . . .
>
> The living organisms of the seabed and subsoil belonging to sedentary species comprised coral, sponges, oysters, including pearl-oysters, pearl shell, the sacred chank of India and Ceylon, the trochus, and plants. . . .

The sponsors of the amendment had agreed that no crustacea or swimming species should be covered by the definition.[242] After seeking clarification

---

241 Marjorie M. Whiteman, Conference on the Law of the Sea: Convention on the Continental Shelf, 52 Am. J. Int'l L. 629, 637 (1958).

242 Marjorie M. Whiteman, Conference on the Law of the Sea: Convention on the Continental Shelf, 52 Am. J. Int'l L. 629, 638-639 (1958).

on the meaning of "harvestable stage" of sedentary species, the United States supported the proposed definition of natural resources, which was approved.[243]

B. Outer Continental Shelf Lands Act Amendments

The oil supply of 1973 through 1974 led to a search for more domestic sources of oil and gas, which in turn focused government attention on greater development of the US OCS. In addition, OCSLA was found to be inadequate over time with regard to leasing practices, evolving use of equipment, protection of the environment, involvement of states in US OCS decisions, and other matters. The Ad Hoc Select Committee on the Outer Continental Shelf reported:

The OCS Lands Act of 1953 has never really been amended and is outmoded. No legislation exists for coordination and compensation for injury to other users of the OCS besides the oil and gas industry. No comprehensive national legislation presently exists for responsibility and liability for the effects of oil pollution resulting from activities on the Shelf. In addition, specific mechanisms are needed to involve states, and local governments within states, in all OCS decisions.[244]

As a result, Congress enacted the Outer Continental Shelf Lands Act Amendments of 1978, which were signed into law on September 18, 1978.[245] Of particular relevance to the present discussion, Congress amended section 4(a) of OCSLA to strike "fixed structures" and add the "permanently or temporarily attached to the seabed" language, which is as it exists today:

The Constitution and laws and civil and political jurisdiction of the United States are extended to the subsoil and seabed of the outer Continental Shelf and to all artificial islands, and all installations and other devices permanently or temporarily attached to the seabed, which may be erected thereon for the purpose of exploring for, developing, or producing resources therefrom, or any such installation or other device (other than a ship or

---

243 Marjorie M. Whiteman, Conference on the Law of the Sea: Convention on the Continental Shelf, 52 Am. J. Int'l L. 629, 640 (1958).
244 H. Rep. No. 95-590, at 53 (1977).
245 Outer Continental Shelf Lands Act Amendments of 1978 (OCSLA 1978), Pub. L. No. 95-372, 92 Stat. 629 (1978).

vessel) for the purpose of transporting such resources, to the same extent as if the outer Continental Shelf were an area of exclusive Federal jurisdiction located within a State.[246]

The 1978 legislative history provides in part:

Section (a) amends section 4(a)(1) of the OCS Act of 1953 by changing the term "fixed structures" to "and all installations and other devices permanently or temporarily attached to the seabed" and making other technical changes. It is thus made clear that Federal law is to be applicable to all activities or all devices in contact with the seabed for exploration, development, and production. The committee intends that Federal law is, therefore, to be applicable to activities on drilling ships, semi-submersible drilling rigs, and other watercraft, when they are connected to the seabed by drillstring, pipes, or other appurtenances, on the OCS for exploration, development, or production purposes.[247]

The United States House of Representatives also adopted an amendment to section 4(e) of OCSLA applying the laws of the United States relating to operation, design, construction and equipment of vessels, training of vessel crews and control of vessel discharges to foreign-flagged vessels, subject to certain exceptions.[248] The section 4(e) amendment applied to any foreign-flagged vessel "conducting any activity pursuant to this Act or in support of any activity pursuant to this Act within the fishery conservation zone or within fifty miles of any artificial island, installation, or other device" referred to in section 4(a) of OCSLA.[249] Although that particular provision was not ultimately adopted by Congress, a similar provision was included in the law regarding safety standards and manning requirements for "any vessel, rig, platform, or other vehicle or structure . . . for activities pursuant to this subchapter."[250]

---

246 43 U.S.C. §1333(a)(1) (2006). Section 4(a)(2), regarding state law, was not amended. Compare id. §1333(a)(1) with id. §1333(a)(2).
247 H.R. Rep. No. 95-590, at 128 (1977), as reprinted in 1978 U.S.C.C.A.N. 1450, 1534.
248 H.R. 1614, 95th Cong. §203(e) (1977).
249 H.R. 1614, 95th Cong. §203(e) (1977).
250 43 U.S.C. §1356(a) (2006).

What is significant about the House amendment to section 4(e) is that the associated legislative history reveals something about congressional thinking on the application of the Jones Act to the US OCS. Apparently recognizing that the amendment overlapped with Jones Act requirements—which would have required vessels to be U.S.-documented and comply with all of the laws being applied to certain foreign-flagged vessels—the House noted the limitations of its amendment:

> The Bureau of Customs has determined that artificial islands and structures, including rigs, are points within the United States and within the coastwise laws of the United States, even though located outside territorial waters.

Under that determination, the transportation of passengers and merchandise between islands, structures, and rigs, or between islands, structures and rigs and the United States while engaged in OCS activities is covered by the Jones Act . . . .

This determination is under review and the committee, by this subsection, does not in any way negate or supersede existing law. This subsection [the amendment to section 4(e)] only applies to allowable transportation by foreign vessels and does not apply to situations when such vessels are banned by the Jones Act, unless the Jones Act is waived under existing laws.[251] The meaning of "this determination is under review" is not clear.

The 1978 Amendments also added several significant definitions to OCSLA. In particular, the Amendments defined each of "exploration," "development," and "production" and in each instance with reference to minerals:

- "Exploration" means "the process of searching for minerals, including (1) geophysical surveys where magnetic, gravity, seismic, or other systems are used to detect or imply the presence of such minerals, and (2) any drilling."[252]

---

251 H.R. Rep. No. 95-590, at 129 (1977).
252 43 U.S.C. §1331(k) (2006).

- "Development" means "those activities which take place following discovery of minerals in paying quantities."[253]
- "Production" means "those activities which take place after the successful completion of any means for the removal of minerals."[254]
- "Minerals" was defined to "include oil, gas, sulphur, geopressured-geothermal and associated resources" and any other "mineral" otherwise specifically authorized by Congress.[255]

C. Application of Federal Law to OCSLA Resources: Oil, Gas, and Minerals

While the phrase "which may be erected thereon for the purpose" appears to be a limitation on artificial islands, installations, and devices, it is also important to discern the meaning of "exploring for, developing, or producing resources therefrom." More simply, is alternative energy such as wind an OCSLA "resource"? Unfortunately, because the word "resource" was not defined in OCSLA, it is necessary to look for evidence of congressional intent.

1. Exploring, Developing, and Producing

The word "resources" in section 4(a) is modified by the terms exploring, developing, and producing in such a way that section 4(a) appears to only apply to resources that can be explored, developed, or produced. In 1953, the terms "exploring," "developing," and "producing" were undefined. But in 1978, Congress defined "exploration," "development," and "production."[256] In each instance, Congress defined the terms exclusively by reference to minerals, including "searching for minerals" and "those activities which take place following discovery of minerals," and "after the successful completion

253 43 U.S.C. §1331(l) (2006).
254 43 U.S.C. §1331(m) (2006).
255 43 U.S.C. §1331(q) (2006).
256 OCSLA 1978 §201, 92 Stat. at 633-34 (codified as amended at 43 U.S.C. §1331(k)-(m) (2006)).

of any means for the removal of minerals."[257] "Minerals" in turn was given to mean essentially "oil and gas" in 1978.[258]

The legislative history of the 1978 amendments provides a glimmer of enlightenment as to whether Congress intended the definitions of the nouns to apply to the respective verbs. One of the House of Representatives reports indicates that the purpose of the "exploration," "development," and "production" definitions "is to identify the point, after exploration and before development, beyond which actively [sic] under a lease cannot proceed without an approved development and production plan."[259] The conference report, however, contains nothing similar and merely states that the "conference report retains new definitions included in both the Senate bill and the House amendment" for a number of terms.[260] Moreover, the leases for which the terms were defined were leases to explore for, develop, and produce oil and natural gas.

The OCSLA findings and declaration of purposes of OCSLA also support the notion that OCSLA was directed toward mineral recovery. Twelve of the fifteen findings expressly relate to oil and gas and none of the remaining three point to other resource objectives on the US OCS or alternative resource technologies.[261] Similarly, the statutory purposes enacted in 1978 are predominantly oil and gas exploration and production purposes.[262] Moreover, where the concept of "new and improved technology" enters the picture, it does not suggest the incorporation of technology for new energy sources, but rather technology to "eliminate or minimize risk of damage to the human, marine, and coastal environments," and "physical obstruction

---

257 OCSLA 1978 §201(k-m), 92 Stat. at 633-34 (codified as amended at 43 U.S.C. §1331(k)-(m) (2006)).

258 OCSLA 1978 §201(q), 92 Stat. at 633-34 (codified as amended at 43 U.S.C. §1331(k)-(m) (2006)).

259 H.R. Rep. No. 95-590, at 126 (1977), as reprinted in 1978 U.S.C.C.A.N. 1450, 1532.

260 H.R. Rep. No. 95-1474, at 78 (1978).

261 OCSLA 1978 §201(q), 92 Stat. at 630-631 (codified as amended at 43 U.S.C. §1331(k)-(m) (2006)).

262 OCSLA 1978 §102, 92 Stat. at 631-632 (codified as amended at 43 U.S.C. §1331(k)-(m) (2006)).

to other users of the waters or subsoil and seabed" from oil and gas related risks such as "blowouts, loss of well control, fires, spillages."[263]

When courts have considered OCSLA in a variety of situations they have tended to consider OCSLA an oil and gas statute. For example, United States Court of Appeals for the Fifth Circuit indicated in 1961 that the "Continental Shelf Act was enacted for the purpose, primarily, of asserting ownership of and jurisdiction over the minerals in and under the Continental Shelf."[264] Then again in 1978, the Fifth Circuit followed up with, "The structure of the Act [OCSLA] itself, which is basically a guide to the administration and leasing of offshore mineral-producing properties, reinforces this conclusion. The Act consists almost exclusively of specific measures to facilitate exploitation of natural resources on the continental shelf."[265]

In the Jones Act context, this interpretation is confirmed by at least one decision, 106 Mile Transport Associates v. Koch.[266] In 106 Mile Transport, a 1987 decision dealing with the offshore dumping of sludge, the United States District Court for the Southern District of New York rejected the notion that the Jones Act applied to all points on the US OCS.[267] Rather, the court found that OCSLA extended Maritime Cabotage Laws "for limited purposes dealing with conservation and exploitation of natural resources."[268] The court concluded, "There is no indication that Congress intended by this statute to extend Federal laws like the Jones Act to sludge dumping sites which are wholly unrelated to the development of natural resources in the seabed of the Continental Shelf."[269]

Even more importantly, CBP appears to have interpreted the Jones Act

263 43 U.S.C. §1332(6) (2006).

264 Guess v. Read, 290 F.2d 622, 625, 1961 AMC 1413, 1415 (5th Cir. 1961), cert. denied, 368 U.S. 957 (1962).

265 Treasure Salvors, Inc. v. The Unidentified Wrecked & Abandoned Sailing Vessel, 569 F.2d 330, 339, 1978 AMC 1404, 1416 (5th Cir. 1978).

266 106 Mile Transport Associates v. Koch, 656 F. Supp. 1474, 1987 AMC 2335 (S.D.N.Y. 1987).

267 106 Mile Transport Associates v. Koch, 656 F. Supp. 1474 at 1482, 1987 AMC 2335 at 2338-2339 (S.D.N.Y. 1987).

268 106 Mile Transport Associates v. Koch, 656 F. Supp. 1474 at 1482, 1987 AMC 2335 at 2338-2339 (S.D.N.Y. 1987).

269 106 Mile Transport Associates v. Koch, 656 F. Supp. 1474 at 1482, 1987 AMC 2335 at 2338-2339 (S.D.N.Y. 1987).

only to apply to "points" on the US OCS involved in the exploration, development, or production of seabed mineral resources. For example, in 1990 the predecessor to CBP ruled that a construction project approximately eight miles off the coast of Massachusetts wholly unrelated to "the exploration, development, or production of natural resources on the seabed of the outer continental shelf" would not constitute a "point" under the Jones Act.[270]

The authorities support the view that the terms exploration, development, and production apply exclusively to mineral activities. Pursuant to that view, if section 4(a) only applies to "resources" for the purpose of mineral exploration, development, and production, then section 4(a) would not apply to a nonmineral "resource" such as offshore wind energy. Nor would it seem reasonable under this view to infer the meaning of "resource" in section 4(a) in a manner broader than its actual application.

2. "Natural Resources" in the Companion Submerged Lands Act

Although the word "resources" was not defined in OCSLA, it was defined in the Submerged Lands Act (SLA). There, the definition for the natural resources conveyed to the states included seabed minerals as well as all marine life, but excluding "water power, or the use of water for the production of power."[271] Because OCSLA is expressly a follow-on statute to the SLA and works in tandem with the SLA (SLA for the navigable waters, OCSLA for the seabed beyond the navigable waters) it is possible to argue that the SLA definition should apply in the OCSLA context.[272]

However, that approach is limited. While the definition of "natural resources" in SLA section 2(e) is referred to in the state territorial grant[273] and the federal U.S. OCS assertion of jurisdiction,[274] the federal assertion and reservation of U.S. OCS jurisdiction did not include all of the "natural resources" contained in the SLA definition. There are two reasons for this.

---

270 CBP, HQ 111098 (Aug. 8, 1990); CBP, HQ 110956 (June 7, 1990).
271 SLA, Pub. L. No. 83-31, §2, 67 Stat. 29 (1953).
272 Carolyn Elefant, Ocean Energy Development in the 1990s, 14 Energy L.J. 335, 343-44 (1993).
273 SLA §3, 67 Stat. at 30 (1953).
274 SLA §3, 67 Stat. at 32-33 (1953).

First, the grant to the states in SLA section 3(a) included title to the land and its resources under the navigable waters and the resources in the navigable waters themselves.[275] The asserted jurisdiction and control of the federal government in SLA section 9, however, included only the U.S. OCS natural resources in the subsoil and seabed.[276] Thus, regardless of the common definition of "natural resources," the SLA did not in fact assert federal jurisdiction and control for the U.S. OCS over all of the same natural resources conveyed to the states. Rather, Congress applied the term "natural resources" to the U.S. OCS in a manner that included only the subset of natural resources within the subsoil and seabed. Interpreting the meaning of OCSLA "resources" to mean the same as "natural resources" in SLA section 2 would therefore contradict how Congress applied that term to the U.S. OCS.

Second, the U.S. jurisdictional assertion over OCS resources in the Truman Proclamation in effect at the time of the SLA was substantially narrower in scope than the definition of "natural resources" in the SLA. As to OCS resources, the Truman Proclamation had asserted jurisdiction and control over the "natural resources of the subsoil and seabed."[277] President Truman's statement releasing the Proclamation further explained that it addressed the "mineral resources of the continental shelf," and that it did not abridge the character of the waters as high seas.[278] The SLA does not suggest an intent by Congress to assert jurisdiction and control over more than the OCS seabed and subsoil resources asserted in the Truman Proclamation.[279]

3. International Understanding of OCS "Resources"

The U.S. involvement with the United Nations Convention on the Law of the Sea (UNCLOS) I from 1950 to 1958 also provides some insight into the meaning of OCSLA "resources." By 1958, the Continental Shelf Convention recognized the rights of coastal states to explore and exploit "natural resourc-

---

275 SLA §3, 67 Stat. at 30 (1953).
276 SLA §3, 67 Stat. at 32-33 (1953).
277 Proclamation No. 2667, 1945 Pub. Papers 352 (Sept. 28, 1945).
278 Proclamation No. 2667, 1945 Pub. Papers 352 at 354 (Sept. 28, 1945).
279 Exec. Order No. 9633, 10 Fed. Reg. 12,305 (Sept. 28, 1945).

es" of the OCS, which it expressly defined as subsoil and seabed minerals and sedentary species.[280] Like the Truman Proclamation and section 3(b) of OCSLA, article 3 of the Continental Shelf Convention expressly disclaims coastal state sovereignty over the water or airspace above the US OCS.

The U.S. delegation at UNCLOS I was adamant both before and after the 1953 enactment of OCSLA that the Continental Shelf Convention should not recognize rights above the seabed and subsoil.[281] Indeed, after OCSLA was enacted, the U.S. delegation to UNCLOS I negotiating the continental shelf provisions cited OCSLA section 3(b) as evidence of the U.S. limited rights position.[282] The U.S. delegation voted in favor of both limited seabed rights and the limited natural resource definition adopted in the 1958 Convention,[283] which the United States signed in 1958 and ratified in 1961.[284]

Considering the contemporaneous position of the United States in support of the 1958 Convention—including specifically as to limited OCS jurisdiction and the subsoil mineral-focused definition of natural resources—interpreting the meaning of "resources" in OCSLA as more expansive than "natural resources" in the 1958 Convention would imply that the U.S. delegation advocated for treaty terms that would not have protected internationally the stated interests of the United States. And it would imply that Congress knowingly consented to a treaty in conflict with domestic law. The alternative, that the contemporaneous understanding of OCSLA resources was consistent with the understanding of UNCLOS I resources, appears more plausible.

Moreover, the Fifth Circuit rejected the notion of a conflict between OCSLA and the 1958 Convention, holding: "To the extent that any of the terms of [OSCLA] are inconsistent with the later adopted Geneva Conven-

---

280 United Nations Convention on the Continental Shelf, Apr. 29, 1958, 15 U.S.T. 471, Art. 3, U.N.T.S. 312

281 Marjorie M. Whiteman, Conference on the Law of the Sea: Convention on the Continental Shelf, 52 Am. J. Int'l L. 629 at 636 (1958).

282 Marjorie M. Whiteman, Conference on the Law of the Sea: Convention on the Continental Shelf, 52 Am. J. Int'l L. 629 at 632 (1958).

283 Marjorie M. Whiteman, Conference on the Law of the Sea: Convention on the Continental Shelf, 52 Am. J. Int'l L. 629 at 637-639 (1958).

284 United Nations Convention on the Continental Shelf, Apr. 29, 1958, 15 U.S.T. 471, Art. 3, U.N.T.S. 312.

tion on the Continental Shelf, they should be considered superseded."[285] In United States v. Ray, the court addressed two related questions: (1) whether the Army Corps had jurisdiction to require a Rivers and Harbors Act section 10 permit for installations on submerged coral reefs in the US OCS, and (2) whether the coral reefs were OCSLA "resources" subject to the exclusive rights of the federal government and thus warranting of injunctive relief.[286]

After finding that the reefs were included within the meaning of "seabed" and "subsoil," and that planned caissons would constitute obstructions to navigation for the purpose of Corps' permit authority,[287] the court addressed whether the federal government had the exclusive right to control the coral, that is, whether coral was an OCSLA resource.[288] Whether coral was an OCSLA "resource" was disputed in part over whether coral was a dead part of the seabed or a living resource not subject to OCLSA.[289] The court resolved the question by applying to OCSLA the definition of "natural resource" in the Continental Shelf Convention.[290]

Applying the approach in Ray, the meaning of resources in OCSLA would be interpreted in a manner consistent with the definition of "natural resources" in the Continental Shelf Convention.[291] That approach would not likely recognize offshore wind as an OCSLA resource.

The 1982 United Nations Convention on the Law of the Sea (UNCLOS III) also provides insight into the meaning of OCSLA "resources." The fact that part V of UNCLOS III recognizes expressly the sovereign rights of coastal states for the purposes of "activities for the economic exploitation and exploration of the [EEZ], such as the production of energy from the water, currents and winds," supports the position that offshore wind energy is now recognized as a resource.[292] But whether the EEZ rights in UNCLOS III

---

285 United States v. Ray, 423 F.2d 16, 21, 1970 AMC 1, 7 (5th Cir. 1970).
286 United States v. Ray, 423 F.2d 16, 18-21, 1970 AMC 1, 3-4 (5th Cir. 1970).
287 United States v. Ray, 423 F.2d 16, 20, 1970 AMC 1, 6 (5th Cir. 1970).
288 United States v. Ray, 423 F.2d 16, 20-22, 1970 AMC 1, 6-8 (5th Cir. 1970).
289 United States v. Ray, 423 F.2d 16, 22, 1970 AMC 1, 8 (5th Cir. 1970).
290 United States v. Ray, 423 F.2d 16, 21, 1970 AMC 1, 7 (5th Cir. 1970).
291 Treasure Salvors, Inc. v. Unidentified Wrecked & Abandoned Sailing Vessel, 569 F.2d 330, 340, 1978 AMC 1404, 1416 (5th Cir. 1978).
292 See United Nations Convention on the Law of the Sea, Dec. 10, 1982, 1833 U.N.T.S. 397 art 56.

should inform the meaning of "resource" in OCSLA—either when enacted or when amended—is a different question with a less clear answer.

As a threshold matter, the United States has not ratified UNCLOS III. The 1958 Convention remains the relevant treaty concerning the continental shelf. Therefore, at least with regard to the approach taken in Ray, UNCLOS III should not inform the meaning of domestic law. Further, the sovereign rights to water and air resources reflected in the UNCLOS III EEZ provisions were plainly not contemplated when either OCSLA or the 1958 Convention were enacted.[293] Indeed, the addition of offshore wind as an exploitable resource in the new EEZ provisions, while separately maintaining the existing and distinct continental shelf provisions, underscores that alternative energy in the water and above the surface was not considered an OCSLA resource at the time of the prior Convention. Thus, it does not appear that the meaning of OSCLA resources at the time OCSLA was enacted should be informed by the later extension of sovereign rights over water and air alternative energy resources recognized in the UNCLOS III EEZ provisions.

4. "Resources" in the US EEZ Proclamation and 2005 OCSLA Amendment

UNCLOS III is not the only recognition of alternative energy as an EEZ resource. In the stead of ratifying UNCLOS III, President Reagan issued the U.S. EEZ Proclamation. Among other things it asserted the U.S. sovereign rights over wind energy in the U.S. EEZ. As discussed earlier, however, the express terms of the Proclamation disclaimed any effect on domestic policy, including with regard to the OCS and OCSLA. The EEZ domestic policy disclaimer has been given similar effect as the domestic policy disclaimer in the twelve-mile proclamation.[294] Maritime Cabotage Laws have only been

---

293 The recognition of sovereign rights over offshore wind energy on the EEZ is structured in UNCLOS III as an expansion of sovereignty over the resources above the seabed and seafloor to the water and airspace above it, neither of which were contemplated in (and indeed were expressly excluded from) the 1958 Continental Shelf Convention.

294 U.S. Customs & Border Protection (CBP), HQ 114715 (June 16, 1999).

extended to the U.S. EEZ pursuant to express congressional action.[295] For example, while the transportation of valueless material within the U.S. EEZ was made subject to the Jones Act, Congress has not extended the application of the Jones Act to other merchandise.[296]

Nevertheless, it has been suggested that the 1983 EEZ Proclamation characterization of offshore wind energy as a resource of the EEZ and the 2005 OCSLA amendment authorizing OCS alternative energy leasing, taken together, demonstrate congressional intent to include wind energy as an OCSLA "resource" subject to all federal laws, including the Jones Act.[297] However, the evidence of such intent is not readily apparent.

While it is well established, as discussed above, that Congress can and has extended certain Maritime Cabotage Laws to the extent of the EEZ, which has not occurred for most Maritime Cabotage Laws. Nor does the plain language of OCSLA, as amended, define "resources" to include alternative energy, nor does it extend OCSLA to encompass the geographical scope or resources reflected in the EEZ Proclamation.

In addition, the absence of a clear OCSLA amendment stands in contrast to the long-standing practice not to apply the EEZ Proclamation domestically, absent legislation.[298] Moreover, the newly amended OCSLA section 8(p)(9) expressly states that "nothing in this subsection displaces, supersedes, limits, or modifies the jurisdiction, responsibility, or authority of any Federal or State agency under any other Federal law."[299] The savings provision suggests that the amendment of section 8 should not be interpreted to imply a jurisdictional expansion and substantive modification of the long-standing application of the Maritime Cabotage Laws by CBP.

It is at least conceivable, however, that the terms of the EEZ Proclamation disclaiming any effect on OCSLA could have been overridden by the

---

295 46 U.S.C. §55110 (2006).

296 46 U.S.C. §55101-55102 (2006) with 46 U.S.C. §55110 (2006).

297 Letter from Rep. James L. Oberstar et al. to Jayson P. Ahern, Acting Commissioner, U.S. Customs & Border Prot. (July 30, 2009) (Comment No. 135 to CBP Notice Regarding Application of the Jones Act, 43 Customs Bull., July 17, 2009, at 54, available at http://foia.cbp.gov/streamingWord.asp?i=32).

298 46 U.S.C. §55110 (2006).

299 43 U.S.C. §1337(p)(9) (2006).

2005 OCSLA amendments. Notwithstanding that such an intent was not expressed in plain language, it does not appear that the legislative history would support that conclusion. The amendment to OCSLA section 8 implies that Congress thought OCSLA already provided a jurisdictional basis to lease OCS land for alternative energy, for example, pursuant to the broad jurisdictional claim in OCSLA section 2(a).[300] But the legislative history does not suggest an intent to alter the administration of US OCS resources to treat alternative energy as an OCSLA resource for all OSCLA purposes, to expand OCSLA to encompass the EEZ Proclamation, or to apply all federal laws to alternative energy activities authorized by section 8(p).

In the Bush Administration's view, OCSLA was a "statutory framework for oil, gas, and other mineral activities" that alternative energy leasing could use as "umbrella statutory authority."[301] Amending section 8 alone was intentional, to "allow the Department to build on many of the provisions already in the Act while tailoring this bill's or this act's relevant provision to innovative alternative energy-related activities."[302] The statements suggest that the intention was not to apply all OCSLA provisions to the proposed alternative energy activities. Moreover, none of the authorities referenced by the Bush Administration (that the proposed section 8(p) would "build on") were OCSLA provisions with stated oil and gas purposes. Rather, each of the referenced authorities—interagency agreements, occupational safety, site access, remedies and penalties, and agency coordination—reflect MMS authority derived from OCSLA provisions of general applicability.[303]

Interagency agreement, occupational safety, and site access authorities are

---

300 OCSLA, Pub. L. No. 83-212, §2(a), 67 Stat. 462 (1953).

301 H.R. 793, 108th Cong.; see Legislative Hearing on H.R. 793 and H.R. 794 Before the H. Subcomm. on Energy and Mineral Resources of the H. Comm. on Resources, 108th Cong. 23 (Mar. 6, 2003) [hereinafter H.R. 793 Hearing] (statement of J. Burton, Dir. of Minerals Mgmt. Serv.).

302 H.R. 793, 108th Cong.; see Legislative Hearing on H.R. 793 and H.R. 794 Before the H. Subcomm. on Energy and Mineral Resources of the H. Comm. on Resources, 108th Cong. 23 (Mar. 6, 2003) [hereinafter H.R. 793 Hearing] (statement of J. Burton, Dir. of Minerals Mgmt. Serv.).

303 H.R. 793, 108th Cong.; see Legislative Hearing on H.R. 793 and H.R. 794 Before the H. Subcomm. on Energy and Mineral Resources of the H. Comm. on Resources, 108th Cong. 23 (Mar. 6, 2003) [hereinafter H.R. 793 Hearing] (statement of J. Burton, Dir. of Minerals Mgmt. Serv.).

contained in section 22 of OCSLA, as amended by section 208 of OCSLA 1978, and apply to any action "promulgated pursuant to this Act."[304] "This Act" refers to OCSLA and, as codified, refers to subchapter III of title 43 of the United States Code (the codification of OCSLA as amended).[305] The referenced civil and criminal penalty authority in section 24 of OCSLA similarly applies generally "to enforce any provision of this Act."[306] And the referenced authority regarding "coordination" in section 21 of OCSLA applies to federal agency coordination "in administration of the provisions of [section 21]."[307] Section 21(c) provides in part for Coast Guard regulation of "unregulated hazardous working conditions" related to "activities on the OCS."[308] Thus, the examples of what section 8(p) would "build on" are provisions of OCSLA that apply generally to all OCSLA activities—pursuant to section 8(p) or otherwise—and therefore do not evidence an intent for oil and gas focused provisions to apply to section 8(p) alternative energy activities.

OCSLA contains other provisions of general applicability,[309] but it also contains provisions that do not apply generally to all OCSLA activities, including provisions specific to oil, gas, and mineral activities. For example, in contrast to the generally applicable section 21(c) noted above, section 21(a) mandated a safety study pertaining only to "the adequacy of existing safety and health regulations and of the technology, equipment, and techniques available for the exploration, development, and production of the minerals of the outer Continental Shelf."[310] Section 21(b) requires the "use of best

---

304 OCSLA 1978, Pub. L. No. 95-372, §208, 92 Stat. 629, 655 (1978) (codified as amended at 43 U.S.C. §1348(a)) (recognizing interagency agreement authority for enforcement "pursuant to this Act"); id., 92 Stat. at 655-56 (codified as amended at 43 U.S.C. §1348(b)(1)) (requiring occupational safety compliance for "any holder of a lease or permit under this Act" at "all places of employment within the lease area"); id., 92 Stat. at 656 (codified as amended at 43 U.S.C. §1348(b)(3)) (noting site access to "the site of any operation subject to safety regulations").

305 43 U.S.C. §1348(a) (2006).

306 OCSLA 1978 §208, 92 Stat. at 659 (codified as amended at 43 U.S.C. §1350(b)) (providing for civil penalties for failure to comply with any "provision of this Act"); see also 43 U.S.C. §1350(c) (providing same for criminal penalties).

307 OCSLA 1978 §208, 92 Stat. at 655 (codified as amended at 43 U.S.C. §1347(f)(1)).

308 43 U.S.C. §1347(c)) (2006).

309 43 U.S.C. §1334 (2006).

310 OCSLA 1978 §208, 92 Stat. at 654 (codified as amended at 43 U.S.C. §1347(a)).

available and safest economically feasible technologies," but only on the "artificial islands, installations and other devices referred to in section 4(a)(1)."[311]

A similar result is reflected in the OCSLA section 23 "citizen suit" and jurisdiction provisions.[312] Section 23(a) authorizes private party causes of action for "any alleged violation" of OCSLA, OCSLA regulation, or OSCLA lease or permit.[313] It thus appears that the "citizen suit" provision generally applies to alleged OCSLA violations, including those related to OCSLA-authorized alternative energy activities. However, the broad grant of the original federal jurisdiction in section 23 is in part limited to mineral resources. OCSLA provides original federal jurisdiction in federal district court for cases arising out of or in connection with:

(A) any operation conducted on the outer Continental Shelf which involves exploration, development, or production of the minerals, of the subsoil and seabed of the outer Continental Shelf, or which involves rights to such minerals, or

(B) the cancellation, suspension, or termination of a lease or permit under this subchapter. Proceedings with respect to any such case or controversy may be instituted in the judicial district in which any defendant resides or may be found, or in the judicial district of the State nearest the place the cause of action arose.[314]

While section 23(b)(1)(B) grants original jurisdiction for certain actions related to OCSLA leases, the broader grant of original jurisdiction in section 23(b)(1)(A) is limited to actions involving exploration, development, or production of minerals.

It is also fairly transparent that the Bush Administration's legislative approach sought a greater degree of regulatory flexibility for administering

---

311 OCSLA 1978 §208, 92 Stat. at 655 (codified as amended at 43 U.S.C. §1347(a)).
312 OCSLA 1978 §208, 92 Stat. at 657 (codified as amended at 43 U.S.C. §1347(a)).
313 OCSLA 1978 §208, 92 Stat. at 657 (codified as amended at 43 U.S.C. §1347(a)).
314 OCSLA 1978 §208, 92 Stat. at 658 (codified as amended at 43 U.S.C. §1347(a)).

alternative energy activities. In response to comments seeking greater state input and environmental review, which critics asserted was provided in existing OCSLA provisions not amended by the section 8 proposal, MMS Director Burton testified:

> We agree these are important considerations, but we also believe by amending the OCSLA, a lot of the framework for these activities are already included in the present law, and these issues, after [the proposed bill] is enacted in to law as an amendment to OCSLA, will be dealt with . . ..[315] Although the language is veiled, it further suggests that the Bush Administration understood that not all OCSLA statutory provisions would apply to alternative energy activities, but that it preferred to "deal with" such concerns post-enactment, presumably through discretionary regulation.

The Bush Administration's contemporaneous view is instructive, but it has only limited interpretive value. It is not direct legislative history, for example, statements of congressional purpose contained in a conference report, and it does not expressly address the specific questions of treating alternative energy as an OCSLA "resource" or the applicability of Maritime Cabotage Laws to alternative energy activities.

Nevertheless, Congress was aware of the Bush Administration's view that only some OCSLA provisions would apply to the alternative energy activities pursuant to the proposed section 8 amendment.[316] Congress was also aware of the criticism that amending section 8 alone would render parts of OCSLA

---

315 H.R. 793, 108th Cong.; see Legislative Hearing on H.R. 793 and H.R. 794 Before the H. Subcomm. on Energy and Mineral Resources of the H. Comm. on Resources, 108th Cong. 23 (Mar. 6, 2003) [hereinafter H.R. 793 Hearing] (statement of J. Burton, Dir. of Minerals Mgmt. Serv.).

316 H.R. 793, 108th Cong.; see Legislative Hearing on H.R. 793 and H.R. 794 Before the H. Subcomm. on Energy and Mineral Resources of the H. Comm. on Resources, 108th Cong. 23 (Mar. 6, 2003) [hereinafter H.R. 793 Hearing] (statement of J. Burton, Dir. of Minerals Mgmt. Serv.).

inapplicable to alternative energy activities.[317] And although the legislation as enacted by section 388 addressed some of the concerns raised by critics of the prior proposals, it retained the form of an amendment to section 8.

Thus, while the available history does not tell us what Congress intended, it does show that Congress was aware that the approach of amending section 8 was viewed by supporters and detractors as having limited scope. Silence in this context does not suggest an intent to treat alternative energy as an OCSLA "resource" for all purposes or to apply the EEZ to OCSLA.

5. "Resources" and "Applicable Laws" in OCSLA Alternative Energy Regulation

The recently enacted regulations implementing the alternative energy leasing program are also unclear on these issues. On one hand, the "natural resources" definition includes wind power.[318] That could suggest the possibility that MMS had interpreted or may interpret OCSLA section 4(a) "resources" using the new regulatory definition implementing OCSLA section 8(p). Similarly, the undefined requirements to comply with "all applicable laws," including as to vessel operations, leaves open the possibility that MMS may view Maritime Cabotage Laws as applicable laws.

On the other hand, MMS's comments on the section 8(p) leasing regulations suggest that MMS did not consider alternative energy a "resource" to the extent that OCSLA section 4(a) would apply to alternative energy activities. Indeed, despite providing jurisdictional comments on many of the laws MMS identified as "applicable," it does not expressly rely on section 4(a) of OCSLA to apply any federal law to US OCS alternative energy activities.[319] Moreover, a review of the laws on the MMS list shows that the majority have an independent jurisdictional basis to apply to any federally

---

317 H.R. 793, 108th Cong.; see Legislative Hearing on H.R. 793 and H.R. 794 Before the H. Subcomm. on Energy and Mineral Resources of the H. Comm. on Resources, 108th Cong. 23 (Mar. 6, 2003) [hereinafter H.R. 793 Hearing] (statement of J. Burton, Dir. of Minerals Mgmt. Serv.).

318 30 C.F.R. §285.112 (2009).

319 74 Fed. Reg. 19,638, 19,647-51 (Apr. 29, 2009).

authorized OCS alternative energy activity, and the rest have an independent jurisdictional basis to apply to at least some OCS alternative energy activity.

The list of applicable laws is comprised of: (1) laws that apply to activities on the US OCS regardless of OCSLA section 4(a) because their jurisdiction covers the contemplated substantive activity, for example, NEPA;[320] (2) laws that apply to activities beyond U.S. navigable waters (that is, into the US OCS) regardless of OCSLA section 4(a) because Congress expressly extended their seaward jurisdiction beyond the traditional three-mile limit, for example, the Magnuson-Stevens Fishery Conservation and Management Act[321] and the Ports and Waterways Safety Act;[322] and (3) laws that apply to activities on the US OCS regardless of OCSLA section 4(a) because Congress expressly extended jurisdiction to the US OCS in independent legislation, for example, 14 U.S.C. § 86 (marking of obstructions),[323] title I of the Clean Air Act,[324] and section 10 of the Rivers and Harbors Act.[325]

The only outlier that appears to lack an independent jurisdictional basis to apply to the US OCS is section 404 of the Clean Water Act.[326] But while section 404 may not apply of its own force beyond navigable waters, it is almost certainly implicated in an OCS alternative energy project in light of shore side transmission line and connection-related dredging. Thus, while the MMS list of applicable laws is by its terms not exclusive, MMS does not appear to have relied on OCSLA section 4(a) as a basis for jurisdiction. That suggests that MMS was not treating alternative energy as an OSCLA section 4(a) "resource" that would trigger the application of all federal laws.

The recently concluded EIS is not especially instructive, but it does convey a mixed message. While the vast bulk of the EIS's analysis of environmental impacts of the proposed project and project alternatives (including

---

320 42 U.S.C. §4332 (2006).
321 The Magnuson-Stevens Fishery Conservation and Management Act asserts "exclusive fishery management authority" in the US OCS and within the EEZ, 16 U.S.C. §1811 (2006).
322 33 U.S.C. §1222(5) (2006).
323 14 U.S.C. §86 (2006).
324 42 U.S.C. §7627 (2006).
325 33 U.S.C. §403 (2006).
326 33 U.S.C. §1344 (2006).

regarding transportation and installation) are silent on these issues, the EIS points out in one section, with respect to vessels, that certain purpose-built vessels may be needed and that "[i]n the early years, such vessels may come from overseas."[327] The EIS does not analyze how foreign vessels could be lawfully utilized on the US OCS, or if the comment refers to activities not within the scope of Maritime Cabotage Laws, how U.S. vessels would later supplant foreign vessels.

In contrast to the ambiguity in the alternative energy EIS, the Final Environmental Impact Statement released by MMS in 2007 for the Oil & Gas Leasing Program expressly addresses the applicability of the Jones Act to OCS oil facilities:

The Merchant Marine Act of 1920 (Jones Act). . . .

The U.S. Customs Service has determined that facilities fixed or attached to the OCS used for the purpose of oil exploration are considered points within the United States. The OCS oil facilities are considered U.S. sovereign territory and fall under the requirements of the Jones Act; so, all shipping to and from these facilities related to OCS oil exploration can only be conducted by vessels meeting the requirements of the Jones Act. Shuttle tankering of oil that is produced at OCS facilities can only be legally provided by U.S.-registered vessels and aircraft that are properly endorsed for coastwise trade under the laws of the United States.[328]

The discussion plainly appears to convey the view that the Jones Act applies only to oil-related OCS facilities. While that is not the same as stating that the Jones Act would not apply to alternative energy activities, that view

---

327 Minerals Mgmt. Serv., U.S. Dep't of the Interior, Programmatic Environmental Impact Statement for Alternative Energy Development and Production and Alternate Use of Facilities on the Outer Continental Shelf, Final Environmental Impact Statement (2007) [hereinafter EIS], available at http://ocsenergy.anl.gov/documents/fpeis/index.cfm. MMS prepared the EIS pursuant to OCSLA section 8(p) (4), (7), and (9), as well as pursuant to the National Environmental Policy Act of 1969 (NEPA), 42 U.S.C. §4321 (2006), Chap. 3 at 23.

328 Minerals Mgmt. Serv., U.S. Dep't of the Interior, Outer Continental Shelf Oil & Gas Leasing Program: 2007-2012, Final Environmental Impact Statement App. D, at 7-8 (2007), available at http://www.mms.gov/5-year/2007-2012FEIS.htm (follow "appendix D" hyperlink under "Volume 2" heading) (last visited April 28, 2014).

gains support considering that (1) MMS addressed the OCSLA Energy Policy Act of 2005 amendment earlier in the same discussion without expanding the scope of the Jones Act discussion, and (2) the alternative energy EIS does not contain a similar Jones Act discussion.[329]

IX.   OCSLA Applied to Alternative Energy Projects

The result of the foregoing analysis appears to be that OCSLA applies federal law to artificial islands, installations, and devices that are attached to the seabed, but probably only in each instance if they are associated with exploring, developing, or producing minerals.[330] Because alternative energy projects involve the antithesis of oil, gas, or mineral extraction, OCSLA appears not to apply federal law to alternative energy artificial islands, installations, or devices located on the US OCS even if they are attached to the US OCS. Because most of the Maritime Cabotage Laws are federal laws, which appear to apply only as a result of the OCSLA extension of federal law, then it would appear that they would not apply to US OCS alternative energy projects.

In addition to artificial islands, installations, and devices erected on the US OCS, OCSLA also applies to "any such installation or other device (other than a ship or vessel) for the purpose of transporting such resources."[331] If the words "exploring," "developing," and "producing" are limited to minerals related activity, then the reference to "such resources" may be equally so limited and "transporting" would mean "transporting minerals." In that instance, the same analysis would apply, and the Maritime Cabotage Laws

---

329 Minerals Mgmt. Serv., U.S. Dep't of the Interior, Outer Continental Shelf Oil & Gas Leasing Program: 2007-2012, Final Environmental Impact Statement App. D, at 2 (2007), available at http://www.mms.gov/5-year/2007-2012FEIS.htm (last visited April 29, 2014).
330 Elizabeth A. Ransom, Note, Wind Power Development on the United States Outer Continental Shelf: Balancing Efficient Development and Environmental Risks in the Shadow of the OCSLA, 31 B.C. Envtl. Aff. L. Rev. 465, 483-484 (2004).
331 43 U.S.C. §1333(a)(1) (2006).

would not apply to the "transporting" of electricity from offshore alternative energy projects on the US OCS.[332]

A. OCSLA Should Not Be Forced to fit the Development of Wind Energy on the OCS

The OCSLA, in its present state, should not be extended to the development of offshore wind farms. The historic developments leading up to the enactment of the OCSLA and the specificity with which Congress defined the terms relating to the activities permitted on the outer continental shelf led to the conclusion that extension of the OCSLA to the development of offshore wind farms is untenable.

Historically, the purposes behind the Truman Proclamation, the SLA and the OCSLA were the extraction of oil and mineral deposits from submerged lands lying in the outer continental shelf.[333] These enactments took Congress over five years to develop a comprehensive program for the proper jurisdiction and purposes relating to the outer continental shelf. No reference is made in these enactments to the development of renewable sources of energy on the outer continental shelf. In fact, nothing but the development of oil and related minerals is discussed.[334] Additionally, the terms "exploration," "development," and "production" do not contain any ambiguities that would include the development of offshore wind technology on the outer continental shelf.[335] Each term is specifically tailored to the development and

---

332 Constantine G. Papavizas & Gerald A. Morrissey III, Does the Jones Act Apply to Offshore Alternative Energy Projects? 34 Tul. Mar. L.J. 377, 425-40 (2010).

333 Proclamation No. 2667, 10 Fed. Reg. 12,303 (1945)).

334 G. Kevin Jones, The Development of Outer Continental Shelf Energy Resources, 11 Pepp. L. Rev. 9 (1983) (tracing "the history of the development of OCS energy resources as well as the official policies underlying federal governmental actions affecting the OCS").

335 G. Kevin Jones, The Development of Outer Continental Shelf Energy Resources, 11 Pepp. L. Rev. 9 (1983) (tracing "the history of the development of OCS energy resources as well as the official policies underlying federal governmental actions affecting the OCS").

extraction of oil and mineral resources from the outer continental shelf.[336] The history of the enactments leading up to the enactment of the OCSLA and the terms specifically defined by Congress therein do not lend themselves to an extension for the development of offshore wind technology on the outer continental shelf. Consequently, new legislation should be drafted, or amendments made to the existing OCSLA to allow for guided development of offshore wind technology and other renewable sources.[337]

Since the OCSLA is substantively insufficient and specifically tailored to oil and mineral resource development, a subsequent issue is whether, without specific legislation on point, the statute the Army Corps is relying upon delegates to the Army Corps' the regulatory authority to issue permits in federal waters of the outer continental shelf.[338]

X. Other Potential Laws that may impact the Installation of Offshore Energy

A. The Migratory Bird Treaty Act

The Migratory Bird Treaty Act (the "MBTA") implements four international treaties that the U.S. government has entered into with other countries to protect birds that migrate across U.S. airspace.[339] The Fish and Wildlife Service ("FWS") of the Department of the Interior administers the provisions of the MBTA. Invoking strict liability, the MBTA makes it unlawful:

[T]o pursue, hunt, take, capture, kill, attempt to take, capture, or kill, possess, offer for sale, sell, offer to barter, barter, offer to purchase, purchase, deliver for shipment, ship, export, import, cause to be shipped, exported, or

---

336 G. Kevin Jones, The Development of Outer Continental Shelf Energy Resources, 11 Pepp. L. Rev. 9 (1983) (tracing "the history of the development of OCS energy resources as well as the official policies underlying federal governmental actions affecting the OCS").

337 Michael Schulz, Questions Blowing in the Wind: The Development of Offshore Wind as A Renewable Source of Energy in the United States, 38 New Eng. L. Rev. 415, 429-34 (2004)

338 Alliance to Protect Nantucket Sound v. United States Dep't of the Army, 288 F. Supp. 2d 64 (D. Mass. 2003) (No. 02-11749).

339 16 U.S.C. § 703(a) (2000).

imported, deliver for transportation, transport or cause to be transported, carry or cause to be carried, or receive for shipment, transportation, carriage, or export, any migratory bird [protected under the four treaties].[340] By its terms, the MBTA only applies to migratory bird species that are "native to the United States or its territories."[341]

Because strict liability attaches for any killing of a migratory bird under the MBTA, wind power developers must carefully examine the presence of migratory birds near their chosen project location. In fact, section 707 of the MBTA provides that:

Any person, association, partnership, or corporation who shall violate any provisions of said conventions or of this subchapter, or who shall violate or fail to comply with any regulation made pursuant to this subchapter shall be deemed guilty of a misdemeanor and upon conviction thereof shall be fined not more than $15,000 or be imprisoned not more than six months, or both.[342] Thus, the MBTA creates a sizable economic disincentive to creating a wind power project that leads to the death of migratory birds.[343]

B. Bald and Golden Eagle Protection Act

Like the MBTA, the Bald and Golden Eagle Protection Act ("BGEPA") may affect the location of wind power projects in the United States due to their potential effect on certain birds. The BGEPA prohibits the taking of any bald eagle or any golden eagle, alive or dead, or any part, nest, or egg thereof, and imposes both civil and criminal penalties.[344] A taking includes any wounding or killing of the protected eagles.[345] In particular, a taking will result in a civil fine of not more than $5,000.[346] Each taking constitutes a separate violation of the Act.[347] One must note, however, that anyone

---

340 16 U.S.C. § 703(a) (2000).
341 16 U.S.C. § 703(b)(1) (2000).
342 16 U.S.C. § 707(a) (1998).
343 Flint Hills Tallgrass Prairie Heritage Found., Inc. v. Scottish Power, PLC, 147 Fed. Appx. 785 (10th Cir. 2005).
344 16 U.S.C. § 668 (2000).
345 16 U.S.C. § 668(c) (2000).
346 16 U.S.C. § 668(b) (2000).
347 16 U.S.C. § 668(b) (2000).

accused of violating the BGEPA must be given notice of, and an opportunity for a hearing, with respect to each such violation before a fine may be assessed.[348]The Secretary of the Fish & Wildlife Service may consider the "gravity of the violation, and the demonstrated good faith of the person charged," in determining the amount of the penalty.[349] In fact, "[f]or good cause shown, the Secretary may remit or mitigate any such penalty."[350] Therefore, while there is no guarantee that a wind turbine project that takes protected eagles will result in a monetary penalty, the potentially steep civil fines may dissuade developers from choosing locations where bald or golden eagles may be affected.

The BGEPA already has resulted in at least one notable effect on U.S. wind power development. The Center for Biological Diversity ("CBD") invoked the BGEPA in a 2004 complaint against a number of companies operating wind turbines as part of California's Altamont Pass Wind Resource Area.[351] The plaintiffs argued that the turbines caused a taking of many birds, including bald and golden eagles, and that the taking amounted to a violation of the public trust doctrine and an unlawful business practice under California law.[352] Although the Alameda Superior Court initially allowed the case to proceed based on this novel pleading, the Court granted the defendants' motion for judgment on the pleadings on October 12, 2006.[353]

---

348 16 U.S.C. § 668(b) (2000).

349 16 U.S.C. § 668(b) (2000).

350 16 U.S.C. § 668(b) (2000).

351 Center for Biological Diversity, Inc. v. FPL Group, Inc., Alameda Case No. RG04183113 (Alameda Super. Ct. Nov. 1, 2004) (unreported), Compl. at 26-27, available at http:// www.biologicaldiversity.org/swcbd/programs/bdes/altamont/complaint9.pdf (last visited April 29, 2014).

352 Center for Biological Diversity, Inc. v. FPL Group, Inc., Alameda Case No. RG04183113 (Alameda Super. Ct. Nov. 1, 2004) (unreported), Compl. at 26-29, available at http:// www.biologicaldiversity.org/swcbd/programs/bdes/altamont/complaint9.pdf (last visited April 30, 2014).

353 Center for Biological Diversity, Alameda Case No. RG04183113, Order Granting Motions for Judgment on the Pleadings (Oct. 12, 2006), available at http://apps.alameda.courts.ca.gov/fortecgi/fortecgi.exe? Servicename =DomainWebService&PageName=Image&ID=1&Parent=12598900&Action=18994682 (last visited April 30, 2014).

CBD announced that it would consider appealing the decision.[354] Despite the unfavorable ruling, Alameda County supervisors earlier that month had "approved a six-month, $600,000 plan to investigate and monitor effect[s] of the Altamont windmills on avian mortality."[355]

While its complaint did not ultimately prevail, the CBD succeeded in calling attention to how wind turbines affect birds—especially bald and golden eagles. Thus, one can expect a proliferation of scientific studies on the effects of wind turbines on all birds and bats, including the fiercely protected bald and golden eagles, as wind power projects become more widespread, even in offshore situations.[356]

C. The Endangered Species Act

The Endangered Species Act (the "ESA"), perhaps the most famous and influential environmental law in the United States, affects wind power development in much the same manner as the MBTA.[357] The ESA seeks to ensure that all federal departments and agencies utilize their authorities to conserve endangered and threatened species, as well as their ecosystems.[358] The Fish & Wildlife Service of the Department of the Interior and the National Marine Fisheries Service of the Department of Commerce administer the law.[359] In addition, the ESA commands all other federal agencies to comply with its provisions, even where such protection conflicts with the agency's primary responsibility.[360] The ESA also requires that the Secretary cooperate to the

---

354 Center for Biological Diversity, Press Release, Judge Dismisses Altamont Pass Bird Kill Lawsuit (Oct. 17, 2006), available at http:// www.biologicaldiversity.org/ swcbd/PRESS/altamont-10-17-2006.html (last visited April 30, 2014).

355 Judge Dismisses Altamont Pass Windmills Bird Deaths Lawsuit, KTVU, Oct. 17, 2006, http://www.ktvu.com/news/10097288/detail.html? rss=fran&psp=news (last visited April 30, 2014).

356 Don Hopey, Aviary Tracking Raptors to Find Safe Sites for Wind Turbines, Pittsburgh Post-Gazette, Jan. 14, 2007, available at http://www.post-gazette.com/ pg/07014/753462-28.stm (last visited April 30, 2014).

357 16 U.S.C. §§ 1531-1544 (2000).

358 16 U.S.C. §§ 1531(c)(1)(2000).

359 16 U.S.C. §§ 1532(15) (2000).

360 16 U.S.C. §§ 1531(c)(1)(2000).

maximum extent practicable with the states, and affords financial incentives to the states for doing so.[361]

The ESA targets species designated as "endangered" or "threatened" due to one of five designated factors: "(1) the present or threatened destruction, modification, or curtailment of its habitat or range; (2) overutilization for commercial, recreational, scientific, or educational purposes; (3) disease or predation; (4) the inadequacy of existing regulatory mechanisms; or (5) other natural or manmade factors affecting its continued existence."[362] Importantly, the ESA allows the Secretary to concurrently designate any habitat of an endangered or threatened species as a "critical habitat."[363] The statute affords the Secretary wide discretion in designating critical habitat, requiring that it be done "to the maximum extent prudent."[364] "A designation of critical habitat is not prudent [whenever] . . . (1) the species is threatened by taking or other human activity, and identification of critical habitat can be expected to increase the degree of such threat to the species, or (2) such designation would not be beneficial to the species."[365]

Particularly relevant to the development of wind power, section 9 of the ESA makes it illegal to "take any such species within the United States or the territorial sea of the United States."[366] Under the ESA, "the term 'take' includes to harass, harm, pursue, hunt, shoot, wound, kill, trap, capture, or collect, or to attempt to engage in any such conduct."[367] Therefore, any activity related to the construction or maintenance of wind turbines could expose an individual or entity to liability where it results in the harming, wounding, or killing of a protected species. While liability would be expressly limited to instances involving certain species expressly designated under the ESA, any wind turbines located within the habitat of such species would be affected. Thus, the ESA would limit the number of locations suitable for wind turbine projects.

---

361 16 U.S.C. §§ 1535 (2000).
362 16 U.S.C. §§ 1533(a)(1) (2000).
363 16 U.S.C. § 1533(a)(3)(A) (2000).
364 16 U.S.C. § 1533(a)(3)(A) (2000).
365 50 C.F.R. § 424.12(a)(1)(i)-(ii) (2006).
366 16 U.S.C.§ 1538(a)(1)(B) (2000).
367 16 U.S.C.§ 1532(19) (2000).

Fortunately for developers, the ESA includes a provision that may allow for wind turbines in areas that would be otherwise prohibited. Thanks to a 1982 amendment, the FWS has the power to issue what is known as an "incidental take permit" under §10(a) of the Act to allow "otherwise lawful state or private actions that would result in the incidental taking of listed species."[368] More particularly, the FWS has the direction to issue an incidental take permit to an entity engaged in an otherwise lawful activity to continue actions that may result in a taking, so long as any taking that occurs is incidental to and not the purpose of otherwise lawful activity.[369] In theory, then, the FWS could issue incidental take permits to entities responsible for wind turbines in order to mitigate any fear that the entities have regarding liability for incidental takings that could result from turbines.[370]

Moreover, the ESA includes another requirement that affects potential wind power development. The ESA requires that any non-federal activities that seek an incidental take permit must include a habitat conservation plan ("HCP") along with the application for the incidental take permit.[371] Throughout this process, the public must be given the opportunity to comment on both the permit and the conservation plan proffered by the applicant.[372] The habitat conservation planning process helps to ensure that there is adequate minimization and mitigation of the effects of the authorized incidental take before a permit is granted.[373] The HCP prerequisite to obtaining an incidental take permit provides a further safeguard against an entity obtaining an incident take permit without first designating how its planned activity will affect the species in question. Drafting an approved HCP also alleviates a

---

368 Christopher Carter, A Dual Track for Incidental Takings: Reexamining Sections 7 and 10 of the Endangered Species Act, 19 B. C. ENVTL. AFF. L. REV. 135, 155, (1992).

369 16 U.S.C. § 1539(a)(1)(B) (1997).

370 U.S. Department of the Interior, Service Interim Guidelines on Avoiding and Minimizing Wildlife Impacts from Wind Turbines 36 (2003), available at http://www.fws.gov/habitatconservation/wind.pdf.

371 16 U.S.C. § 1539(a)(2)(A); see also U.S. Fish & Wildlife Service, Habitat Conservation Plans: Section 10 of the Endangered Species Act (2005), available at http://www.fws.gov/Endangered/hcp/HCP_Incidental_Take.pdf.

372 16 U.S.C. § 1539(a)(2)(B) (2000).

373 16 U.S.C. § 1539(a)(2)(B) (2000).

private landowner's uncertainty regarding potential liability or increased regulation.

The Secretary also has the power to grant an exemption from the permit process to a private party based on an "undue economic hardship" arising from the listing of the endangered or threatened species, including "substantial economic loss resulting from an inability . . . to perform contracts . . . [or] substantial economic loss to persons who . . . derived a substantial portion of their income from the [otherwise] lawful taking of any listed species . . . [or] curtailment of subsistence taking."[374] The exemption is limited, however, to one year from publication in the Federal Register.[375]

One of the greatest benefits of drafting a HCP is that doing so will provide for a "no surprise assurance" through section 10(a)(1)(B).[376] A "no surprise assurance" is tantamount to a governmental guarantee to non-federal landowners that the FWS will not require the commitment of additional land, water, or financial compensation; or place additional restrictions on the use of land, water, or other natural resources beyond the level otherwise agreed to in the HCP without the consent of the permittee, should "unforeseen circumstances" arise.[377] In fact, the government will honor these assurances as long as the permittee implements and maintains the terms and conditions of the HCP, permit, and other associated documents in good faith.[378] The government, in turn, benefits by receiving consistent behavior from the landowner, with any potential effects on listed species already having been reviewed.

D. The National Environmental Policy Act

The National Environmental Policy Act of 1969 ("NEPA"), invoked in the Cape Wind litigation by the Alliance, will affect any wind power development project that requires federal action significantly affecting the quality

---

374 16 U.S.C. § 1539(b)(1)-(2) (2000).
375 16 U.S.C. § 1539(b)(1) (2000).
376 16 U.S.C. § 1540(a)(1)(b) (2000).
377 16 U.S.C. § 1540(b)(2000).
378 16 U.S.C. § 1539(a)(2)(A) (2000).

of the human environment.[379] The purpose of NEPA is to create a national policy that promotes better harmony between mankind and the environment, particularly in regards to environmental damage caused by society.[380] This broad applicability makes NEPA an important piece of legislation that must be considered by anyone proposing a wind power project.[381]

Under NEPA, federal agencies must include in every major federal action significantly affecting the quality of the human environment (including recommendations or reports on proposals for legislation) an "economic impact statement" ("EIS") detailing the environmental impact of the proposed action, any adverse environmental effects which cannot be avoided should the proposal be implemented, alternatives to the proposed action, the relationship between local short-term uses of man's environment and the maintenance and enhancement of long-term productivity, and any irreversible and irretrievable commitments of resources involved in the proposed action should it be implemented.[382] The Council on Environmental Quality, created by NEPA, has established regulations in 40 C.F.R. 1500-1508 that describe how to prepare an EIS.[383]

E. The National Wildlife Refuge Systems Administration Act

Wind power development may occur on lands owned by the federal government that are designated as a national wildlife refuge. The National Wildlife Refuge Systems Administration Act ("NWRSAA") governs the National Wildlife Refuge System (the "System"), with the purpose of administering a national network of lands and waters for the conservation, management, and where appropriate, restoration of the fish, wildlife, and plant resources and their habitats within the United States for the benefit of present and future generations of Americans.[384]

Particularly important to the development of wind power on wildlife

---

379 42 U.S.C. §§ 4321-47 (2004).
380 42 U.S.C. §§ 4321 (2004).
381 42 U.S.C. § 4331 (2004).
382 42 U.S.C. § 4332(c) (2004).
383 42 U.S.C. § 4321 (2004).
384 16 U.S.C. § 668dd(a)(2) (2004).

refuge land, the NWRSAA prevents any person from taking or possessing any fish, birds, mammals (including bats) and other wildlife within any refuge area, unless by activities that are otherwise permitted by law, proclamation, regulation, or executive order.[385] The Act allows, however, for an exemption to permit the use of any area within the System for any purpose, including but not limited to hunting, fishing, public recreation and accommodations, and access whenever such uses are compatible with the major purposes for which such areas were established.[386] Accordingly, any wind power development on refuge land must be compatible with the major purpose for which the refuge was established.[387] It is important to note that the NWRSAA already permits easements in, over, across, upon, through, or under any areas within the System for purposes including, but not limited to, the construction and maintenance of power lines, telephone lines, pipelines, and roads.[388]

As a result, the NWRSAA may allow for wind power development on wildlife refuge space in limited circumstances given its similarity to other approved uses. The Fish and Wildlife Service has published guidelines for the consideration of wind turbines located on easement lands in Region 6.[389] The guidelines are intended for use by Refuge Managers and Wetland District Managers for site-by-site consideration of compatibility determinations for individual right-of-way requests for wind turbine use on easement lands.[390] The guidelines seek to prevent the alteration or destruction of grassland habitat that could result from the construction of wind turbines on easement

385 16 U.S.C. § 668dd(c) (2004).
386 16 U.S.C. § 668dd(d)(1)(A) (2004).
387 Memorandum from Deputy Dir., Fish and Wildlife Serv., U.S. Dep't of the Interior, to Reg'l Dirs., Service Interim Guidance on Avoiding and Minimizing Wildlife Impacts from Wind Turbines, at 36 (May 13, 2003).
388 16 U.S.C. § 668dd(d)(1)(B) (2004).
389 Memorandum from Deputy Dir., Fish and Wildlife Serv., U.S. Dep't of the Interior, to Reg'l Dirs., Service Interim Guidance on Avoiding and Minimizing Wildlife Impacts from Wind Turbines, at 40-41 (May 13, 2003).
390 Memorandum from Deputy Dir., Fish and Wildlife Serv., U.S. Dep't of the Interior, to Reg'l Dirs., Service Interim Guidance on Avoiding and Minimizing Wildlife Impacts from Wind Turbines, at 40-41 (May 13, 2003).

land.[391] The guidelines are subject to future revision and modification due to ongoing research and monitoring of the effects of wind turbines on wildlife populations.[392]

In particular, the guidelines restrict turbine frequency to a quota of one turbine per every 160 acres of easement tract.[393] Current biological information indicates that this density will not materially interfere with or detract from the purposes of the easement.[394] Wind power industry spacing recommendations also advise a distance of not less than 2000 feet between turbines, and a distance of 2000 from an occupied building, in order to prevent clumping of the turbines.[395] Turbines also shall not be constructed on wetlands, including lakes, ponds, sloughs, swales, swamps, and potholes.[396] Additionally, turbine owners must update bird strike avoidance equipment and implement techniques to reduce the disturbance to nesting birds at turbine sites.[397] Of course, any turbines on refuge land must still comply with other environmental laws and regulations, including the ESA and NEPA.

While this law is more applicable to on land wind farms, the impact may not be as farfetched as it appears. A question could be asserted regarding the impact of offshore wind farms on protected land. If the wind farms are

---

391 Memorandum from Deputy Dir., Fish and Wildlife Serv., U.S. Dep't of the Interior, to Reg'l Dirs., Service Interim Guidance on Avoiding and Minimizing Wildlife Impacts from Wind Turbines, at 40-41 (May 13, 2003).
392 Memorandum from Deputy Dir., Fish and Wildlife Serv., U.S. Dep't of the Interior, to Reg'l Dirs., Service Interim Guidance on Avoiding and Minimizing Wildlife Impacts from Wind Turbines, at 40-41 (May 13, 2003).
393 Memorandum from Deputy Dir., Fish and Wildlife Serv., U.S. Dep't of the Interior, to Reg'l Dirs., Service Interim Guidance on Avoiding and Minimizing Wildlife Impacts from Wind Turbines, at 40-41 (May 13, 2003).
394 Memorandum from Deputy Dir., Fish and Wildlife Serv., U.S. Dep't of the Interior, to Reg'l Dirs., Service Interim Guidance on Avoiding and Minimizing Wildlife Impacts from Wind Turbines, at 40-41 (May 13, 2003).
395 Memorandum from Deputy Dir., Fish and Wildlife Serv., U.S. Dep't of the Interior, to Reg'l Dirs., Service Interim Guidance on Avoiding and Minimizing Wildlife Impacts from Wind Turbines, at 40-41 (May 13, 2003).
396 Memorandum from Deputy Dir., Fish and Wildlife Serv., U.S. Dep't of the Interior, to Reg'l Dirs., Service Interim Guidance on Avoiding and Minimizing Wildlife Impacts from Wind Turbines, at 40-41 (May 13, 2003).
397 Memorandum from Deputy Dir., Fish and Wildlife Serv., U.S. Dep't of the Interior, to Reg'l Dirs., Service Interim Guidance on Avoiding and Minimizing Wildlife Impacts from Wind Turbines, at 40-41 (May 13, 2003).

shown to impact the wildlife or any other feature of the refuge, there could be an asserted violation of the act.

F. The National Historic Preservation Act

One additional federal statute that may have implications on the future of wind power development in the United States is the National Historic Preservation Act ("NHPA"). The NHPA promotes the federal government's role in historic preservation through programs and activities, encourages agencies and individuals undertaking preservation by private means, and seeks to assist state and local governments and the National Trust for Historic Preservation in the United States in expanding and accelerating their historic preservation programs and activities.[398]

The NHPA can affect wind power development by requiring, similar to the NEPA, that federal agencies take into account the effects that actions will have on items or sites listed, or eligible for listing, in the National Register of Historic Places.[399] In particular, federal agencies will need to determine the effects that any proposed development will have on listed sites where the development is built, funded, or permitted by a federal agency.[400] This statute may become more important as technology advances allow for wind turbines to be placed in offshore settings affecting the esthetics. Other statutes may be invoked as equally unique circumstances arise.[401]

---

398 16 U.S.C. §§ 470-470b, 470c-470n (2004).

399 Memorandum from Deputy Dir., Fish and Wildlife Serv., U.S. Dep't of the Interior, to Reg'l Dirs., Service Interim Guidance on Avoiding and Minimizing Wildlife Impacts from Wind Turbines, at 36 (May 13, 2003).

400 Memorandum from Deputy Dir., Fish and Wildlife Serv., U.S. Dep't of the Interior, to Reg'l Dirs., Service Interim Guidance on Avoiding and Minimizing Wildlife Impacts from Wind Turbines, at 36 (May 13, 2003).

401 Another statute that could affect wind power development in a small number of areas is the Coastal Barrier Resources Act ("CBRA"). Section 5(a)(1) of the CBRA, 16 U.S.C. § 3501(a)(1), could possibly prevent future construction of wind power projects near congressionally designated undeveloped coastal barriers on "the Atlantic and Gulf coasts and along the shore areas of the Great Lakes of the United States and the adjacent wetlands, marshes, estuaries, inlets and near shore waters..."

Table 5: More Federal Laws and Regulations Potentially Applicable to Offshore Wind Power and Aquaculture[402]

Law or Regulation	Agency	Action	Subject Jurisdiction	Potential Applicability
1. Rivers and Harbors Act (RHA), 33 U.S.C. § 403 and Outer Continental Shelf Lands Act (OCSLA), 43 U.S.C. § 1333	Army Corps of Engineers	Analyze compatibility w/other uses; consult/coordinate w/other agencies (e.g., NOAA, MMS, and EPA) and make "public interest" determination	Obstructions in navigable water	Both
1a. Clean Water Act (CWA), 33 U.S.C. § 1344	Army Corps of Engineers (Lead) & U.S. EPA (Veto)	Permit	Dredging and filling	Both if within three miles of shore, but depends on action (concurrently with RHA permit)
1b. National Environmental Policy Act (NEPA), 42 U.S.C. § 4332	Lead Agency - Army Corps of Engineers	Environmental evaluations (EAs and EISs)	Major federal actions significantly affecting the environment	Both (as part of RHA permit)
1c. Fish and Wildlife Coordination Act, 16 U.S.C. §§ 661-666c	U.S. FWS	Formal consultation	Fish and wildlife consultation	Both (part of RHA permit process)
1d. Magnuson-Stevens Fishery Conservation and Management Act, 16 U.S.C. § 1855	NOAA/NMFS	Formal consultation	Essential fish habitat consultation	Both (part of RHA permit process)

402 Jeremy Firestone, Willett Kempton, Andrew Krueger, Christen E. Loper, Regulating Offshore Wind Power, and Aquaculture: Messages from Land and Sea, 14 Cornell J.L. & Pub. Pol'y 71, 78 (2004).

Law or Regulation	Agency	Action	Subject Jurisdiction	Potential Applicability
1e. Endangered Species Act (ESA), 16 U.S.C. § 1536	NMFS and/or U.S. FWS	Formal consultation	Species jeopardy or adverse critical habitat modification consultation	Both (part of RHA permit process)
1f. MPRSA, 16 U.S.C. § 1434	NOAA	Formal consultation	Marine sanctuary consultation	Both (part of RHA permit process); presently three on Atlantic coast.
1g. Marine Mammal Protection Act (MMPA), 16 U.S.C. §§ 1361 et seq.	NMFS and/or U.S. FWS	Coordination	Marine mammal takes prohibited	Potentially applicable to both (part of RHA permit process)
1h. Migratory Bird Treaty Act, 16 U.S.C. §§ 703 et seq.; Migratory Bird Conservation Act, 16 U.S.C. §§ 715 et seq.	U.S. FWS	Coordination	Migratory birds takes prohibited	Wind (part of RHA permit process)
1i. National Historic Preservation Act (NHPA), 16 U.S.C. § 470f	State Historic Preservation Officer; Advisory Council on Historic Preservation	Formal consultation	Historic shipwrecks; archaeological sites; views from historic districts	Both, but jurisdiction limited to state waters and land (part of RHA permit process)
1j. Coastal Zone Management Act (CZMA), 16 U.S.C. § 1456	Affected States	Certification	Actions affecting land, water use of natural resources of coastal zone	Both, but only if "affects"
1k. CWA, 33 U.S.C. § 1341	State	Water quality certificate	State water quality standards	Both, if within three miles of shore
2. 14 U.S.C. § 83, 85 and 33 C.F.R. Parts 66 and 67	Coast Guard	Authorization	Private aids to navigation	Both (also generally part of RHA permit)

Law or Regulation	Agency	Action	Subject Jurisdiction	Potential Applicability
3. Federal Aviation Act of 1958, as amended, 49 U.S.C. § 44701; 14 C.F.R. Part 77	FAA	Notice, marking, and lighting	Notice if over two hundred feet high or near runway. If greater than five hundred feet (or under other conditions), considered an obstruction.	Wind (address potential impacts by type/direction of lights)
4. CWA, 33 U.S.C. §§ 1342 and 1343	U.S. EPA	Permit	Pollutant discharge in territorial sea, contiguous zone, or ocean	Possibly both, but greater consequence for aquaculture
5. Federal Power Act, 16 U.S.C. §§ 824, 824d.	FERC	Rate setting (does not involve environmental issues)	Sale and transmission of electricity between producer and wholesaler	Wind (no authority over wind farm permitting/operation)
6. Marine Protection, Research and Sanctuaries Act (MPRSA), 33 U.S.C. § 1412	U.S. EPA	Permit	Ocean dumping	Probably neither (definitely not needed if CWA 402 permit)
7. MPRSA, 33 U.S.C. § 1413	Army Corps of Engineers	Permit	Transportation for ocean dumping	Probably neither

XI. The OCS and Wind Resources: Proposed Legislation: H.R. 793 and H.R. 5156

A bill was placed before Congress that would consolidate the authority to "approve and regulate new and existing energy activities on the Outer Continental Shelf with the Minerals Management Service (MMS), which is under the Department of the Interior."[403] The bill was submitted in recognition that "mechanisms do not currently exist by which an applicant can obtain approval from the Federal Government to utilize the Outer Continental Shelf for non-oil and gas related activities."[404] Although the original version (H.R. 5156) failed in Congress due to widespread opposition, the reintroduced version (H.R. 793) remains substantially the same.[405] The bill would have transferred to the Secretary of the Interior the "authority to [g]rant an easement or right-of-way for alternative energy on the OCS, including renewable energy projects, such as wave, wind, or solar projects. . . ."[406]

Proponents of this piece of legislation mentioned a couple of benefits from its enactment.[407] "First, it will clarify the regulatory process considerably."[408] When a project is proposed by the private sector, there is a starting point for the permitting process which eliminates confusion.[276] The private sector would be able to start at a definite point, while in the current situation, the private sector may be "forced to 'agency shop' in an attempt to identify an authority that will allow them to move forward on a creative new ven-

403 Mary Helen Yarborough, Bill Would Broaden MMS Authority Over OCS Energy Projects, Inside Energy, July 29, 2002, at 12.

404 Letter from Rebecca W. Watson, Assistant Secretary of Land and Minerals Management, to Honorable Richard B. Cheney, President of the Senate 1 (June 20, 2002) [hereinafter Letter to Vice President Cheney], available at http://www.mms. gov/ooc/newweb/congressionalaffairs/letter%20to%CCC20VP%20-% 20Jun% 202002.pdf (last visited April 30, 2014).

405 Outer Continental Shelf Lands Act and Federal Coal Resources Act: Hearing on H.R. 793, 794, and 5156 Before the House Resources Comm. Subcomm. on Energy and Mineral Resources (2003) (testimony of Peter Shelley, Conservation Law Foundation), 2003 WL 11715984.

406 Outer Continental Shelf Lands Act and Federal Coal Resources Act: Hearing on H.R. 793, 794, and 5156 Before the House Resources Comm. Subcomm. on Energy and Mineral Resources (2003) [hereinafter Burton Testimony] (testimony of Johnnie Burton, Director, Minerals Management Service), 2003 WL 11715980.

407 Outer Continental Shelf Lands Act and Federal Coal Resources Act: Hearing on H.R. 793, 794, and 5156 Before the House Resources Comm. Subcomm. on Energy and Mineral Resources (2003) [hereinafter Burton Testimony] (testimony of Johnnie Burton, Director, Minerals Management Service), 2003 WL 11715980.

408 Outer Continental Shelf Lands Act and Federal Coal Resources Act: Hearing on H.R. 793, 794, and 5156 Before the House Resources Comm. Subcomm. on Energy and Mineral Resources (2003) [hereinafter Burton Testimony] (testimony of Johnnie Burton, Director, Minerals Management Service), 2003 WL 11715980.

ture."[409] Also, notice to other federal agencies will facilitate a timely review and consideration.[410] A second benefit that it would provide one agency within the federal government with "the tools to comprehensively address in one statute the array of issues associated with permitting and overseeing alternative energy-related uses on the OCS."[411] The reasons given for the Department of the Interior's lead role is that it is "the primary agency in the federal government to oversee development of our Nation's federal energy resources."[412]However, this proposed piece of legislation is not without its weaknesses.

Although the proposed legislation set out a framework for unification under one agency and clarifies the process by which a private corporation may attain the requisite property rights from the federal government, it only superficially addressed how the agency would allocate the submerged land for these activities.[413] The proposed materials state that by unifying under one federal agency, it will ensure that proposed activities, such as offshore wind development, are conducted in a "safe and environmentally sound

409 Outer Continental Shelf Energy Leasing Act: Hearing on H.R. 5156 Before the House Resources Comm. Subcomm. on Energy and Mineral Resources (2002) (testimony of Johnnie Burton, Director, Minerals Management Service), 2002 WL 25098173.

410 Outer Continental Shelf Lands Act and Federal Coal Resources Act: Hearing on H.R. 793, 794, and 5156 Before the House Resources Comm. Subcomm. on Energy and Mineral Resources (2003) [hereinafter Burton Testimony] (testimony of Johnnie Burton, Director, Minerals Management Service), 2003 WL 11715980.

411 Outer Continental Shelf Lands Act and Federal Coal Resources Act: Hearing on H.R. 793, 794, and 5156 Before the House Resources Comm. Subcomm. on Energy and Mineral Resources (2003) [hereinafter Burton Testimony] (testimony of Johnnie Burton, Director, Minerals Management Service), 2003 WL 11715980.

412Outer Continental Shelf Lands Act and Federal Coal Resources Act: Hearing on H.R. 793, 794, and 5156 Before the House Resources Comm. Subcomm. on Energy and Mineral Resources (2003) [hereinafter Burton Testimony] (testimony of Johnnie Burton, Director, Minerals Management Service), 2003 WL 11715980.

413 See Minerals Management Service, U.S. Dep't of the Interior, Draft Legislation (n.d.), at http:// www.mms.gov/ooc/newweb/congressionalaffairs/ Approved%20 Alternate%CCC20Energy%CCC20leg%CCC%-%2005-24-02.pdf (last visited April 29, 2014).

manner."[414]However, the proposed legislation lacks substance in providing exactly how or in what manner easements and rights of way will be granted in submerged land and to whom.[415] This may explain why it gained no traction and ultimately failed.

One way to be more specific in how submerged land is allocated would be to consider a system such as the leasing program found in the OCSLA.[416] This statute contains a mechanism through which a private company may enter into a lease with the federal government for federally owned submerged land.[417] Through this type of system, once an area has been identified and properly studied as suitable for development, private companies may enter into competitive bids to lease the land from the federal government.[418]The draft legislation set before Congress only stated that easements or rights of way will be granted "on a competitive or noncompetitive basis."[419] Although the government would be compensated under this provision, it is inadequate when compared to the lease program of the OCSLA because the bids may not be competitive and the areas proposed would not have to be scoped out for the resources.[420]

---

414 Letter from Rebecca W. Watson, Assistant Secretary of Land and Minerals Management, to Honorable Richard B. Cheney, President of the Senate 1 (June 20, 2002) [hereinafter Letter to Vice President Cheney], available at http://www.mms.gov/ooc/newweb/congressionalaffairs/letter%20to%CCC20VP%20-%20Jun%202002.pdf (last visited April 29, 2014).

415 See Minerals Management Service, U.S. Dep't of the Interior, Draft Legislation (n.d.), at http:// www.mms.gov/ooc/newweb/congressionalaffairs/ Approved%20Alternate%CCC20Energy%CCC20leg%CCC'%-%2005-24-02.pdf (last visited April 29, 2014).

416 43 U.S.C. § 1337 (2000).

417 43 U.S.C. § 1337 (2000).

418 43 U.S.C. § 1337 (2000).

419 Minerals Management Service, U.S. Dep't of the Interior, Draft Legislation (n.d.), at http:// www.mms.gov/ooc/newweb/congressionalaffairs/Approved%20Alternate%CCC20Energy%CCC20leg%CCC'%-%2005-24-02.pdf (last visited April 29, 2014).

420 Minerals Management Service, U.S. Dep't of the Interior, Draft Legislation (n.d.), at http:// www.mms.gov/ooc/newweb/congressionalaffairs/Approved%20Alternate%CCC20Energy%CCC20leg%CCC'%-%2005-24-02.pdf (last visited April 29, 2014).

XII. Conclusion

The foregoing discussion confirms that all of the Maritime Cabotage Laws apply to activities undertaken within U.S. navigable waters regardless of whether the activity is a traditional oil, natural gas, or an alternative energy project. Outside of U.S. navigable waters, however, there is some uncertainty about the application of the Jones Act, the Passenger Act, and the Towing Statute because all of those laws rely upon OCSLA for their jurisdiction and OCSLA appears, at least at first blush, to be limited to mineral extraction-related activities. Because many offshore alternative energy projects may be undertaken outside of U.S. navigable waters on the US OCS, and it has been alleged that the Maritime Cabotage Laws may impede those projects because of the alleged lack of qualified U.S.-flagged vessels, the issue of whether those laws apply is a significant one. However, many individuals in the U.S. wind energy industry are strong believers in the implementation of the Jones Act.[421] The potential to train offshore oil workers, to retool vessels used in the Gulf Oil industry, and the potential revitalization of the U.S. maritime industry are strong reasons to support this notion, however the further delay, added expense, and uncertainty of course are the risk.

The United States and South Carolina are primed for an "all of the above" energy plan, however the over regulation and legalization of every avenue of energy have forced a national reliance on energy resources from outside of US territory. As shown below, wind energy is plentiful however as illustrated above the regulations, laws, process, and construction have made the cost for wind energy unsustainable without government subsidy. The current wind cost is about $1.00 per kwh, verses $0.07 kwh for oil and $0.05 for coal:[422]

---

421 Elizabeth Colbert-Busch, Clemson Innovation Center, Interview on April 16, 2014.
422 Chris Caravelle, Southern Alliance for Clean Energy in Charleston, South Carolina, April 14, 2014.

Table 6: South Carolina Offshore Wind Speed Graph[423]

Mean Annual Wind Speed of South Carolina at 100 Meters

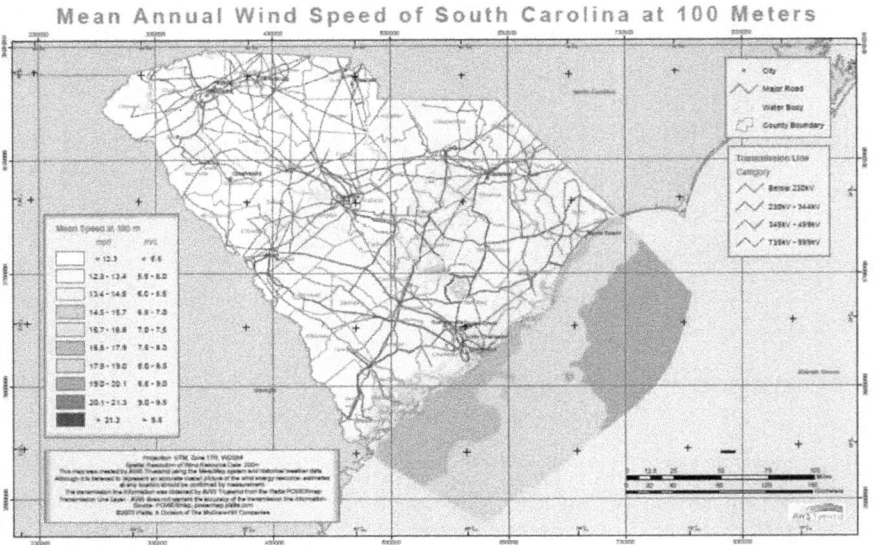

The trajectory for the State of South Carolina is to prepare for the implementation of wind, natural gas, and an "all of the above" energy plan, however companies are still submitting applications for seismic testing in the Atlantic. A BOEM record of decision issues is expected in May 2014, meanwhile three companies have resubmitted their previous applications.[424] During this time the previously mentioned studies are completed, along with an application for an Incidental Harassment Authorization (IHA) to National Marine Fisheries Service (NMFS) is filed which takes 4 to 8 months for NMFS to complete, companies in East coast states will be asked to review the proposed permits under the Coastal Zone Management Plans – by regulation this is a 60 day review, but could be longer or shorter, and BOEM conducts site specific environmental analysis.[425] Once these steps are completed BOEM issues a permit. Best case would be a permit being

---

423 http://www.boem.gov/uploadedFiles/BOEM/Renewable_Energy_Program/State_ Activities/SC%20Offshore%20 Wind%20Initiatives_Energy%20Office_Vanden-Houten.pdf (last visited April 30, 2014).
424 Interview with State Representative Stephen Goldfinch, April 21, 2014.
425 Interview with State Representative Stephen Goldfinch, April 21, 2014.

issued by end of 2014 with survey starting sometime in first half of 2015,[426] and the first windmill being built in 2017.[427]

The economic impact of the wind industry has already been felt on South Carolina. Currently, 1,134 jobs in South Carolina are related to wind energy or services that support that industry with 1,797 positions generating through indirect and induced wind energy efforts.[428] This accounts for $530 million in economic output for South Carolina in 2012, with $29 million in state revenue, and $21 million in local government revenue.[429]

Should offshore energy become a reality the farms, services, and construction will change the South Carolina landscape in potentially prime South Carolina for prosperity not felt for centuries.

Table 7: Wind Industry Economic Impact in 2016[430]

Employment	1,106 jobs
Private Non-Farm Employment	1,008 jobs
Total Compensation	$54.1 million
Total Impact (Output)	$164.7 million
State GDP	$87.8 million
Net Local Govt. Revenue	-$0.15 million
Net State Govt. Revenue	$1.6 million

426 Interview with State Representative Stephen Goldfinch, April 21, 2014.
427 Elizabeth Colbert-Busch, Clemson Innovation Center, Interview on April 16, 2014.
428 http://www.energy.sc.gov/files/OSWPhase2Feb-27-2014FINAL.pdf (last visited April 28, 2014).
429 http://www.energy.sc.gov/files/OSWPhase2Feb-27-2014FINAL.pdf (last visited April 28, 2014).
430 http://www.nwf.org/~/media/PDFs/Global-Warming/Reports/NWF_2012Off-shoreWind_Final.ashx (last visited April 28, 2014).

Table 8: Wind Industry Economic Impact per Year for 2017 - 2036[431]

Employment	13 jobs
Private Non-Farm Employment	11 jobs
Total Compensation	$1.2 million
Total Impact (Output)	$3.2 million
State GDP	$1.8 million
Net Local Govt. Revenue	-$63,000
Net State Govt. Revenue	$14,000

Unfortunately, no matter the economic implications or the willingness of the people,[432] with the aforementioned compilation of regulations, laws, studies, applications, permits, leases, combined with the high cost of wind energy, necessity of subsidies, and general risks associated with a novel application the window for this renewable resource may close before it is even opened to the United States and South Carolina. Ironically, many of the laws and regulations, conservation and environmental groups fought to introduce throughout the last century are now delaying the primary alternative energy resource the U.S. possesses.

Much like the implementation of any new crop from Carolina Gold Rice to offshore energy there will be trial and error. Moments of insecurity will arise during its growth, but if a harvest is to flourish then a willingness to plant is a necessity. However, until a concise process and a clear plan are

---

431 http://www.nwf.org/~/media/PDFs/Global-Warming/Reports/NWF_2012Off-shoreWind_Final.ashx (last visited April 28, 2014).

432 Clemson University Restoration Institute Wind Turbine Drivetrain Testing Facility: On October 2010
Clemson broke ground on the world's largest turbine drivetrain testing facility on the former Charleston Navy base. This state-of-the-art facility is supported by $98 million in public and private funding ($45 million U.S. DOE grant, $53 million from other public and private sources). The 7.5-megawatt test rig is scheduled to begin commissioning this fall, with the 15-megawatt rig to follow.

introduced, the enigma of the U.S. Energy Policy will continue to deter and delay the potential of offshore energy in South Carolina and the U.S. whether it be natural gas and oil or renewable resources like wind.

Attorney Thomas W. Winslow is the founding partner of Winslow Law, LLC in Pawleys Island, South Carolina. He has vast experience with medical malpractice and personal injury cases.

He has also worked with employment law, criminal matters, homeowners' associations, police and jail misconduct, maritime law, and products liability. Throughout his practice—whether defending the criminally accused, litigating a contentious claim, or researching and preparing legal documentation—he exhibits an ability to represent clients with the highest degree of competence and professionalism.

Tom is licensed to practice in state and federal court in South Carolina (Active) and Washington DC (Inactive). This honor allows him access to over seventeen state courts through the reciprocity process. He has also been admitted to practice in Georgia, North Carolina, Pennsylvania, Cherokee Reservation, and Tennessee. Along with practicing law, Tom is a certified Notary and Mediator in the State of South Carolina. Mediation is a conflict resolution process in which Attorney Winslow helps aggrieved parties settle their differences and resolve disputes.

In high school, Tom met his wife Lauren, and they quickly became best friends. They married 12 years later in 2006 and moved from Columbia to Georgetown, SC. Lauren was the Parish Administrator at Prince George Episcopal Church before deciding to stay at home with daughter Lea and son William. Together, the Winslows serve their community through many charitable and civic organizations.

Prior to attending Law School, Tom worked at the National Advocacy Center—the designated training center for all federal prosecutors located in Columbia, South Carolina. Mr. Winslow then earned his law degree from Loyola School of Law and his B.A. in International Studies from the University of South Carolina. After his graduation, Mr. Winslow joined the Bell Legal Group with a focus on professional malpractice, criminal law, and personal injury. He was soon admitted to practice in the Federal District Court of South Carolina. In 2011, Tom joined the Graham Law Firm, P.A. and handled their medical malpractice litigation department, which included birth injury litigation.

Tom accepted a partnership with Goldfinch Winslow in 2012. This role allowed him the opportunity to apply his knowledge and experience in helping the people of his community. During this time, Mr. Winslow earned an advanced degree in maritime law from the Charleston School of Law.

In his current work at Winslow Law, LLC, Tom's involvement with clients often results in a relationship that lasts well beyond the case. He attentively listens and cares about each client.

> We value our clients and our community; that is why we fight for both. Since 2005, I have been helping people and businesses by litigating for those that need an advocate. I have worked on complex litigation with both the plaintiff and the defendant. The practice of law is exciting, and every day motivates me to do the best I can for my clients.
>
> —*Tom Winslow*

When not at work, Tom has served as a Board of Director for the Winyah Auditorium, YMCA, SOS, Winyah Gym, Patriots Club, St. Francis Animal Center, Georgetown County Library, and the Tara Hall Home for Boys. He was appointed to the State Pilotage Commission which governs all the state maritime pilots. He is a frequent guest speaker, presenter, and lecturer throughout the state. He enjoys the outdoors, skiing, cooking, exercising with his wife, and family time with their young daughter and son.

Tom's children's book, *Firefly Forest*, was recently published and dedicated to his children. His second book, *The Art of Law*, was published for attorneys, judges, paralegals, etc.

www.ingramcontent.com/pod-product-compliance
Lightning Source LLC
Chambersburg PA
CBHW040851210326
41597CB00029B/4805